Doctors and Their Crimes

Doctors and Their Crimes is a compelling and meticulously researched exploration of doctors who commit criminal acts. Written by two experienced general practitioners, the book examines high-profile cases of medical malpractice, fraud, manslaughter, sexual misconduct, and abuse of power. Combining forensic analysis with professional insight, it reveals how these crimes unfold within the trusted structures of healthcare, where authority and access can be misused.

Drawing on real-world cases and insights from the authors' clinical experience, the book examines the ethical dilemmas, legal consequences, and societal impact of these betrayals of trust. It explores how systemic failures within healthcare and legal frameworks can enable such crimes, while also addressing sensitive issues like racism, justice, and professional accountability. Through expert analysis, it provides a nuanced understanding of the pressures and vulnerabilities that contribute to these breaches, offering valuable reflections on how trust in the profession can be restored.

Going beyond individual stories to consider the wider consequences of these crimes, including their impact on public trust, healthcare policy, and the relationship between medicine and the law, this book highlights the growing importance of trusted, independent sources of knowledge in addressing these challenges. By confronting medicine's darkest moments, *Doctors and Their Crimes* sheds light on how established systems can fail and how understanding these failures is essential to restoring trust in the profession. An essential resource for healthcare professionals, academics, and general readers alike, the book delivers a thought-provoking and nuanced examination of the ethical complexities and societal implications of professional misconduct in medicine.

Doctors and Their Crimes

Hiding Behind the White Coat

Clare Gerada and Zaid Al-Najjar

CRC Press
Taylor & Francis Group
Boca Raton London New York

CRC Press is an imprint of the
Taylor & Francis Group, an **informa** business

Designed cover image: Getty Images

First edition published 2027
by CRC Press
2385 NW Executive Center Drive, Suite 320, Boca Raton FL 33431

and by CRC Press
4 Park Square, Milton Park, Abingdon, Oxon, OX14 4RN

CRC Press is an imprint of Taylor & Francis Group, LLC

ISBN: 978-1-041-34189-5 (hbk)
ISBN: 978-1-041-31861-3 (pbk)
ISBN: 978-1-003-78106-6 (ebk)

DOI: 10.1201/9781003781066

Typeset in Minion
by KnowledgeWorks Global Ltd.

Contents

Acknowledgement **vii**

About the Authors **ix**

1 Introduction: Doctors and their crimes 1
2 Murder: Harold "Fred" Shipman 4
3 The Public Inquiry and its aftermath 16
4 Medical serial killers: Exploration of common themes 26
5 Serial killers: Michael Swango 33
6 Serial killers: A series of firsts 41
7 When medicine becomes murder 50
8 Gross negligence manslaughter: A dangerous intersection 64
9 Assault in medicine 74
10 Doctors, drugs, and crime 95
11 From victim to vector: Doctors and pills 105
12 Sexual misconduct in medicine 120
13 Specific cases of professional sexual misconduct 128
14 Sex, drugs, and doctors 141
15 Why do doctors transgress sexual boundaries? 148
16 Doctors, fraud, theft, and corruption 154
17 Addiction, opportunity, and descent into crime: Reflections from Dr Namasivayam Thiagalingam 162
18 Final thoughts 166

Index **171**

Acknowledgement

We are grateful to Dr Pallavi Bradshaw for her contribution to the chapter on fraud. We also thank Dr Namasivayam Thiagalingam and Jonathan Coe for their contributions to the book.

About the Authors

Baroness Clare Gerada PRCGP FRCPsych has been a doctor for more than 40 years working predominantly in mental health, including the mental health issues of doctors, and has set up and, together with Zaid, led the NHS Practitioner Health Programme. Professor Dame Gerada has extensive experience supporting doctors who have transgressed their professional boundaries, which is where the genesis of this book came from, and became a life peer in November 2025.

Zaid Al-Najjar FRCGP MBA LLM DOccMed DCP has been a doctor for over 20 years working in primary care, medicolegal practice, and the mental health of healthcare professionals. He is currently Medical Director at NHS Practitioner Health, which he has led alongside Professor Dame Clare Gerada, supporting health and care staff with mental health and addiction problems. Before joining Practitioner Health, he advised and supported doctors through complaints, inquests, claims, criminal proceedings, and regulatory proceedings at a major medical defence organisation.

1

Introduction: Doctors and their crimes

CLARE GERADA AND ZAID AL-NAJJAR

Doctors hold a unique position. They are invited into the most private aspects of people's lives, entrusted with their bodies, secrets, and often their survival. When doctors abuse this power, the consequences can be devastating. This book examines those rare yet disturbing cases in which doctors misuse their authority to commit crimes. The authors, who have spent decades working as general practitioners, expert witnesses, and advocates for doctors in difficulty, share their insights. We have cared for thousands of medical professionals, including some who, due to illness, have engaged in criminal behaviour, and others whose criminal acts have led to mental breakdowns. We have seen good doctors ruin themselves through serious lapses in judgement, and dishonest doctors conceal their misconduct until it can no longer be hidden.

Entering medicine requires not only academic excellence but also an impeccable behavioural record. Individuals with a criminal past rarely succeed in entering medicine; criminality and medicine are seen as fundamentally incompatible. Less than half of 1% of doctors in the United Kingdom have a criminal conviction, compared with roughly 16% of the general population. Most of these doctors receive convictions for driving offences.

But even these small figures translate into real numbers: in 2020, about 1,500 practising doctors had criminal records, including convictions for violence, sexual offences, manslaughter, and even child abuse imagery.

Their motives differ, as do the personal vulnerabilities and psychological factors that contribute to their behaviour. Yet all share one common feature: the abuse of power.

Our aim in writing *Doctors and Their Crimes* is not to sensationalise but to understand: why do a small number of doctors stray so far from their professional ideals?

DOI: 10.1201/9781003781066-1

In these pages, we explore various forms of misconduct, from dishonesty and fraud to sexual offences and, in the most serious cases, murder and manslaughter. We investigate the psychological roots, systemic pressures, and personal vulnerabilities involved. We hear from doctors who have faced sanctions or imprisonment and analyse how this affects their lives. We also consider the impact on their victims. Most importantly, we examine how the qualities that make medicine a noble profession, its intimacy, authority, and promise of healing, can, under certain circumstances, become the conditions that cause harm.

THE ARCHETYPE OF THE HEALER AND ITS SHADOW

The doctor–patient relationship is more than just a transactional interaction; it holds symbolic significance and serves as an archetype that has endured for thousands of years, recognised across all cultures and ethnicities. The healer archetype, in its ideal form, represents skill, wisdom, compassion, and a commitment to relieve suffering. However, every archetype has a shadow. The Swiss psychologist Carl Jung observed that the brighter the light of an archetype, the darker its shadow becomes, as it contains the repressed, destructive aspects of the personality lurking beneath the surface. For doctors, this shadow can appear as arrogance, a desire for control, or an exaggerated sense of superiority. If left unchecked, it can interfere with communication, undermine patient autonomy, and lead to serious misconduct.

Some of the most powerful forces in medicine operate unseen. The British psychiatrist and psychotherapist, renowned for his work on therapeutic communities, Dr Thomas Main, described the "unconscious phantasy" between doctor and patient: the patient yearns for healing, even to be rescued from death; the doctor may be unconsciously or consciously drawn to the power of being the one who can save or harm. The doctor might seem motivated to care, whilst secretly gaining emotional satisfaction from dependence, admiration, or the subtle fear they evoke in their patient. For some, these unconscious motives can go even deeper. Medicine offers access to intense human experiences such as suffering and dying, and for some individuals, these are not seen as a privilege but a temptation to exploit. The chance to control or even create these moments can be highly seductive. As a result, a doctor's public image may appear altruistic, but privately, they might be driven by a need for dominance or constant validation of their importance, or a sense of mastery over uncertainty. These motivations are seldom recognised. It may only be after a boundary is crossed, a law is broken, or a patient is harmed that the doctor and those around them begin to see the hidden forces shaping their behaviour.

Literature has explored this theme. In Jules Romano's 1923 satirical play *Knock ou le Triomphe de la médecine*, Dr Knock persuades the healthy residents of a village that they are all ill, medicalising everyday life for profit and influence. The work satirises both medical ambition and public complicity. It is hard not to see echoes of this in many of the doctors in this book, whose motives may have included the pathological transformation of the healthy into the dying (Hurwitz, 2015).

The misuse of medical authority is not limited to the past, notorious outliers, or specific specialities. It can happen wherever the patient's needs align with the doctor's opportunity for misuse. The white coat, the surgical mask, the doctor's reassuring voice can conceal exploitation just as easily as they can show compassion.

OUR APPROACH

Writing this book has been challenging and painful. As doctors, we cannot ignore the impact of these stories. They evoke deep shame and personal discomfort as they reveal members of our profession, people who trained with us, swore similar oaths, and worked alongside us, betraying everything that our profession represents. Even if their offences are rare, the harm to the profession's reputation is considerable, affecting all of us who practise. We have had to revisit distressing, sometimes tragic cases that are always complex. In doing so, we are reminded that doctors are human, flawed, fallible, and sometimes fatally compromised.

The research for this book draws on information readily available from public sources, as well as our experiences with patients who have attended our service. When necessary, details have been altered, but the core of each case remains accurate.

Categorising the crimes in this book has often been challenging. Many of the crimes we highlight cross different areas of criminal activity: an assault resulting in death could be seen as manslaughter, just as a repeated poisoner might be classified amongst serial killers. This ambiguity serves as a reminder that human behaviour rarely fits neatly into categories. Motives overlap, boundaries become blurred, and the line between healer and criminal is never as clear-cut as we might wish.

We have not discussed crimes committed as part of wartime atrocities.

This book has been written with the medical profession in mind, although we have made it accessible in language to lay audiences.

We have not included cases where the doctor has obtained a criminal record without directly abusing their position as a medical professional. For example, theft, drink-driving, or being convicted of assault outside the doctor–patient relationship are not covered.

The book, whilst involving cases drawn from around the world, focuses mainly on UK (NHS) policy, practices, and regulation.

REFERENCE

Hurwitz, B. (2015). Medical humanities and medical alterity in fiction and in life. *Journal of Medical Ethics*, *41*(1), 64–67. https://doi.org/10.1136/medethics-2014-102300

2

Murder: Harold "Fred" Shipman

CLARE GERADA

KNOWING WHERE TO START

Knowing where to begin a book about doctors and their crimes isn't simple. It's not due to a lack of cases; quite the opposite. From Victorian poisoners like Dr William Palmer, the first person convicted of murder by strychnine, to more recent doctors who assaulted patients for pleasure, medicine has always had a dark side. One might start with the most gruesome, such as Marcel Petiot, named *The Butcher of Paris,* or with those who are egotistically brazen, like American neurosurgeon Christopher Duntsch, one of many doctors in this book dubbed "Dr Death" for the destruction he caused in the operating theatre. Some, like Dr Thomas Cream, were hanged for their crimes; he was the last person publicly executed in Britain. Others received multiple life sentences, such as American oncologist Dr Farid Fata, who fabricated cancer diagnoses to defraud insurers and subjected healthy people to unnecessary chemotherapy. Or Dr Swango, who, if he pleaded guilty, exchanged the death penalty for life imprisonment. He murdered colleagues, patients, and even friends. All these doctors, and many more, feature in this book. However, we have chosen to start with the case that most profoundly shaped our professional careers: Dr Harold Frederick Shipman, known as "Fred," possibly the most prolific serial killer in peacetime history. Shipman transformed British medicine to such an extent that in 2004, Dr Richard Smith, editor of the *British Medical Journal*, wrote in Shipman's obituary:

> Few doctors have left as enduring a mark on British medicine as Harold Shipman. The scope of his influence and legacy is beyond measure.

Dr Harold "Fred" Shipman (1946–2004) was the general practitioner (GP) whom everyone admired. One relative of a patient he was to murder said that being accepted onto his list was "like winning the lottery. He went above and

DOI: 10.1201/9781003781066-2

beyond, making home visits at night even when he could use a GP deputising service, rarely taking holidays, and seldom employing locums. His patients valued him so highly that even after his crimes were exposed and his victims' bodies were being exhumed, they sent him cards, flowers, money, and letters of support. Once in practice, Shipman quickly rose through the ranks of general practice, taking on roles in both local and national leadership. These positions granted him influence and a degree of protection, allowing him to continue killing without arousing suspicion. He was seen as authoritative, knowledgeable, and trustworthy. For decades, no one suspected that he might be murdering his patients.

When Shipman was practising his deadly skills, I was starting my career as a GP in South London. In 1996, as part of my duties, I became a special adviser to the Department of Health, responsible for improving how doctors managed controlled drugs such as morphine, diamorphine, and pethidine. The role placed me at the intersection of policy and practice. That is why, in early 2000, a pink A4 folder marked "confidential" was placed on my desk. Inside were Shipman's prescribing records. By then, he had been convicted of 15 murders and the forgery of Mrs Grundy's will, although the full scale of his crimes was still unknown. I was not the first, nor the last, to review his prescriptions, but my review was part of the process leading to the Public Inquiry.

What I discovered was alarming.

It wasn't just the quantity of drugs he prescribed but also their type and potency. I was familiar with controlled drugs, not only through my role at the Department of Health but also because I now led a service for patients who used heroin. I had seen first-hand how my drug-using patients could acquire large amounts of drugs on the black market, some diverted from unscrupulous prescribing doctors. I knew that these patients could consume doses far higher than non-drug users due to their tolerance. However, nothing prepared me for what I saw. Shipman's prescribing was extraordinary. He preferred to prescribe high-strength opiates, especially diamorphine. He would prescribe dozens of 30 mg or 100 mg ampoules of diamorphine to a single patient, which are exceedingly high doses even for those with pancreatic cancer, and few of his patients were terminally ill. For one patient, he prescribed 1,000 mg of diamorphine daily for 10 days. These quantities are staggering and would typically be needed in a hospice. He also personally collected these medications from the pharmacist, claiming he would deliver them himself to his patients. Even without hindsight, these prescribing patterns should have raised concerns. The problem was that dispensing pharmacists were so focused on ensuring the prescriptions met legal requirements (such as being written correctly, with the dose spelt out in words and figures, and properly dated) that they overlooked whether the medicines themselves were clinically appropriate. Kay Roberts, a pharmacy expert who later testified at the Public Inquiry, noted that it was a classic case of not seeing the wood for the trees.

As it turned out, Shipman had been systematically prescribing large quantities of these drugs, often collecting unused ampoules from patients' homes after their deaths or not delivering them at all, and stockpiling them to kill. This kind of deception defined Shipman's career. His skill in manipulating those around him, both professionally and personally, enabled him to carry out his murders unnoticed for three decades.

EARLY LIFE

To understand how he became the most prolific serial killer in modern history, it might be helpful to examine the influences that shaped him, from his early years in a working-class family in Nottingham to his marriage to Primrose and, subsequently, to his work as a GP.

Shipman was a baby boomer, born on the Bestwood Council Estate in Nottingham on 14 January 1946. He was the second son among three children, and his father was a truck driver. Both his parents were devout Methodists. He was raised amidst echoes of the Second World War. Nottingham had suffered extensive damage from German bombs, and rationing continued until he was ten. He grew up in a loving, close-knit family home. His mother had high aspirations for the brightest (and the favourite) of her three children, hoping he would be the first in their family to attend university. She died of lung cancer when Fred was only 17. Much later, people speculated that witnessing her dying and seeing her receive morphine to ease her pain led him to imitate this method of killing. However, many doctors have experienced personal trauma, and for some, this influenced their decision to pursue medicine. But, unlike Shipman, they became caring healers, not killers.

The young Shipman excelled academically and athletically. He passed the crucial 11-plus exam and, after completing his grammar school education, studied medicine at Leeds University. He qualified in 1970 and became fully registered in 1971. His medical training appeared routine, and there were no early concerns about his patient care. Although hints that he might have misused pethidine as a medical student emerged much later, nothing suspicious was evident at the time. Shipman met his wife, Primrose, on a bus during his first year at medical school. She was 17 and became pregnant within a few months of their meeting. They married shortly afterwards, and once he qualified as a GP, she embodied the typical general practitioner's wife. She drove him on home visits, answered the phone when he was out, helped as a part-time receptionist at the surgery, and managed the practice accounts. She was devoted to him and remained loyal until the very end, visiting him daily in jail and being the first to arrive and the last to leave during his trial. She never believed her husband was guilty, and until compelled by police, she did not reveal the contents of the large box of trinkets, jewellery, and personal effects Shipman had collected from his victims. To many relatives' dismay, she was never questioned under oath. Although police sought to interview her, her lawyer stated she would only agree to questioning if she were arrested, which never happened. When asked questions after the trial, she said she "couldn't remember" or "wasn't sure" about what had happened. As one senior officer remarked, "Primrose has been in denial since the beginning, and it hasn't changed."

TODMORDEN AND PETHIDINE ADDICTION

After finishing his house jobs, Shipman became a GP at Abraham Ormerod Medical Centre in Todmorden, Yorkshire, where he became the junior partner. As he had during his house jobs at Pontefract, he made a positive impression on patients and colleagues. He worked diligently, took on extra responsibilities such as managing controlled drugs, and fully engaged in general practice. Everything seemed to go well until, just over a year into his role, concerns arose about the recording of pethidine. At that time, it was common for practices to keep reasonable stocks of strong painkillers for use during home visits or occasionally for patients on the practice premises. The legal requirement then (as now) was for the practice to maintain a controlled drug register recording each new supply and each administration to patients. Practices were also required to store these drugs in a locked cabinet unless they were being taken out to administer them at a patient's home.

In June 1975, a routine inspection by a Home Office inspector at a wholesale supplier uncovered significant drug shipments to Boots Pharmacy in Todmorden. During the visit, the inspector examined the drug register and discovered that most of the drugs had been supplied to Dr Shipman. When he interviewed the doctors at the practice, Shipman claimed ignorance to explain the discrepancy between the drugs received and those administered. He said he did not know how to record medication use for patients but denied any misconduct. This explanation seemed plausible, as later, when I supervised improvements in how controlled drugs were monitored, a common mistake by practices was failing to record drug receipts and disposals accurately. The practice was warned and told that the inspector would continue to monitor them to prevent recurrence. However, a few months later, one of the partners noticed an invoice indicating the practice had again purchased large quantities of pethidine ampoules, ostensibly for surgical stock, none of which had been recorded as "received" in the practice's drugs register.

When confronted, Shipman admitted to using the drug himself, offered his resignation, which was accepted, and was reported to the police.

He was to spend 3 months at a residential treatment service, The Retreat in York.

He admitted to the police that he was injecting pethidine every 2 to 3 hours up to 700 mg per day, which is a massive amount considering the standard dose is only around 50 mg. He said he used it to combat depression. Besides using supplies from the surgery, he also told the police that he obtained drugs by signing prescriptions in patients' names and forging staff signatures at a local nursing home, making it seem as if they had authorised the collection of prescriptions, which he used for himself. At the time, his treating psychiatrist noted how depressed he was, with Shipman expressing very negative comments about himself, saying he felt like a complete failure in his personal and professional life and *believing that he should be in prison for punishment, not in a hospital for treatment.*

This was prophetic, considering what was to follow later.

Shipman was to plead guilty to eight offences of unlawful possession of pethidine. At his trial, he also requested that a further 74 offences be considered, all relating to the fraudulent acquisition of drugs. His legal team obtained two psychiatric assessments, one of which was by a forensic psychiatrist. Both reports were very favourable, stating that his drug use was not so deeply rooted as to cause dependency, that he had insight, had sought treatment, and would seek appropriate help if he became depressed again. Shipman also wrote to the magistrate, confirming he had no intention of returning to general practice or work in a setting where he could access supplies of pethidine. He was to break both of these assurances. Given the testimonials and his contrition, Shipman avoided a custodial sentence and was fined.

As was standard practice, the General Medical Council (GMC) was informed of his criminal charges, and they had to decide what sanction, if any, to impose. Before reaching a decision, they gathered evidence and reports from those familiar with Shipman: employers, colleagues, and psychiatrists. All reports reached the same conclusion: Shipman had undergone treatment, had good insight, was now well, and posed minimal risk of reoffending. He received a warning letter (the lowest of all possible sanctions) and was permitted to continue practising without restrictions, including no limitations on his ability to prescribe controlled drugs. His prognosis was regarded as favourable, and the treating psychiatrist stated that the chances of relapse into *drug dependence or anything similar* were low. One suspects this doctor never thought *anything similar* would include murder. At the time, the psychiatrist informed the GMC committee that "as far as I am concerned, Dr Shipman is extremely well, and it would be to his advantage if he were allowed to continue practising, and conversely, it would be catastrophic if he were not."

Much later, during the Public Inquiry into the Shipman case, Dame Janet Smith, its chair, criticised the GMC's response to Shipman's addiction. Her recommendations, which followed the inquiry, transformed how the GMC managed doctors with health issues. This included the authority to impose specific conditions on the doctor, such as regular monitoring, hair or urine tests, reports from treating and supervising psychiatrists, and, if relevant, reports from their workplace supervisors. This supervision would continue for at least 5 years. At any time, the doctor could have their licence to practise revoked, either temporarily or permanently, if they failed to comply.

During his time at Todmorden, Shipman signed 22 death certificates, more than double the amount of the next highest partner, with suspicions that at least six (including three who died on the same day) were questionable.

DONNEYBROOK PRACTICE

> I remember the time [he] gave to my Dad. He would come around at the drop of a hat. He was a marvellous GP, apart from the fact that he killed my father.
>
> (Rudol C, Barkham, P. The Shipman report. *The Times*, 20 July 2002).

In 1977, after a brief period working again as a hospital doctor, Shipman became a GP partner at Donneybrook House in Hyde, Greater Manchester. The practice was aware of his prior history but, on the advice of the Home Office and the GMC, was reassured that he could practise without any restrictions.

At Donneybrook, Shipman again earned a reputation for being diligent and was well-liked by his patients. He spent 14 years at this practice. It was estimated that he murdered at least 71 patients while working there, with a further 30 suspicious deaths.

In January 1992, Shipman left Donneybrook to become a sole practitioner at a nearby practice. This was an unusual decision, especially as the trend in general practice was shifting from small, individual clinics to group practices. He cited several reasons for his departure: a dislike of the new computer system the practice was adopting, and a desire to avoid managing budgets for patient care, which GPs were beginning to be encouraged to take on. Regardless of his stated reasons, working alone reduced the risk of other doctors discovering his overprescribing and the pattern of his patients' deaths. His new practice prospered, his list grew, and he continued to build a reputation as an attentive and compassionate doctor. His popularity increased, particularly because he was willing to make home visits to elderly patients.

At the Inquiry, Paul Spencer, a patient whose signature he forged on the will of his last victim, stated,

> I genuinely thought he was a great doctor, very intelligent. I went to see him with different things, and he always had time to talk... there was a year-long wait to get onto his list: he was the most popular doctor in Hyde.

THE WHISTLE IS BLOWN (BUT NOT HEARD)

In March 1998, unease began to stir across the road from Shipman's surgery.

Dr Linda Reynolds, a GP at the neighbouring practice, noticed something unusual. Like most doctors in Hyde, she signed cremation forms for colleagues – a routine courtesy to prevent delays for grieving families if doctors from further afield needed to sign the necessary paperwork. Usually, it involved a brief phone call: a quick chat about the patient's medical history, the cause of death, and other relevant details. Shipman, however, handled things differently. He would arrive in person, medical records under his arm, and give detailed, lengthy accounts of his patients' final days. His thoroughness seemed excessive, almost rehearsed, as if he wanted to eliminate any doubt before it could even arise. However, what disturbed Dr Reynolds was the sheer number of forms she was asked to sign, 16 in just 3 months. In comparison, her own practice, with a patient list more than three times as large, recorded only 15 deaths during the same period. The pattern was too obvious to ignore.

For the first time, someone was openly questioning what many in Hyde had whispered about but never dared confront: why were so many of Harold Shipman's patients dying?

Other details heightened her unease. Every one of Shipman's victims appeared to share the same profile: older women, often living alone, whose deaths were attributed to strokes or heart disease. Strangely, many of them died in Shipman's presence or were found lifeless shortly after he had left their homes.

For most GPs, an occasional unexpected death at home was part of the job, especially in deprived communities where patients often did not have landlines and emergency help was not always easy to summon. After more than a decade in practice, Dr Reynolds was no stranger to such events. But even considering these factors, the numbers didn't add up. When she raised her concerns with her partners, their reaction left her more unsettled. They, too, had noticed the unusual death rate among his patients, but they brushed it aside, attributing it to his caseload, which mainly consisted of elderly patients. To Dr Reynolds, the pattern seemed to be something far more sinister.

Eventually, Dr Reynolds raised her concerns beyond her practice. She contacted the local coroner, who then passed her worries to the police. A covert investigation was launched. To avoid any hint of scandal, a fellow GP, Dr Alan Banks, was asked to discreetly review the notes of seventeen of Shipman's recent deaths. It was merely a paperwork exercise. Dr Banks never spoke to families, never visited their homes, and never questioned the circumstances of those deaths. The police also held back, wary of causing alarm. After all, Harold Shipman was not just any doctor in Hyde. By that time, he had established a reputation as a respected senior figure, a leader within the local medical community. To suggest that he might be killing his patients was unthinkable.

Dr Reynolds was not the only one to notice something strange. Around the same time, local undertaker Alan Massey started to feel uneasy. He, too, had observed Shipman's patients dying at an unusually high rate, but it was not just the frequency that troubled him; it was the way the bodies were found. Time and again, when Massey arrived to collect the deceased, the scene looked eerily similar. The patient would be fully clothed, often seated neatly in a chair or reclining on a sofa, as if sleep had overtaken them mid-afternoon. The scene was too tidy, too consistent. In Massey's experience, this was not how people usually died. Those with terminal illnesses typically pass away in their beds, often surrounded by signs of decline: syringe drivers, pill bottles, commodes, dressings, and the silent witness of their suffering. Families were usually at the bedside. Sudden deaths also had their own familiar signs: a body found on the floor after a collapse, or in bed following a final heart attack during the night, or sometimes in the bathroom. What he did not expect, what felt profoundly unnatural, was this repeated pattern of women, fully dressed, upright in their chairs, as though death had tapped them on the shoulder while they sat comfortably in their living room.

Alan Massey, uneasy about what he perceived as the strange pattern of deaths, decided not to approach the coroner or the police. Instead, he arranged a routine appointment at Shipman's surgery, and when the time came, he expressed his concerns directly to him, saying,

> "We seem to be getting a lot of deaths of elderly ladies," he said carefully. "Fully clothed, sat up, or just back from shopping. It seems strange."

Shipman's response was swift. He rose, moved across the room, and retrieved the heavy death register from his cupboard. Flipping through its pages, he pointed to names as if the book and the record of the deaths themselves proved innocence. He then confidently told Massey that there was nothing to worry about, saying, "*Anybody can see this book.*"

The message was clear: everything was in order, all deaths had been properly recorded, and nothing was amiss. Massey left the surgery not entirely convinced but also not ready to push further. Shipman had projected an air of authority, reassurance. Who was he, an undertaker, to challenge the word of a senior doctor?

Meanwhile, the report commissioned by the police into the 17 deaths found that there was nothing that *could support allegations of impropriety.* No further action was taken, and the case was subsequently dropped.

Shipman's reputation stayed intact. Yet his patients continued to die.

The circle of unease widened even further. John Shaw, a local taxi driver, began noticing something odd. Many of his regular fares, older women who depended on him for trips to appointments, shopping, or visits with friends, were dying suddenly, and nearly all of them were patients of Dr Shipman.

By now, the deaths had established a pattern. On average, Shipman was killing one person every week. It was a steady, relentless cycle, hidden in plain sight and masked by his reputation as a dedicated family doctor. However, even a predator can sense when the chase has attracted too much attention. For several months, he slowed his pace, perhaps realising how close he had come to exposure after Dr Reynolds' warnings (which he had gained knowledge of), Massey's suspicions, and Shaw's observations. But the pause was temporary. Within weeks, Shipman reverted to his old routine, and this time, it was the death of Kathleen Grundy that finally shattered the veil of professional trust and community respect that had protected him for so long.

THE WHISTLE IS BLOWN (AND HEARD LOUD AND CLEAR)

On 24 June 1998, the body of Kathleen Grundy was found in her tidy red-brick house in Hyde, Greater Manchester. The former mayoress was 81 but still sprightly. She was known locally for her intellect and tireless community work. She had been seen only the day before, well-dressed, walking down the main high street, seeming her usual self. Friends were concerned when she didn't attend a planned luncheon and went to her home, horrified to find her slumped in an armchair, obviously dead. They contacted Dr Harold Shipman, who arrived within minutes. Calm, courteous, and reassuring, he briefly examined the body before declaring life extinct. He explained there was no need for further investigation. He recorded the cause of death as "old age" and left the house.

It may have ended there as just another quiet passing in a northern town, except that, days later, a solicitor opened a handwritten will leaving nearly all of Kathleen Grundy's estate to Dr Shipman himself. That single document would spark a police investigation that uncovered not only a forged will but also one of the most prolific murder sprees in modern history. The will awarded Shipman a substantial inheritance of £400,000. Grundy's daughter, Angela Woodruff, a solicitor, raised the alarm and contacted the police. Shipman's crimes began to unravel. Grundy's body was exhumed in August 1998, and a post-mortem revealed she had died from a lethal dose of morphine administered within hours of her death. Once suspicion fell on Shipman, the process of uncovering his deception moved swiftly. The will left to him was shown to be a crude forgery, with a blatant imitation of her signature, and the document was marked with his fingerprints. It had also been typed on Shipman's own typewriter, a coincidence he tried to dismiss by claiming Mrs Grundy had borrowed it, along with the pen used to sign her name.

When the net began to tighten, Shipman tried to cover his tracks. After the exhumation order for Kathleen Grundy's body but before his arrest, he altered her medical records, both paper and electronic. In them, he inserted a new story: that the 81-year-old former Mayoress of Hyde was an intravenous drug user. It was a grotesque fabrication, designed to explain the morphine that would inevitably be found in her body. To the police, he later insisted there was a serious drug problem in Hyde, which was true enough, and that Mrs Grundy might have been a secret heroin addict. But there were no morphine vials or syringes in her home, no hidden paraphernalia tucked away in drawers, no needle marks on her arms. The autopsy revealed none of the telltale signs of long-term drug use. Hair analysis showed no trace of opiate abuse. The claim was as desperate as it was insulting, an attempt to blacken the reputation of a respected widow to protect his own. For those who knew Kathleen Grundy, and for any doctor with even passing experience of drug addiction, the idea was absurd. Yet it revealed something chilling about Shipman: the arrogance to believe that his word alone, as a doctor, might still carry more weight than all the evidence stacked against him.

Mrs Grundy's death led to a police investigation into other fatalities. Nine bodies were exhumed and found to contain significant and lethal levels of morphine. One body was exhumed in Malta; the patient had died in Manchester but was buried on the Island. None of those exhumed had died of natural causes. The police searched Shipman's home, and upon entering, they were shocked by the chaos. One officer remarked it was a place where you wiped your feet on the way out, not on the way in. The house was filthy, with grill pans covered in thick bacon fat, dirty dishes piled in the sink, and carpets so grime-coated that visitors' shoes stuck to them. Inside his home, the police found containers of medical records, many stored in the garage or kept in Kleenex boxes, along with large quantities of ampoules of diamorphine.

On 7 September 1998, Greater Manchester Police moved in.

Police Officers arrived at his surgery on Market Street, Hyde, and arrested Shipman on suspicion of murdering 14 patients between March 1995 and July 1998, as well as on suspicion of fraud. The family doctor, the man who delivered babies, comforted the sick, and signed many death certificates, was taken away in handcuffs.

The criminal investigations revealed a clear pattern in Shipman's behaviour. His victims were mainly women over 65. His method involved planning visits to patients' homes, sometimes arranged in advance but often unplanned, under the guise of routine checks such as blood tests or blood pressure readings. In many cases, he falsely told relatives that the deceased had requested a home visit, a claim contradicted by surgery records showing no such request. On three occasions, he fabricated statements claiming the patients had called his surgery complaining of chest pains, which was easily disproved by telephone records indicating no such calls. Shipman never attempted resuscitation nor sought help, even when the patient was believed to have become unwell in his surgery, where staff would have been available to assist. When patients appeared unwell at their homes, he never called 999, even though he claimed to have done so in some cases. He advised relatives against post-mortems for their deceased loved ones, even though all the deaths, being sudden and unexpected, should have been referred to the coroner, who would then decide.

Harold Shipman had been an integral part of Hyde, a reassuring presence in his smart suit, carrying his doctor's bag from door to door.

THE TRIAL

On 5 October 1999, Harold Shipman's trial commenced at Preston Crown Court, the so-called "Old Bailey of the North." The world's press flocked to the scene, their cameras and notebooks focused not only on the accused but also on the broader implications of the case.

For me, it was not something I could observe with detached curiosity. Shipman was one of us, a general practitioner accused of betraying the most sacred trust in medicine. His crimes cast a long shadow over the entire profession. It felt as though every GP in the country now bore a measure of his guilt.

At the time, I was advising the Department of Health and serving on the Council of the Royal College of General Practitioners, the professional body representing GPs in the UK. Shipman had never been a member of the College, but that detail hardly mattered. In the public eye, his stethoscope was ours; his consulting room, a reflection of ours. We all felt tainted.

Shipman pleaded not guilty to the fifteen murders and to forging the will.

At the trial, opening the prosecution case, Richard Henriques QC said of Shipman:

> The defendant killed these fifteen people because he enjoyed doing so. He exercised the ultimate power of controlling life and death and repeated it so often that he must have found the drama of taking life to his taste.

In the weeks that followed, Preston Crown Court hosted an extraordinary procession of witnesses. Relatives of the deceased stood alongside experts in medicine, pharmacy, and toxicology, each contributing to the unravelling of Shipman's crimes. Over a hundred witnesses were called for the prosecution. For the defence, there were only two: a fingerprint expert and Shipman himself.

The evidence against him was overwhelming, although all circumstantial, as he had never been seen killing any patient. A receptionist from his practice recalled a specific day when a 62-year-old patient came for an appointment. This patient was never to leave alive. The receptionist described how Shipman continued seeing three other patients while the other one lay dead in his treatment room. When he finally emerged, he looked flushed and unsettled. To the police, he later claimed she had died of natural causes whilst an ECG was being conducted. However, the post-mortem revealed a different story: a lethal injection of morphine. Shipman had dismissed her as a "*nuisance patient.*"

When Shipman stepped into the witness box, he was no longer the confident figure who had sat impassively through weeks of evidence. Reporters described him as a shadow of the man he once appeared to be, his voice thin, his manner subdued, so much so that the judge had to ask him more than once to speak up.

For 5 days, he testified, denying every charge. Case by case, he dismissed the deaths as natural, coincidences, or misunderstandings. He showed no flicker of doubt in his own innocence, nor any concession to the mountain of evidence against him.

The cross-examination lasted a gruelling 7 days. Patiently, relentlessly, Henriques put the facts to him. "*You had both the means and the opportunity to kill Kathleen Grundy, didn't you?*" he asked.

Shipman's reply was flat: "*I don't think I did, and I didn't.*"

But when questioned about the six missing ampoules of diamorphine, part of a box of ten prescribed for a patient who had died and were later recovered from his own home, Shipman could not explain. He denied, denied, denied. His stance remained unchanged throughout. He was resolute, even when faced with evidence that was overwhelming to everyone else.

Shipman's defence rested on a single, fragile line of attack: the unreliability of toxicology. His barrister, Miss Nicola Davies QC, told the jury that the entire case against him stood on one foundation stone, and that stone could not be trusted. "*The prosecution's case is built on toxicology,*" she said. "*Without that, there is no case.*"

It was a tactic with echoes of an earlier era. In the nineteenth century, Victorian poisoners often avoided conviction by exploiting gaps in forensic science, claiming that chemical tests were too primitive and ambiguous to prove guilt beyond doubt. Shipman's defence employed the same approach more than a century later, trying to create just enough doubt among twelve jurors. But this was not the 1850s. Forensic toxicology had progressed, and in Shipman's case, the evidence was unequivocally clear. Repeatedly, the findings indicated morphine overdoses, lethal doses given to patients with no medical need for the drug.

When the summing-up concluded, the jury of seven men and five women retired to deliberate. For 6 days, the nation waited. Then, on 31 January 2000, the court reconvened. The press benches were packed, the public gallery filled, and a tense silence fell as the foreman of the jury rose to speak. The verdicts were unanimous: guilty on fifteen counts of murder and one of forgery.

Shipman stood on the dock flanked by two prison officers. He did not flinch. He showed no emotion, no crack in the mask he had worn throughout. Beside him in the gallery, his wife Primrose sat dressed head to toe in black, as unreadable as her husband. Their sons, one seated at her side, the other just behind, lowered their eyes to the floor, avoiding the gaze of the world.

On that day, 31 January 2000, Harold Shipman, GP of Hyde, the family doctor with the black bag and calm bedside manner, was uncovered as Britain's most prolific serial killer.

After the jury delivered its verdicts, Mr Justice Forbes turned to address the man in the dock. His words were measured but impactful.

> You have finally been brought to justice by this jury's verdict. You murdered every one of your victims in cold blood. You took advantage of your position and grossly abused the trust of your patients. You were, after all, their doctor. I have little doubt that many of your victims smiled and thanked you as they submitted to your deadly ministrations.

Following that, he received fifteen life sentences for murder and a further 4 years for forging Kathleen Grundy's will.

Shipman's removal from the medical profession that once protected him was quick and anticlimactic. The General Medical Council held a special session; his name was erased from the register, and he was never to return.

On 13 January 2004, the day before his 58th birthday, Harold Shipman was found dead in his cell at Wakefield prison, having taken his own life. The man who had earned the trust of a community, only to betray it in the most chilling way imaginable, had chosen to end his story on his own terms. His suicide sparked public and political debate, mainly because it deprived victims' families of further answers and denied them potential insights into his motives.

Shipman is not the only UK doctor to be accused of murdering his patients. When news of Shipman's murders became public, many people thought of Dr John Bodkin Adams (1899–1983), a GP from Eastbourne, who in 1957 faced trial for killing one of his patients. Rumours circulated that he had murdered many more, using morphine to "*ease the passing*" of elderly patients. The similarities with Shipman are striking, and it is hard to imagine that Shipman was unaware of Adams. Adams was said to have inherited money, jewellery, cars, and antiques, from at least 132 patients, many of whom died soon after altering their wills. Yet, at his sensational Old Bailey trial, he was acquitted. He claimed simply to be relieving suffering, and the prosecution made the fatal error of bringing only one case to trial. With Shipman, the police avoided that mistake. They pursued multiple charges, ensuring that the weight of evidence could not be dismissed.

Shipman's crimes were so grave that a Public Inquiry was unavoidable, and it is this Inquiry that forms the basis of the next chapter.

REFERENCES

Shipman Inquiry. (n.d.) https://www.the-shipman-inquiry.org.uk/bg_chronology.asp

Whittle, B., and Ritchie, J. (2009) *Harold Shipman – Prescription for Murder: The True Story of Dr Harold Frederick Shipman*. Hachette.

3

The Public Inquiry and its aftermath

CLARE GERADA

In 2001, the Public Inquiry following Shipman's trial took place in the grand Victorian setting of Manchester Town Hall, with its vaulted ceilings and carved stone pillars lending an air of gravity to each session. In that imposing chamber, Dame Janet Smith and Professor Esmail, a GP in Manchester (Esmail, 2005), presided from an elevated table, a visible manifestation of the moral weight of their task: to uncover how a family doctor had managed to kill so many, undetected for so long (Shipman Inquiry, 2002).

The Inquiry looked beyond Harold Shipman's murders to broader issues such as professionalism, general practice, the doctor–patient relationship, and the healthcare systems in which he worked. His crimes forced the medical profession, especially GPs, to confront a distressing truth: the core qualities of good general practice, continuity, autonomy, and trust, could, in rare and tragic cases, be manipulated to cause harm. The Inquiry's work uncovered cultural blind spots within the profession and demonstrated how patterns of deference, professional courtesy, and an almost instinctive hesitation to suspect foul play sustained these problems.

The Inquiry investigated four main areas (https://webarchive.nationalarchives.gov.uk/ukgwa/20090808155123/http://www.the-shipman-inquiry.org.uk/bg_termsofref.asp):

1. The extent of Shipman's unlawful activities.
2. The actions taken by statutory bodies and other organisations involved in the procedures and investigations following the deaths of Shipman's patients.
3. The performance of statutory bodies and other organisations responsible for monitoring primary care provision and the use of controlled drugs.
4. What measures should be implemented to safeguard patients in the future.

DOI: 10.1201/9781003781066-3

From 2001 to 2005, the Inquiry carefully examined every aspect of Shipman's story. They investigated his methods, potential motives, and the systemic failures that protected him, interviewing or obtaining statements from hundreds of individuals, organisations, and government bodies. The findings were released gradually, with each report revealing another layer of the tragedy. The first report appeared in 2001, and the final one was published on 27 January 2005. The six reports contained over 100 recommendations covering coroners, controlled drugs, death certification (Dyer, 2004), complaints procedures, appraisal, medical regulation, and monitoring of doctors.

EXTENT OF SHIPMAN'S UNLAWFUL ACTIVITIES

The First Report of the Shipman Inquiry (published in July 2002) concentrated on uncovering what Shipman had done, the facts of his crimes, and how he managed to evade detection for so long.

Amongst these, the most critical "fact" that needed to be established was how many patients Shipman had murdered (*The Shipman Inquiry. First Report. Death Disguised*, 2002). The task of determining this was assigned to Professor Richard Baker, who reviewed all patient records from 1974 to 1998 where Shipman had signed death certificates. This was an enormous task, requiring him to sift through hospital and general practice records, both paper and electronic (Baker, 2001; Ramsay, 2001). Based on Baker's findings, suspicious deaths were then investigated by the police. Where possible, witnesses provided statements, but many of the deceased had no witnesses, given the time elapsed since their deaths. Professor Baker's findings were almost unfathomable: at least 215 people were killed over nearly three decades, the first on 17 March 1975 and the last in June 1998.

The numbers were uneven, with troughs when Shipman lay low and spikes when his confidence presumably surged, but the pattern was unmistakable (Sibbald, 2001). On average, this amounted to ten killings a year. Between 1990 and 1993, he killed "only" three people, but in 1996, at least 30, and in 1997, at least 37. The times when he was not killing appeared to coincide with near misses with respect to him being discovered. For example, there were no deaths between November 1979 and April 1981, believed to be due to Shipman's failure in his attempt to kill a patient. After informing the daughter that her mother was dead and that no post-mortem was necessary, the patient, Alice Gorton, let out a loud groan, though she died a few days later, never having regained consciousness. Shipman had, in essence, proclaimed her to be dead when she was in fact still alive.

A patient, Mr Kenneth Smith was one of the few men Shipman murdered. Shipman visited Mr Smith at his home, and he then died suddenly at 3 pm, with only Shipman present. Shipman recorded the cause of death as a heart attack, and although he was there according to his records, he did not call 999. Decades later, a local window cleaner, who had cleaned Mr Smith's windows for 8 years, testified to the Inquiry as to how shocked he was to hear of the death, having seen Mr Smith a few days earlier, looking fit and well whilst fixing an outside fence. Many of the witnesses, as with this window cleaner, did not raise concerns at the time.

What was most striking about Baker's analysis was not only the cold arithmetic but also the ordinariness of the settings where the murders took place: living rooms, sitting rooms, front parlours. Victims dressed, seated upright in their chairs, sometimes just back from shopping. Death seemed natural, even mundane, until you looked closely.

The final estimate was that Shipman murdered between 215 and 236 patients. One occurred in Todmorden, West Yorkshire; 71 whilst Shipman worked in Donneybrook, Hyde, Greater Manchester. The remaining victims were killed during his 6 years at the Market Street surgery, also in Hyde (Ashraf, 2002).

Whatever the precise number, this makes Shipman the most prolific serial killer during peacetime (Kinnell, 2000).

Baker estimated that Shipman was 25 times more likely than comparable GPs to be present at the time of death, attending in 20% of cases compared with a norm of 0.8%. Relatives were present at 40% of his patients' deaths, versus 80% for deaths attended by other doctors (Sibbald, 2001).

HOW DID SHIPMAN GET AWAY WITH THE MURDERS?

The first report also investigated how Shipman was able to go unnoticed for such a long time. This is a fair question, considering he had been killing his patients for almost 30 years, and the joking around amongst his staff focused on the high number of deaths amongst his patients. They even nicknamed him "*Dr Death.*"

Detective Inspector Smith, who led the initial investigation, spoke about being blindsided as in

> In all quarters of the civilised world, doctors do not deliberately kill their patients.

This belief allowed Shipman to enter patients' homes unannounced and administer lethal doses of diamorphine without arousing suspicion. He was skilled at covering his tracks, creating fake phone calls or pretending that the patient had requested the visit. His control over the death certification process further protected him from scrutiny, as he often cited plausible causes of death such as heart attacks, old age, or strokes. Relatives rarely questioned him, especially as Shipman, using his authority, discouraged them from requesting post-mortems.

The Inquiry noted that Shipman knew how to manipulate both paper and computerised medical records. The disorganisation of his paper notes, coupled with his often-illegible handwriting, may have been a deliberate tactic to obscure his false additions. He kept records of deceased patients in his garage at home, beyond the reach of routine scrutiny. He understood how to obtain controlled drugs, how to oversupply them, and how to retrieve unused quantities later. He also knew what to say to pharmacists to justify requests for high-strength diamorphine.

Dame Janet Smith concluded that Shipman's reputation as a conscientious and caring doctor, combined with the trust placed in GPs, the lack of scrutiny of death certification, and the absence of effective systems for monitoring unusual death patterns, allowed him to act unchecked for years. It raised concerns about the death certification process, controlled drug record-keeping, and failures in local oversight, all of which she would investigate further in her later reports.

Finally, certain attitudinal beliefs about older people may have led to the concealment of his actions. Deaths amongst the elderly are often seen as unavoidable and are rarely scrutinised. These cultural views possibly contributed to a reduced sense of concern regarding the deaths under Shipman's care.

WHAT LED SHIPMAN TO BECOME A SERIAL KILLER?

Explaining *how* Shipman killed is much easier than explaining *why*. The methods are straightforward: lethal injections of morphine, administered under the guise of medical authority. But the question of motive remains much less clear.

Who was this man who twisted his professional code to become such a killer? What drove this quiet, popular, intelligent, and seemingly kind and capable doctor to commit such heinous acts?

Chapter 4 explores in greater depth the psychology of serial killers, from those who are sadistic and psychopathic, deriving pleasure from suffering, to those for whom murder is less about cruelty than about control.

Some researchers suggest that serial murder may share similarities with addictive behaviour (Ressler et al., 1988). Just as individuals with substance use disorders feel compelled to repeat taking drugs, Shipman may have experienced killing as his *drug of choice*. The repetitive nature of serial murder supports this model: offenders develop a *modus operandi*, a consistent method, and sometimes even a *signature*, a personal hallmark that links their crimes. Shipman's "signature" was staging his victims: dressed, upright, often seated in their living rooms, in the most ordinary surroundings. His relentless work ethic, large patient list, and habit of making house calls at any hour gave him repeated opportunities to kill.

Dame Janet Smith herself explicitly linked Shipman's earlier reliance on pethidine to his subsequent compulsions.

> I think it is likely that whatever it was that caused Shipman to become addicted to pethidine also led to other forms of addictive behaviour... it is possible that he was addicted to killing.

Professor Aneez Esmail, who assisted Dame Janet Smith, echoed this in his article *Physician as Serial Killer – The Shipman Case* (Esmail, 2005):

> *He may have become addicted to killing, experiencing a "buzz" of pleasure from the association with death and the power and control that it gave him.*

Whether viewed as psychopathy, control, or addiction, the unsettling truth is that Shipman's motives may never be fully understood. What is certain is that his murders followed a pattern of compulsion, repetition, method, and signature, more akin to habit than isolated acts of malice.

At least five formal assessments were carried out during Shipman's lifetime, yet their conclusions varied significantly. The first two occurred in the 1970s, after he was charged with theft related to his pethidine misuse. Both were pre-trial reports for the Court. The General Medical Council then commissioned two more assessments to determine whether he was fit to continue practising. Across all four, the findings were primarily unremarkable: depression, drug misuse, but no major psychiatric disorder. Could Shipman have manipulated these assessments? It is possible. He was intelligent, articulate, and would have known how to present himself favourably. However, it stretches credibility to think he could have deceived four different psychiatrists, along with the many professionals overseeing him during his time at the hospital, the York Retreat. The final evaluation occurred in 1998, after his arrest, when Dr Michael Badcock, an experienced forensic psychiatrist, examined him as part of the pre-murder trial proceedings. Badcock's report was the most damning. He described Shipman as exhibiting necrophiliac traits: a sadistic indifference to suffering, an apparent enjoyment in watching his victims die, and perhaps even deriving sexual gratification from the act. He speculated that Shipman's choice of medicine as a career might have been influenced by these tendencies, possibly rooted in the trauma of witnessing his own mother die of cancer during adolescence. By taking lives, Shipman may have sought to reenact that primal scene of loss, this time with himself in control, elevated to a position of absolute authority over life and death.

From his prison cell, Shipman bitterly complained to the General Medical Council (GMC) [the UK medical regulator] about Badcock, accusing him of breaching confidentiality by speaking to the press. Whether or not Badcock's conclusions were correct, the clash highlights a deeper problem: psychiatry could describe Shipman, but it could not truly explain him.

The Inquiry appointed four forensic psychiatrists to assess Shipman. He refused to meet them. They relied on records, testimonies, and third-party accounts to build a profile of the man. They concluded that Shipman's outward confidence, his composure, and his apparent certainty were likely masks for deep insecurity. They suggested he had a personality disorder: enduring patterns of behaviour so rigid and deviant from social norms that they can be harmful. Some went further, proposing that Shipman exhibited pathological narcissism. Narcissists crave admiration, have an exaggerated sense of self-importance, and lack empathy for others. In this context, Shipman's conduct fits all too clearly. He manipulated patients and families, killed without remorse, and saw those who trusted him not as people but as objects or props to feed his sense of power and entitlement. His impassive demeanour during the trial and his refusal to admit guilt reinforced the impression of a man consumed by self-regard. Years later, the release of his private prison letters seemed to confirm this view. In his correspondence, Shipman sought recognition, boasting of himself as a "*medical God*." The phrase revealed what perhaps mattered most to him: not the lives he ended, but the absolute control he wielded over them, and the dominance he claimed over life and death itself.

One of the more charitable theories suggests that Shipman was a misguided mercy killer, releasing older women from the hardship of institutional care or prolonged decline. His senior practice clerk recalled him once saying that "*anybody over seventy was a survivor,*" a phrase some interpret as evidence of his belief that death at home, at his hands, was a form of kindness. However, the facts do not support this. Some of his victims were not terminally ill or particularly unwell. Many were active, independent, and even thriving. Several had been seen shopping or gardening just hours before their deaths. These were not patients facing a painful, undignified end. They were individuals with years of life still ahead of them. If mercy influenced Shipman's actions, it was unrecognisable. The large number of deaths, the consistent methods, and the careful staging of bodies suggest not compassion but obsession and control.

Some commentators suggest that early life experiences such as physical or emotional abuse, isolation, and abandonment may contribute to serial killing. Childhood trauma is a recurring theme, although it is rarely sufficient on its own to make someone a murderer. Shipman's own trauma was the death of his mother when he was still a teenager. Watching her die of cancer whilst she was receiving morphine may have had a deep impact on him. However, this alone does not account for the extent or nature of his crimes. His victims were not merely substitutes for his mother: some were men, and many were significantly older than she had been.

Ultimately, attempts to explain Shipman's murders through mercy, trauma, or addiction only go so far. There is little more to say beyond Dame Janet Smith's own conclusion. With her extensive experience as a High Court judge, overseeing numerous murder trials, she was well placed to compare Shipman with other killers.

Dame Janet Smith expressed her perplexity in a lecture given to the Royal College of General Practitioners (Hurwitz, 2015):

> *I still do feel it was unspeakably dreadful, just unspeakable and unthinkable and unimaginable that he should be going about day after day pretending to be this wonderfully caring doctor and having with him in his bag his lethal weapon ...which he would just take out in the most matter of fact way.*

During her Inquiry, she reviewed all the theories discussed in this chapter, including psychological gratification from exerting total control over life and death and a potential narcissistic or psychopathic personality structure. She observed during the trial his arrogance, manipulativeness, and lack of empathy. Smith ultimately concluded that Shipman's motive "*remains obscure*" and that "*there is no evidence that financial gain, mercy killing, or sexual motives played a significant part.*"

She believed his killings were likely driven by a mix of power, control, and compulsive behaviour, rather than compassion or greed. The Sixth Report, which synthesised the Inquiry's findings, again noted that "*it is impossible to know what made him kill*" and that Shipman appeared to gain satisfaction from the act itself, from deceiving others and asserting his authority as a doctor.

Smith explicitly resisted speculative psychologising, stating that although the public might wish for an explanation, the Inquiry's role was not to diagnose but to reform the systems that allowed such crimes to go undetected.

Her words were stark in their humility:

> I regret to say that I can shed very little light on why Shipman killed his patients.

It is not easy to disagree.

Despite the Inquiries, the psychiatric reports and the endless theories, the truth is that Shipman remains, at his core, inexplicable. That is what makes his case so unsettling yet compelling. It is not just the enormity of his crimes, but the void of meaning behind them. His motives, as with many of the doctors in this book, defy understanding and are akin to what the Lithuanian-born French philosopher Emmanuel Levinas has described as "radical evil," such that the perpetrator of violence reduces the *Other to the Same*, in denying the face and humanity of another person (Bernstein, 2002).

THE AFTERMATH

As is a theme throughout this book, it was not only what Shipman did but also what others failed to do that allowed him to escape justice for so long.

Dame Janet Smith's Fifth Report (December 2004) – "*Safeguarding Patients: Lessons from the Past – Proposals for the Future*" – was the most critical volume, highlighting individual and systemic failings. The Greater Manchester Police were criticised for their investigation in 1998 after concerns had been raised. The Inquiry stated the police had failed to conduct a proper investigation, had not sought independent medical advice promptly, and had effectively accepted Shipman's explanations at face value. Dr Banks (Shipman's GP colleague and later medical adviser to the police inquiry) was also criticised. Dame Janet Smith concluded that Banks' clinical opinion which reassured the police that Shipman's prescribing and practice were not unusual, was inadequate and misleading. She found that his advice "*played a significant part in the decision to close the investigation*" and therefore represented a serious failure. Dr Banks was to be referred to the GMC based on this investigation.

The Fifth Report also examined how complaints about doctors were handled, how concerns were investigated, and whether regulation through the GMC and revalidation processes adequately protected patients. Smith found serious weaknesses in the systems for raising concerns, particularly about GPs. Complaints from patients, families, or staff were often ignored or poorly investigated, and primary care organisations lacked effective mechanisms for monitoring performance. A prevailing culture of deference towards doctors meant that patterns of misconduct or poor practice were rarely identified.

The GMC faced intense criticism in the report. Smith argued that it had historically prioritised doctors' interests over patient safety and had operated without enough transparency or accountability. She concluded that its proposals for revalidation, the periodic relicensing of doctors, had become diluted, shifting from a real test of fitness to practise into a softer form of professional appraisal. This, she said, blurred the line between developmental support and strict assessment.

Her report recommended extensive reform. Complaint and whistle-blowing systems needed strengthening, with more robust clinical governance in general practice. She felt that the GMC itself should be restructured to be more transparent, patient-centred, and subject to external scrutiny, including parliamentary oversight. Cultural change was central to her belief: doctors must embrace openness, accept scrutiny, and prioritise patient safety over professional loyalty. Without such change, Smith warned, oversight failures like those that allowed Shipman's crimes could happen again. The report sparked parliamentary debate and led to reforms in medical regulation, revalidation, and professional accountability, shaping UK health policy and medical governance ever since, including establishing a Care Quality Commission.

The most noticeable legacy was the introduction of revalidation in 2012. Although long debated, it was Shipman who made it politically unavoidable. For the first time, every licensed doctor was required to undergo regular appraisal and 5-yearly revalidation, demonstrating that their competence and professionalism were up to date. However, as many of us acknowledged at the time, Shipman himself would almost certainly have been able to pass. He was diligent and meticulous in staying informed about medical knowledge. He conducted audits well before they were mandated, attended courses and conferences, prescribed responsibly aside from his misuse of opiates, and received warm praise from patients. In essence, he was the epitome of a modern GP. His crimes were not concealed by professional complacency but by his ability to appear exemplary.

Another reform concerned the process of death certification. Shipman's complete control over his patients' death certificates was a pivotal reason he was able to escape justice for so long. Until then, it had been sufficient for a single doctor, or two in cases where the deceased was to be cremated, to certify death. The Inquiry highlighted how risky that system was. In 2024, the introduction of Independent Medical Examiners added a new layer of oversight. Today, every death not referred to a coroner is reviewed by a doctor outside the immediate care circle, a process that would almost certainly have uncovered Shipman far earlier.

COULD IT HAPPEN AGAIN?

The lingering question is whether such an atrocity could ever happen again (Horton, 2001). The answer is complex.

As Professor Richard Baker and the academic, Professor Brian Hurwitz have argued,

> Killing can only ever be routine where obstacles to its accomplishment have been fully annulled, where all, or almost all, health service and civil systems for monitoring… around the time of a patient's death, are so inadequate as to allow murder in the same way, by the same means, by the same man, to become repeated and established over decades.
>
> *(Baker & Hurwitz, 2009)*

Shipman acted as a warning sign, exposing systemic vulnerabilities, especially around the prescribing of powerful painkillers. Whilst it is unlikely another doctor could now avoid scrutiny in the same way, new risks have appeared. In the United States, pharmaceutical companies aggressively marketed opioids, incentivising doctors to prescribe them, and establishing "pill mills" in deprived communities (discussed in Chapter 11). The result has been disastrous: widespread addiction, countless deaths, and a public health crisis where fatalities from prescribed painkillers now surpass those from illicit drugs. If Shipman showed how one doctor could weaponise medicine against patients, the opioid epidemic demonstrates how an entire system can drift into medicalised disaster.

This chapter concludes with Esmail's wise words, delivered in a speech titled "Rethinking Medical Professionalism, Lessons from the Shipman Inquiry." (Esmail, 2006).

> *There is a war memorial in Hyde, and it is incredible to understand that Shipman's victims are almost as many as are on that war memorial. Shipman chose his victims. He went out of his way to murder them, doing home visits unannounced to kill someone. I remember one case, Joseph Bardsley, who was murdered on April 15, 1984. He was 83 years old and lived on his own. There was little wrong with him. Shipman visited him around 1.30 pm on his way home from another visit and murdered him. I remember sitting next to Janet Smith in the Town Hall and thinking, 'What sort of man can do that?'. There was a doctor trained to save lives, and on a Sunday, without being asked to go and visit, when he could have gone home and had his dinner, he took a detour and went and killed someone. There were many more cases like Mr Bardsley.*
>
> *About Shipman, people keep telling me not to talk about it any more. It is all in the past. We should move forward. But we cannot be allowed to forget. He was a product of our system, our NHS, of our education.*

FURTHER READING

Ashraf, H. (2002). At least 215 people killed by UK doctor, says official inquiry. *The Lancet, 360*(9329), 317. https://doi.org/10.1016/S0140-6736(02)09573-9

Baker, R. (2001). *Harold Shipman's Clinical Practice, 1974–1998: A Review Commissioned by the Chief Medical Officer.* Stationery Office.

Baker, R., & Hurwitz, B. (2009). Intentionally harmful violations and patient safety: The example of Harold Shipman. *Journal of the Royal Society of Medicine, 102*(6), 223–227. https://doi.org/10.1258/jrsm.2009.09k028

Bernstein, R. (2002). *Radical Evil, a Philosophical Interrogation* (p. 11). Polity Press.

Dyer, C. (2004). Shipman inquiry recommends tighter rules on controlled drugs. *BMJ : British Medical Journal, 329*(7459), 188. https://doi.org/10.1136/bmj.329.7459.188-b

Esmail, A. (2005). Physician as serial killer—The Shipman case. *The New England Journal of Medicine, 352*(18), 1843–1844. https://doi.org/10.1056/NEJMp048331

Esmail, A. (2006). Rethinking medical professionalism: lessons from the Shipman Inquiry. Inaugural lecture, University of Manchester, 4 October 2006. Available at: http://www.aneezesmail.co.uk/PDF%20files/Inaugural.pdf

Horton, R. (2001). The real lessons from Harold Frederick Shipman. *The Lancet, 357*(9250), 82–83. https://doi.org/10.1016/S0140-6736(00)03532-7

Hurwitz, B. (2015). Medical humanities and medical alterity in fiction and in life. *Journal of Medical Ethics, 41*(1), 64–67. https://doi.org/10.1136/medethics-2014-102300

Kinnell, H. G. (2000). Serial homicide by doctors: Shipman in perspective. *BMJ (Clinical Research Ed.), 321*(7276), 1594–1597. https://doi.org/10.1136/bmj.321.7276.1594

Ressler, R. K., Burgess, A. W., & Douglas, J. E. (1988). *Sexual Homicide: Patterns and Motives.* Simon and Schuster.

Sibbald, B. (2001). The epidemiology of murder: UK physician responsible for 345 deaths? *CMAJ: Canadian Medical Association Journal, 164*(4), 535.

The Shipman Inquiry. First Report. Death Disguised. (2002). http://www.the-shipman-inquiry.org.uk/firstreport.asp

4

Medical serial killers: Exploration of common themes

CLARE GERADA

BACKGROUND

A serial killer is often imagined as a shadowy figure in a dark alley, knife in hand. But the most prolific killers in history have not lurked on the streets. They have walked in brightly lit hospital corridors, dressed in white coats and other uniforms of trust. Their victims were not strangers lured into danger, but patients seeking care. Sadly, doctors who have killed others, even their patients, have existed since medicine was first practised. However, what is probably a much more recent phenomenon is doctors who are serial killers. The prominence of these individuals would have increased with the proliferation of means of killing in large numbers: poisons, potent medicines, anaesthetic gases, and the hypodermic syringe. We have already discussed one medical serial killer, Harold Shipman, in Chapter 2, suspected of murdering at least 200 of his patients (Kinnell, 2000). He used morphine and its derivatives. Dr Swango, who was murdering around the same time, and discussed in Chapter 5, was America's equivalent to Shipman. He used, amongst other things, arsenic and ricin. There are others, many of whom we will encounter in the following chapters: *poisoners, suffocators, reckless experimenters.*

A serial killer is typically defined as someone who kills multiple victims on separate occasions. However, there is no consensus on the exact number, which can range from two to three or more.

Regardless of the exact definition, the medical profession has played a significant role in this phenomenon. Overall, the toll caused by doctors who kill exceeds that of many of the most notorious murderers outside the medical field. This chapter will explore their motives, the circumstances that enable

DOI: 10.1201/9781003781066-4

them, and the psychological connections that might be linked to this troubling group.

Definition

Several terms have been used to describe serial killing committed by health professionals. The first, mainly for those not from the medical field, is the term Care-Assisted Serial Killing, or CASK. Another term, used for any health professional, is "Quiet Killing." Quietly as death occurs, not with the noise of guns or knives but through the silent lethality of insulin, potassium chloride, or even a tiny bubble of air slipped into a vein (Thunder, 2003). The term, "clinicide," first used by Australian forensic psychiatrist Robert Kaplan, refers to the unnatural death of multiple patients during treatment by a doctor (Kaplan, 2007).

Kaplan believes it is useful to distinguish between CASK and clinicide. Both groups have access to vulnerable patients and potent drugs, but their motives and methods of avoiding suspicion can vary significantly. He considers the key distinction to be that the ultimate responsibility usually lies with the doctor, which is very important for understanding how doctors "get away with murder." Typically, the doctor holds the highest authority within the team. They decide which treatment to administer, when to withhold it, and sometimes whether a death should be investigated. Shipman exploited this authority, signing death certificates, discouraging post-mortems, conducting unannounced home visits, and concealing his murders behind the pretence of "natural causes." Other doctors, when challenged, have used the same defence: a natural death, even if sudden and unexpected, is not a crime. Doctors kill covertly, hidden behind a shield of professional authority. Their decisions are seldom questioned, and their explanations, supported by training, titles, and trust, can delay suspicion for years. Historically, nurses and other health workers, on the other hand, rarely commanded such authority and therefore do not have the same protection as doctors. Their killings often become evident through patterns: excessive deaths in one shift, or alarms repeatedly sounding with the same individual nearby.

Irrespective of the term used, the number of those killed by healthcare professionals is shocking.

Between 1970 and 2006, ninety healthcare workers across twenty countries were prosecuted as serial killers. Nearly half of these were from the United States, not necessarily because Americans kill more, but due to differences in scale and record-keeping practices. Forty-four convictions were obtained, linked to 2,113 suspicious deaths. Doctors accounted for about 12% of these deaths; nurses, 86%. Investigators still believe these figures only scratch the surface. Most of the killers managed to evade suspicion for decades before their crimes were uncovered (Kaplan, 2007; Yorker et al., 2006).

In 2001, an investigation by the Virginia State Crime Commission indicated that up to 65% of deaths among those over 65 were not natural; instead, death resulted from over-medication, poisoning, suicide, choking, or even arson (Thunder, 2003).

One reason why CASK and clinicide reach such high figures is that they occur mainly in settings where deaths are expected and where there is an opportunity to kill many victims without suspicion (Stark et al., 2001). The victims are almost always the most vulnerable: those with dementia, the terminally ill, and voiceless patients with no family to ask difficult questions. Some nurse-killers also target the very young. Detection is notoriously difficult. A patient dies in the hospital; who is surprised? Even post-mortem examinations may find nothing. As time passes, evidence disappears, drugs are broken down and become undetectable, and cremations destroy any remaining traces.

Although this book focuses on doctors, nurses who commit murder also deserve attention, as it may shed light on medical serial killings. When investigators examined the backgrounds of twenty convicted nurse-murderers, clear patterns emerged. Their most effective tool was not strength or stealth but proximity: constant, close access to vulnerable patients and an unlimited supply of potent drugs. Mental illness was often present among the nurses who killed, and in half of the cases, a personality disorder was diagnosed. The gender imbalance was notable. Men make up only about 6% of the nursing workforce, yet they accounted for 44% of murder prosecutions. This pattern mirrors that of serial killers outside medicine, where solitary men tend to predominate. A common pattern was that the nurses volunteered for night duty when staffing was thin and scrutiny was minimal. They were almost always present when death occurred, sometimes even predicting it with unsettling accuracy. They raised alarms, participated in resuscitation efforts, and played the hero. And when suspicion grew too strong, many left, moving between hospitals and starting anew in different places with new victims. Yet, and this is crucial, none of these factors is exclusive to killers. Millions of nurses work night shifts, handle syringes, and care for the dying. They do this with compassion, not cruelty. What distinguishes the murderer is not the job or access, but the dark mindset that exploits the tools to kill.

MOTIVES: WHY DOCTORS MURDER?

With every doctor examined in these pages, the recurring question remains: why? Why would someone sworn to heal choose to harm instead? The answers are rarely straightforward. After all, doctors are not immune to the impulses that lead others to cross ethical boundaries. They too suffer from greed, lust, and jealousy, all of which play a role. For many medical serial killers, however, the motivation is often about control: the Godlike thrill of deciding who lives and who dies (Menshawey & Menshawey, 2023). Others kill for financial gain. Some, like the earlier Victorian serial killers, defraud insurance companies; others alter their victims' wills, suddenly altered to favour the doctor's inheritance. Often, gambling debts are at the centre of motives. Some kill for darker reasons, reasons that defy logic. For instance, they may target patients they find "difficult," those who irritate or drain their time. For these killers, death becomes a form of punishment, or sometimes simply a matter of convenience. In a few cases, the motive is purely sadistic: deriving perverse pleasure from watching life ebb away (Kinnell, 2000).

CLASSIFICATION

The American criminologists Ronald M. Holmes and Stephen T. Holmes have written the book, *Serial Murder,* which is one of the standard criminological texts on serial homicide. It provides a mix of theory, criminological typologies, psychological profiling, and case examples.

Their work has influenced the understanding of the often-chaotic motives of those who commit clinicide (Holmes & Holmes, 2009).

These criminologists categorised serial killers into four main archetypes to understand psychological motivations rather than just behavioural evidence, helping to bridge criminology, forensic psychology, and investigative practice.

As a reminder, an archetype is a universal pattern, symbol, or character type that recurs across cultures, stories, and human psychology.

The four groups they describe can and do frequently overlap.

The first group described is the so-called *Visionary Killers,* who are often psychotic or suffer from severe mental illnesses and hold delusional beliefs about their victims. They commit murder believing they are following commands from an inner or outer source, such as voices or visions. Victims may be chosen seemingly at random, with no clear pattern to the choice of person. The killer's internal logic, often psychotic in nature, guides their decision-making. Crime scenes are often described as "disorganised" by forensic standards, with little effort to conceal evidence or organise the crime. Impulsiveness often plays a role. In the 1970s, Italian psychiatrist Dr Giorgio Coda (1924–1988) was sentenced to 5 years imprisonment. Known as "The Electrician," because of his excessive use of electric shock treatment (often without anaesthesia), claimed he was treating patients with a divine purpose. However, he strapped patients to machines and administered electric shock therapy so intense that many never recovered. He believed he was chosen, but his patients described it as torture.

The next group is the *Mission-Oriented Killers*, whose aim is to eliminate a target or address a specific problem group. Shipman was widely regarded as having a "mission" element to these killings, believing he was protecting elderly patients from future suffering.

The third group consists of *Hedonistic Killers* who murder for pleasure. Some do it out of lust, while others seek the thrill.

Finally, Holmes and Holmes's categories include those who kill mainly for *Power and Control*, aiming to dominate their victims. Dr Michael Swango (Chapter 5) poisoned patients and colleagues, seemingly enjoying the control it gave him over the lives of others.

While their framework offers a single classification type, Robert Kaplan went further, especially with medical serial killers. Kaplan proposed that clinicide can be categorised into three broad groups (Kaplan, 2007).

The first, "*Medical Serial Killers*," are doctors who deliberately kill patients, often motivated by sadism, a desire for control, or other psychological reasons.

These offenders resemble traditional serial killers but *operate* within a medical environment.

The second category is "*Treatment Killers*," who cause patient deaths during medical procedures. In these cases, it is not immediately apparent that the doctor intended for the patients to die. The key feature is that treatment continues despite increasing evidence of harm. Motivation often arises from grandiosity, vanity, or a delusional belief in the correctness of their methods. Patients may be seen more as objects serving the doctor's theories or ambitions than as individuals entitled to safe healthcare. In Chapter 9, we explore examples of treatment killers such as Dr Harry Bailey, who practised "deep sleep therapy" in Australia with disastrous outcomes (Chapter 9), Dr Duntsch, and Dr Jayant Patel (Chapter 9), the surgeons whose reckless procedures led to numerous deaths. For these doctors, the deaths of their patients did not result from a clear intention to kill but stemmed from hubris, detachment, and a refusal to accept failure. However, this does not mean the deaths should be dismissed. The fact that the doctors ignored the deaths of patients under their care repeatedly is inexcusable.

The third and final group described by Kaplan is "*Political Mass Killers*," clinicians involved in killings sanctioned by the state or political regimes, such as medical participation in Nazi concentration camps. Here, murder is rooted in ideology and policy rather than individual pathology.

Peter Smerick, a former FBI criminal profiler, provides a different perspective on medical killers, although there is significant overlap with both Kaplan's and Holmes and Holmes classifications. Smerick describes the "*Hero Doctor*," who intentionally triggers emergencies. A patient is deliberately pushed into cardiac arrest, perhaps by overdosing on insulin, potassium, or morphine, so the doctor or nurse can appear as a hero. The resuscitation team rushes in, yet the "hero" is already at the bedside, leading the effort, often reviving the very crisis they caused. If the patient survives, they are praised for quick thinking. If the patient dies, no blame is assigned; they *did their best*. It creates a dangerous cycle: the addictive nature of applause, the thrill of playing God, like an arsonist who starts fires only to join in the rescue.

The second group is known as the "*Mercy Killer*" or "*Angel of Mercy*." Their justification is based on compassion, or at least the appearance of it. The doctor claims to end suffering, relieve pain, and speed up the inevitable. When the patient is terminally ill, suspicion is minimal, and post-mortems are uncommon. For these killers, the line between assisted dying and murder is not just blurred; it is crossed, often multiple times, under the guise of kindness.

PERSONALITY DISORDER, PSYCHOPATHY, AND THE SERIAL-KILLING DOCTOR

When considering doctors who become serial killers, it is important to distinguish between mental illness and personality disorder. While some were thought to suffer from affective disorders such as bipolar disorder, the more common thread across cases is the presence of enduring maladaptive traits consistent with a personality disorder.

The term psychopathy is not recognised as a formal psychiatric diagnosis, but in forensic and criminological literature, it is often used to describe a group of traits: superficial charm, manipulativeness, deceitfulness, lack of empathy, callousness, absence of remorse, and a craving for control. These traits closely resemble antisocial and narcissistic personality disorders and frequently appear in accounts of doctors who kill. Shipman, for instance, was widely described in psychiatric commentary as psychopathic; his detached manner, cold calculation, and lack of conscience fit the profile with unsettling precision.

PSYCHOLOGICAL FACILITATORS

A common psychological defence mechanism used by doctors, not just those who kill, is the process of compartmentalisation. For example, a junior doctor in the emergency department is involved in an unsuccessful resuscitation of a young trauma victim. Within minutes, she must move to the next patient, a child experiencing an asthma attack, who requires calm reassurance. By mentally "boxing off" the grief and distress from the failed resuscitation, she can be fully present for the next patient. Later, when recounting her day to her friends, she revisits and processes her emotions and sheds several tears. In this context, compartmentalisation acts as a protective mechanism: it helps her cope in the moment while still leaving space for later reflection. However, this defence can be maladaptive. Consider this case: a senior surgeon develops a habit of walling off not only the emotional strain of losing patients, but all feelings linked to error or uncertainty. He convinces himself that complications are simply inevitable, even when colleagues raise concerns about his practices. Over time, this rigid separation fosters emotional detachment and an inability to acknowledge mistakes. Such compartmentalisation allows doctors who harm patients, even repeatedly, to maintain an internal image of themselves as competent and caring.

Closely related to this is the process of "dehumanisation." Isabel Menzies-Lyth, a British psychoanalyst, described this phenomenon as a defence mechanism organisations use to shield themselves from the emotional burden of caring (Menzies, 1960). For instance, when referring to patients as "cases," "beds," or "conditions," nurses and doctors can create emotional distance from their patients' suffering. A junior doctor might refer to patients by their diagnoses, such as "the liver in bed 10." This approach has a function. It helps the doctor manage a demanding workload, prioritise tasks, and maintain clinical objectivity. Outside ward rounds, the doctor still engages with patients as individuals, listening to their concerns and showing empathy. Here, dehumanisation therefore functions as a practical tool, without immediately stripping away their humanity. However, if circumstances allow, it can become exaggerated. An intensive care doctor might, for example, see patients mainly as mechanical bodies to be managed, rather than as individuals with stories, families, and dignity. He refers to them as "ventilators" or "dialysis cases." Families notice the lack of compassion; junior staff imitate his language, thereby perpetuating a sense of detachment. Dehumanisation, therefore, exists on a continuum. On the one hand, it offers a pragmatic approach to managing workload in complex clinical settings. On the other hand, it risks eroding empathy, undermining professional values, and diminishing patient dignity. In rare but serious cases, entrenched dehumanisation has been identified as a psychological enabler of medical harm and serial killing. By objectifying the patient, the killer-doctor erodes the moral barrier that typically protects patients against harm (Lifton, 1986). Dehumanisation repeatedly appears in testimonies surrounding medical killers: their victims are described as faceless, interchangeable, or unworthy of care.

The next chapter will examine some of the most infamous medical serial killers. Collectively, their crimes span more than 150 years. Almost all are men, a fact that might change as more women enter the medical profession.

REFERENCES

Holmes, R., & Holmes, S. (2009). *Serial Murder* (3rd ed.). SAGE.

Kaplan, R. (2007). The clinicide phenomenon: An exploration of medical murder. *Australasian Psychiatry, 15*(4), 299–304. https://doi.org/10.1080/10398560701383236

Kinnell, H. G. (2000). Serial homicide by doctors: Shipman in perspective. *BMJ (Clinical Research Ed.), 321*(7276), 1594–1597. https://doi.org/10.1136/bmj.321.7276.1594

Lifton, R. J. (1986). *The Nazi Doctors: Medical Killing and the Psychology of Genocide*. Basic Books.

Menshawey, R., & Menshawey, E. (2023). Brave Clarice-healthcare serial killers, patterns, motives, and solutions. *Forensic Science, Medicine, and Pathology, 19*(3), 452–463. https://doi.org/10.1007/s12024-022-00556-4

Menzies, I. E. P. (1960). A case-study in the functioning of social systems as a defence against anxiety: A report on a study of the nursing service of a general hospital. *Human Relations, 13*(2), 95–121. https://doi.org/10.1177/001872676001300201

Stark, C., Paterson, B., & Kidd, B. (2001). Opportunity may be more important than profession in serial homicide. *BMJ (Clinical Research Ed.), 322*(7292), 993.

Thunder, J. M. (2003). Quiet killings in medical facilities: Detection & prevention. *Issues in Law & Medicine, 18*(3), 211–237.

Yorker, B. C., Kizer, K. W., Lampe, P., Forrest, A. R. W., Lannan, J. M., & Russell, D. A. (2006). Serial murder by healthcare professionals. *Journal of Forensic Sciences, 51*(6), 1362–1371. https://doi.org/10.1111/j.1556-4029.2006.00273.x

5

Serial killers: Michael Swango

CLARE GERADA

Whilst some killers in this book have concealed themselves in shadows, Dr Michael Swango is not one of them. He took centre stage, was flamboyant, an attention seeker and willing, if challenged, to drop to the ground and perform 100 press-ups during ward rounds. Always available, he was attentive and eager to "go the extra mile" to care for the sickest patients. The dutiful doctor, Swango, often made extra rounds at night to check on his patients, or in the afternoon when he was off duty. Blond, blue-eyed, tall, with a broad, confident smile, he projected the image of a reassuring doctor. However, behind this facade, he evaded justice for decades, committing murders across continents, with institutions failing to stop him for far longer than they should have. By the time he was finally caught, as many as sixty patients, colleagues, and even friends were dead, most poisoned not for money, ideology, or revenge, but seemingly driven by the pure urge to do so. Some suggest the actual number could have reached two hundred, making Swango America's most prolific serial killer (Woods, 2000).

He is undoubtedly one of the strangest killers in this book.

EARLY LIFE AND MEDICAL CAREER

From early on during medical school, colleagues thought Swango was odd. He would wear military dress and combat boots to lectures, as if going to war. Concerns were raised once he was allowed onto the wards. Nurses observed him interfering with intravenous lines. Fellow students nicknamed him "Double-0 Swango," ominously implying he had a licence to kill. He seemed almost to enjoy death, writing "DIED" on the blackboard in the nurses' station with satisfaction as soon as a patient had died. He displayed a morbid interest in death, murder, and the Holocaust. There was a standing joke amongst the students that if they wanted to get rid of a patient, they should assign them to Swango, as it would not be unusual for the patient to suddenly "code," and even after resuscitation attempts, die. Supervisors were worried about his dishonesty and reckless attitude towards patient care.

DOI: 10.1201/9781003781066-5

All these concerns were valid, but ignored, as despite them and, during his career, time spent in prison, forged documents, a name change, and a clear trail of suspicion, Swango was repeatedly permitted to continue practising.

THE MAN AND THE DOCTOR

Michael Swango was born in 1954 and raised in Quincy, Illinois. He was the son of a career military officer, a Vietnam veteran, and an authoritarian and violent man who eventually died of alcoholic cirrhosis. Swango was clever, though, something that helped him escape his troubled upbringing. He excelled at school, graduating as valedictorian, and was described as gifted both academically and musically.

On paper, Swango's life reflected the American ideal of rising through talent and effort.

After serving in the Marines, he returned home with an honourable discharge and pursued medicine with fierce determination. Swango exaggerated his military prowess and lied about being a decorated Vietnam veteran. By 1979, he had completed his undergraduate studies at Quincy College, graduating *summa cum laude* in chemistry and biology, and gained admission to Southern Illinois University School of Medicine. His final-year thesis was a detailed examination of an unusual topic: the murder in 1978 of Georgi Markov, the émigré Bulgarian writer. He was attacked on London's Waterloo Bridge and killed with the tip of a ricin-impregnated umbrella (much later, Swango attempted to manufacture ricin, and it is suspected he also used it in some of his murders).

It was during medical school that troubling patterns in Swango's behaviour began to emerge. His classmates and supervisors noticed a side of him that did not fit the image of a diligent young doctor. He was obsessively competitive, what Americans call a "gunner," but socially isolated and viewed with suspicion. His fellow students used the term "Swango-ing" to describe his odd behaviour. There were concerns about dishonesty, including finding novel ways of cheating in exams. At one point, he faced dismissal from medical school. He was found to have made up his patient's academic assessment during his obstetric rotation. After failing this attachment, a faculty committee reviewed his record and heard testimony from colleagues and senior staff about his dishonesty and incompetence. At a meeting with senior staff members to discuss the next steps, several of those present voted to expel him from training, but one influential teacher argued that he deserved a second chance. That reprieve proved decisive. Swango retook the failed course, completed the additional requirements, and graduated in 1983 with his record officially "clean."

This decision highlights a recurring pattern in the Swango story: the institutional tendency to give him the benefit of the doubt and to pass problems on, rather than address them directly. It is easy with hindsight to argue that he should have been expelled, but this pattern of not doing so is familiar to anyone in the medical field. Concerns about a colleague are often dismissed, minimised, or turned into remedial measures rather than decisive action. As a result, Swango was able to qualify and undertook further training at Ohio State University, a prestigious role that involved significant responsibility for patient care.

POISONINGS AND CONVICTIONS

After graduating in 1983, Swango took up an internship in surgery. It was meant to be the start of a successful career. Instead, it marked the beginning of his slide into notoriety.

Shortly after starting his training, nurses and fellow residents noticed worrying patterns. Stable patients would suddenly worsen after encounters with him. One nurse saw him tamper with an IV-line moments before a patient had a seizure and suffered a respiratory arrest. The patient survived, but suspicions grew. Within months, five unexplained deaths on the ward had been causally linked to his presence. Yet despite this rising concern, hospital leaders carried out only superficial reviews. Interviews took place, suspicions were noted, but no decisive action was taken. The conclusion: Swango was innocent. The problem, they said, lay in "gossip" amongst nurses.

By early 1984, Ohio State quietly ended his appointment at the conclusion of his internship. Notably, the termination letter did not specify the actual reason. There was no formal record of suspected poisoning, nor was there a blemish on his file. In fact, the institution even recommended him for medical licensure. This reluctance to confront the truth, favouring administrative tidiness over transparency, allowed Swango to depart with a clean paper trail, leaving others to face the consequences.

Back in Quincy, Illinois, Swango moonlighted as a paramedic. Here, his murderous tendencies became increasingly difficult to conceal. Colleagues who shared meals and drinks with him began to fall mysteriously ill. One day, he brought a box of doughnuts to work; shortly afterwards, several co-workers experienced severe nausea and vomiting. On another occasion, a colleague who drank a soda Swango had given him became violently ill, with arsenic later detected in his system. Jokes about Swango "poisoning" people circulated nervously amongst the ambulance crew, who had allegedly fed them arsenic-laden pizza. However, the pattern was too consistent to ignore, and the police investigated accusations of poisonings.

A few days after the doughnut incident, Swango received a call at work asking him to visit the County Sheriff's Office to provide some information; Swango had applied to become a deputy coroner, and the Sheriff indicated that he was close to securing the position. However, when he arrived, he was arrested, read his rights, and he allowed the police to search his flat.

What was discovered was described as a mini laboratory of poisons: pest control chemicals, syringes, and recipes for deadly substances like ricin, arsenic, and cyanide. Scrapbooks filled with cuttings about disasters, poisonings, and violent deaths completed the picture of a man obsessed with killing.

The police also confiscated a small cache of weapons, including a twelve-gauge pump-action shotgun with a combat stock and a revolver. When investigators visited the local library, they found that Swango had recently borrowed a non-fiction book about a doctor who kills his wife and a novel about the poisoning of a city's water supply.

In 1985, Swango was tried and convicted for the non-fatal poisoning of his colleagues. The judge who presided over the case reflected on the contradiction: an articulate, well-presented young doctor who appeared earnest and polite, yet whose actions revealed cold-blooded calculation. The court concluded he had deliberately administered arsenic, not necessarily to kill, but to observe suffering.

Swango was sentenced to 5 years in prison, but because of good behaviour, served just two before being released on parole.

This period of imprisonment meant that the legal system had caught up with him, but only temporarily and only for crimes committed against colleagues rather than patients. Suspicious deaths that had occurred on hospital wards remained unprosecuted, partly because evidence had been mishandled or discarded. In one notorious incident, a nurse preserved a syringe she had seen Swango use moments before a patient collapsed. Instead of being analysed, the hospital authorities dismissed the nurses' accusations, and the syringe was thrown away. There were patients who were exhumed, such as the concern about unnatural deaths. But even here, Swango escaped retribution. The autopsy of one exhumed body revealed a wad of hospital gauze lodged in the throat of the individual. Swango had been the attending doctor. The hospital authorities dismissed this as a mortician's error, though the mortician himself flatly denied placing it there. Repeatedly, suspicious circumstances clustered around Swango: patients deteriorating without warning, collapsing suddenly, or dying unexpectedly when he was at their bedside. However, each case was dismissed for lack of "conclusive evidence."

These failures reveal how inadequately hospitals and the authorities within them were prepared to confront the possibility that a doctor might intentionally harm patients. Suspicious patterns were dismissed as mere clinical misfortune. Investigations were superficial, evidence was mishandled, and lawyers focused on limiting liability rather than safeguarding patients. As one prosecutor later expressed, "They didn't want to know. They just wanted him out of the hospital."

CAREER RESURRECTION AND INTERNATIONAL CRIMES

Whilst in prison, Swango lost his licence to practise medicine in both Ohio and Illinois. However, this did not deter him. Accompanied by his girlfriend, he moved to Hampton, Virginia, where he applied unsuccessfully for a licence to practise medicine. When he could not restart work as a doctor, he instead obtained a job as a counsellor at the Career Development Centre, which helped students gain entry to medical and other professional schools. He was dismissed in mid-1989, reportedly after three of his colleagues became violently ill. Police investigated, but no charges were laid.

Swango then found employment as a laboratory technician and proved to be an exemplary worker. Colleagues did fall unexpectedly ill, but their symptoms were never thought to be connected to Swango.

However, he was not to be defeated in his endeavour to return to work as a doctor, and to do so, he used subterfuge.

Swango officially changed his name to David Jackson Adams and, in 1992, obtained a position at a university hospital in Sioux Falls, South Dakota. He presented himself as a young doctor who had made mistakes, served his time, and was now eager for rehabilitation. He even admitted to being convicted of poisoning his colleagues but insisted that the evidence was flawed and that he was the victim of a miscarriage of justice. His charm, intelligence, and apparent honesty convinced those responsible for hiring him. Hospitals, eager to fill residency posts, accepted his paperwork at face value.

Once again, he was trusted with patient care.

Predictably, otherwise healthy patients started dying unexpectedly. Nurses observed that his presence often preceded sudden collapses. As rumours about his past spread more widely, he was dismissed. However, this was not the end. He forged more documents and references, changed his name to Dr Kirk (named after the Star Trek character), and sought work elsewhere.

With false documents, Swango was accepted as a psychiatry resident at the State University of New York at Stony Brook, Long Island, in 1993. He began as a resident at the Veterans Administration hospital. It did not take long before he reverted to his usual behaviour, and once again, colleagues became suspicious. Families of patients also raised concerns.

The wife of one patient, a man with mental health problems, found Dr Kirk injecting something into the vein of her husband's neck.

"*What's this*?" she asked.

"*Vitamins*," replied Dr Kirk, who then removed the syringe.

Later, when a nurse arrived, the wife mentioned that the doctor had given her husband a vitamin injection.

"*You must be mistaken*," said the nurse. "*Doctors do not give injections, that's a nurse's job*."

The patient became unconscious and was placed on a respirator the following day, only to die soon after.

Swango's overconfidence, like that of many others in this book, led to his downfall. Despite changing his name to hide his past, he wrote to the mother of an ex-girlfriend at the VA hospital, after the girl had recently taken her own life, saying he was working as a doctor again, "somewhere in New York." She reported him to the authorities, who traced him to his current job.

In October 1993, Swango was suspended from his training programme. On the same day, a tabloid newspaper devoted its entire front page to the story "*Poison in His Past: Hospital Fires MD. After Learning, He Fed an Ant Killer to the Paramedics*." Oddly enough, he was not arrested, at least not until a year later, even though it was now clear that he had obtained work using false documents, a criminal offence.

Facing increasing scrutiny in the United States, Swango shifted his focus overseas. In 1994, a year after he was suspended from the New York hospital, he fled to Zimbabwe and found work at a mission hospital in the rural district of Mnene. There, patients under his care began dying suddenly, often after receiving injections. More patients died during the month he was there than in the entire previous year. Nurses raised concerns, and rumours spread throughout the community. Swango was briefly arrested but managed to avoid conviction. He reappeared in neighbouring countries, including Namibia, where further unexplained deaths took place.

By the mid-1990s, Swango had become an international fugitive. He was wanted in the United States on fraud charges for providing false information on official documents, but his movements across Africa made him difficult to track. In 1997, he applied for a position in Saudi Arabia. To obtain a visa, he had to return to the United States. Travelling under his real name, at Chicago's O'Hare Airport, he was finally arrested.

Although he was initially charged with relatively minor fraud offences, investigators soon connected him to patient deaths at the Veterans Administration hospital in New York. Exhumations uncovered lethal substances in the bodies of patients he had cared for.

At his trial, prosecutors read from Swango's diaries, which showed him to have been a devotee of books such as The Torture Doctor and other thrillers in which doctors believed they had God-like powers over life and death.

In 2000, Swango pleaded guilty to three murders, admitting guilt to avoid the death penalty. He was given three consecutive life sentences without the possibility of parole. Additional charges in Ohio connected him to the death of a young patient, Cynthia McGee, who had died in 1984 after being hit by a car and admitted to the hospital for recovery. Swango was seen at her bedside shortly before her sudden collapse.

When asked to explain Swango's motive, the lead prosecutor responded:

Dr Swango liked to kill people.

He is serving three life sentences at the federal supermax prison in Florence, Colorado.

As with Shipman, the actual number of his victims may never be known. The FBI has suggested it could be dozens, possibly more. What is certain is that, for nearly two decades, Swango operated across multiple states and continents.

SYSTEMIC BLIND SPOTS AND THE "PROBLEM PEER"

Serial killing is the hallmark of a psychopath, divorced from empathy, compassion, and remorse, and driven solely by self-gratification. If there ever was a perfect example of a medical psychopath, it was Michael Swango. He displayed these traits in abundance: lack of remorse, grandiose self-confidence, intolerance of frustration, and a fascination with cruelty and violence. From his earliest days at medical school, these characteristics were plainly evident.

What makes the Swango case so disturbing is not just his pathology but also the fact that he managed to operate openly for so long. Time and again, warnings were ignored, minimised, or dismissed with levity, allowing him to persist. Colleagues expressed concerns, patients died under suspicious circumstances, and yet he was permitted to continue. The system refused to face the truth.

Most doctors encounter colleagues whose behaviour raises concerns, whether through incompetence, impairment, dishonesty, or negligence. However, medicine has not promoted openness. Doctors are trained to be resilient, self-reliant, and protective of each other. Reporting a colleague can feel like a betrayal.

Institutions, for their part, often prefer discreet solutions: shifting someone elsewhere, arranging early retirement, or offering remedial training instead of addressing the root issue.

Swango exemplifies this dilemma at its most extreme. He was not merely impaired or negligent but actively malevolent. Yet, the same cultural blind spots persisted wherever he worked. At Southern Illinois, his nickname was a joke masking real fear. At Ohio State, nurses reported him tampering with IV lines, only to be dismissed as indulging in "female gossip." In Zimbabwe, suspicions arose when deaths followed his injections, but again, little was done. In every setting, concerns were raised; in every setting, action was weak, fragmented, or absent.

The parallels between Swango and Shipman are unmistakable. Two doctors, working within different healthcare systems and specialities, but with similar failures allowed them to continue. In both cases, concerns were raised but not addressed. Swango was quietly dismissed and then reappointed elsewhere. Coroners and police investigated Shipman, yet suspicions were never communicated or thoroughly examined. Fragmented communication created dangerous blind spots.

Both men concealed themselves behind their medical identities. Swango utilised charm to foster misplaced confidence; Shipman depended on his reputation in a small town. Both exploited the dangerous illusion that professional status guarantees moral reliability. Swango crossed international borders; Shipman remained in one place but exploited the boundaries of trust within the locality. Together, they emphasise the need for oversight that extends beyond borders, both geographical and professional.

Both doctors refused, once their murders had been uncovered, to be examined by psychiatrists or psychologists. Shipman never gave a reason for this, but Swango felt it was unnecessary as, even after pleading guilty, he said he had not done anything wrong. Maybe both refused, as they were intelligent enough to know what an assessment would find.

AFTERMATH

Just as Harold Shipman's crimes in the United Kingdom changed how doctors were regulated and their performance scrutinised, so too did the case of Michael Swango in the United States.

Swango's ability to move repeatedly between states, hospitals, and even countries despite a trail of suspicion showed the porous boundaries of American medical regulation at the time. Self-regulation, valued as a mark of professional integrity, became a way of hiding problems when senior officials within institutions failed to share concerns, fearing litigation if they did. Swango worked in a system where medical licensing and credentialing of doctors was fragmented across different jurisdictions meaning that there was no national system of validating doctors training, competencies or qualifications. Swango exploited the gaps easily. As with Shipman in the United Kingdom, his case became a turning point, forcing US medicine to face the limits of professional autonomy and the urgent need for stronger, centralised mechanisms of accountability.

The exposure of Swango's crimes prompted one of the most searching re-evaluations of medical credentialing and oversight in the United States. Although no formal Public Inquiry was convened, a series of institutional reviews and policy reforms followed, aimed at closing the gaps that had allowed a known risk to move freely through the system (Stewart, 1999). The case demonstrated how professional deference, fragmented record-keeping, and fear of litigation could combine to conceal dangerous conduct.

The most notable changes focused on the National Practitioner Data Bank (NPDB), a federal repository established in 1990 to record malpractice payments, disciplinary actions, and loss of privileges. Many hospitals had failed to query or report to this authority. After the Swango revelations, the Department of Health and Human Services increased compliance efforts.

Parallel reforms addressed the credentialing process itself. There was the introduction of stricter verification requirements, including mandatory cross-checking of educational and employment histories, criminal background checks, and investigations of unexplained employment gaps. The focus shifted from reliance on peer references to documented evidence. These changes formalised what had previously been assumed: that trust must be supported by verification.

Swango's case also revealed the harmful culture of silence in medicine. Hospitals failed to report him not only due to inadequate systems but also because of professional anxiety about litigation and reputation. In response, many states enhanced whistleblower protections and clarified immunity for reporting of unsafe colleagues provided in good faith. Mandatory reporting laws were widened, and "fitness to practise" assessments became more formalised within hospital governance structures.

An additional outcome was enhanced inter-state coordination, rectifying the previous anomaly that a doctor could lose a position in one state and apply elsewhere.

Beyond regulation, the Swango affair catalysed a broader cultural reckoning. Medical schools began using his case to teach professional accountability and the perils of uncritical collegiality. Together, these reforms and reflections have created a more transparent and legally responsible system. However, as legal scholars continue to observe, oversight mechanisms are only as effective as the willingness of institutions to employ them (Egan, 2004; Waters et al., 2003)

REFERENCES

Egan, E. (2004). Lessons from the worst-case scenario. *Virtual Mentor, 6*(3), 150–152. https://doi.org/10.1001/virtualmentor.2004.6.3.oped2-0403

Stewart, J. B. (1999). *Blind Eye: The Terrifying Story of a Doctor Who Got Away with Murder.* Simon and Schuster Paperbacks.

Waters, T. M., Parsons, J., Warnecke, R., Almagor, O., & Budetti, P. P. (2003). How useful is the information provided by the National Practitioner Data Bank? *Joint Commission Journal on Quality and Safety, 29*(8), 416–424. https://doi.org/10.1016/s1549-3741(03)29050-x

Woods, D. (2000). US doctor may have killed 60. *BMJ: British Medical Journal, 321*(7262), 657. https://doi.org/10.1136/bmj.321.7262.657

6

Serial killers: A series of firsts

CLARE GERADA

Shipman and Swango were individuals who abused their skills, authority, and access to patients to commit murders on a shocking scale. What follows now are more of the most notorious examples of serial killers recorded in history.

Their crimes ranged from the poison-filled streets of Victorian London to a starvation sanatorium in Washington and the chaos of wartime-occupied Paris. Some killed for profit, others experimented under the guise of science, and still others murdered out of greed, sadism, or sheer arrogance. Each case reveals a different aspect of the same phenomenon: the healer who becomes the predator.

THOMAS NEILL CREAM (1850–1892): *THE LAMBETH POISONER*

London, 1891. The streets between Blackfriars and Waterloo were thick with fog, gas lamps flickering and casting long shadows over rain-slick cobblestones. Today, it is a fashionable area, but by the end of the nineteenth century, it was marked by severe poverty, with overcrowded slums and streets frequented by the homeless, destitute, and sex workers. Somewhere amidst those streets, a well-dressed, tall, handsome man in a top hat, carrying a medical bag, searched for his next victim. Inside his bag, alongside the usual medical instruments, were small glass vials labelled *STRYCHNINE* and this poison, in its purest form, *NUX VOMICA*.

For Dr Thomas Neill Cream, these were not tools for healing; they were instruments of theatre, agony, and death.

Thomas Neill Cream was born in Glasgow in 1850 and raised in Canada as the privileged son of a prosperous shipbuilder and timber merchant. This privilege gave him access to an elite education. He chose medicine not out of a passion for healing, but perhaps because of what the profession would allow him to hide, namely his murderous tendencies. He began his criminal activities as a medical student. Deep in debt from gambling, he set fire to his room to claim insurance

DOI: 10.1201/9781003781066-6

money. This act marked his transition into a life where medicine served not as a way to heal but as a gateway to crime.

At McGill University in Montreal, where he attended medical school, he developed a keen interest in poisons. His final thesis in 1876 was titled: "The Use of Chloroform and Other Anaesthetics." In it, he examined the administration of chloroform, ether, and various agents used in surgery. A suitable subject, considering his later use of these drugs and other poisons in the murders he committed. The address delivered to that year's graduates by the Dean of the Faculty was on "The Evils of Malpractice in the Medical Profession," which is again a strange coincidence considering Cream's later fate.

Once qualified, Cream persuaded his father to fund further postgraduate studies at St Thomas's Hospital in South London. His father agreed, and Cream prepared to leave Canada for London. Everything was progressing as planned until he met Flora. Miss Flora Brooks, a beautiful young woman, quickly became the object of his affection. They grew close, and when Flora became pregnant, Cream, who was only 26 and had his career ahead of him, did not want to be burdened with a child. He persuaded her to have an abortion, and he operated on her himself after learning about the procedure during medical school. Soon after the operation, Flora became seriously ill. Her father, upon discovering what Cream had done, was furious and, at gunpoint, forced Cream to marry his daughter, which he duly did; the ceremony took place on 11 September 1876. That night, whilst all were asleep, he hurried onto a waiting passenger ship bound for London, England. The following year, he received a telegram informing him of Flora's death, and as her legal husband, he demanded his share of her inheritance, which he received. Her death would later be viewed with suspicion since Cream had prescribed medicine for her before he left and told her to take nothing else and tell no one (Murder by Gaslight, 2010).

Once in London, he enrolled as planned to continue his studies at St Thomas's Hospital. Alongside studying, he began a lucrative practice performing illegal abortions, using chloroform to sedate patients. He completed his training in Scotland, earning a double first at the Royal College of Physicians and Surgeons in Edinburgh in 1877. By this time, like many doctors of his generation, he was addicted to morphine, starting the drug to treat severe headaches, which he believed were caused by syphilis contracted from a prostitute.

Cream's career now became a voyage across continents and crimes.

He left London, England, and headed to London, Ontario. His reasons for moving were many, but two were most notable. The first was his appearance: tall, strikingly handsome, impeccably dressed, with a gleaming top hat and a horseshoe tiepin. His smooth Canadian-Scottish accent only enhanced the image of a well-to-do gentleman wherever he went. Yet, given his striking looks, he felt he could never go unnoticed as he prowled the side streets of South London in search of prey, those he chillingly called the *filthy harlots that walked the streets near my Lambeth lodgings.*

The second reason was more practical: his addiction to morphine. By that time, his dependence had become so severe that he required large daily amounts, which were easier to access in Canada. In London, England, there were stricter regulations, and the pharmacist measured doses carefully whilst asking uncomfortable questions. Canada provided greater liberty to sustain his habit.

Moving to Ontario, he established his offices at *Dr Creams Clinic for Women*, in a less-than-reputable area, offering terminations of pregnancy and treatments for sexually transmitted infections. His practice quickly became profitable with minimal effort. Women arrived discreetly, their eyes shyly scanning and their hands nervously fidgeting. The true purpose of the clinic was clear: it was a place where women could obtain an abortion.

It was during this period, in 1879, that Cream committed his first documented murder. Katherine "Kate" Gardener, a 19-year-old woman, came seeking his services. Unable to afford her treatment, she became his victim, whether out of rage, frustration, or cruelty. Cream suffocated her with chloroform. Her body was later found behind his office, with a bottle of chloroform beside her.

The next day, two detectives from Ontario arrived to investigate the death. At the inquest, her housemate, Sarah Long, testified that Kate had been pregnant and had visited Dr Cream to "bring her right." Cream claimed he was treating her for "senescence" and had not administered an abortifacient. He concluded that her death was a suicide.

The coroner's verdict was that she had died from chloroform, administered by an unidentified person. The verdict also stated that it was impossible to kill oneself with chloroform, as it would cause unconsciousness before a lethal dose could be inhaled. Suspicion fell on Cream, who denied this; however, with insufficient evidence against him, he was not charged with her murder. Nevertheless, press reports about her death and his potential involvement tarnished his reputation, prompting Cream to leave Ontario and cross into America, heading for Chicago.

There, amidst the vibrancy of this city, he managed to restart his professional practice and, after securing accommodation, opened a clinic in the city's red-light district. Once again, due to its location, he attracted many patients, and his practice prospered, with a steady stream of women seeking help for their unwanted pregnancies. By this time, he was not only addicted to morphine but also using strychnine and cocaine.

Part of Cream's medical repertoire included offering new treatments that he invented; one was a pill he claimed not only protected women from venereal diseases but also served as a "morning-after pill." Both pills contained strychnine and, instead of curing his so-called patients, killed them.

By 1880, Cream was becoming well known to the Chicago police as an abortionist, sometimes assisted by an African-American midwife named Hattie Mack.

In August of that year, one of his patients, Mary Ann Faulkner, was found decomposed in an apartment owned by Hattie Mack. Mack was arrested and named Cream as the main culprit. However, the prevailing racial and gender prejudices of the time protected him from prosecution. Cream was acquitted of the charges and, undeterred by how narrowly he had escaped justice, resumed his deadly experiments with increased boldness. Another woman, Ellen Stack, died after taking one of his pills. Once again, he became the subject of a murder enquiry, was arrested, and interviewed. There was insufficient evidence to convict him, and after a few days, he was released without charge.

Later that month, another of Cream's patients died after taking the medication he had been prescribed. He tried to shift the blame and extort money from Frank Pyatt, the pharmacist who filled the prescription. Pyatt reported this to the police, but the investigation was again inconclusive.

After these narrow escapes, Cream changed his approach and started selling a morphine-based elixir marketed as a treatment for epilepsy. Although many dismissed it as a quack remedy, the foul-tasting potion still attracted a steady flow of desperate patients. His business prospered, even as sceptics ridiculed him.

Cream's vanity and recklessness soon betrayed him. In 1881, one of his patients, Daniel Stott, began to suspect Cream's excessive attention towards his much younger wife. Cream responded with typical malice: he laced Stott's medicine with strychnine and murdered him.

The suspicious circumstances surrounding Stott's death might have gone unnoticed but for Cream's overconfidence. He sent a telegram to the coroner stating: *"SUSPECT FOUL PLAY. WILL WRITE IMMEDIATELY. DR. CREAM."* He then wrote letters implicating both Stott's wife and a local pharmacist in the alleged crime. The coroner dismissed the telegram as a prank, but Cream persisted and contacted the District Attorney. Cream demanded that Stott's body be exhumed; it was, and four grains of strychnine were found in his stomach. When investigators pressed Stott's wife, she confessed not only to her affair with Cream but also to his scheme to murder her husband. The case became a sensation. In court, Cream's medical expertise, his adulterous relationship, and his elaborate attempt to frame another man painted a damning picture. He was convicted of Daniel Stott's murder and, in September 1881, was sentenced to imprisonment at the Illinois State Penitentiary, with 1 day each year in solitary confinement, "for the rest of his natural life."

Yet he served only 10 years, his sentence shortened due to good behaviour. During his prison time, his father died, leaving him a substantial inheritance. It is believed that payments were made by Cream's brother to prominent Illinois politicians to secure his release. With money and freedom regained, Cream's deadly career was far from over.

In September 1891, Cream travelled to Liverpool, England, aboard the SS Teutonic with his suitcase full of drugs for both personal and less-than-personal use. The dark, rainy evening of 5 October 1891 marked Cream's return to London, where he maintained a façade of respectability and adopted a new alias, "Dr Thomas Neill." He again secured accommodation near St Thomas's Hospital, and the triangle of South London bordered by Blackfriars Road, Lambeth Road, and the river became his hunting ground.

Under his new alias and dressed in his usual attire of a top hat and a silk-lined cloak, Cream befriended his victims and offered them medication laced with strychnine, supposedly to cure rashes, venereal diseases, or spots. He murdered four women over 7 months. A fifth intended victim escaped death by refusing to take the strychnine-laced pills he offered her.

Cream's reign of terror earned him the moniker "The Lambeth Poisoner" as more young women fell victim to his poison, suffering agonising deaths.

The net began to tighten as one woman, Matilda Clover, was brought in a nearly dead state to St Thomas's Hospital. She told the attending staff that a strange man had given her some pills, which she then took. She was to die, and her post-mortem revealed that she had both strychnine and arsenic in her system.

By now, Cream's confidence had developed into arrogance. No longer content with killing quietly, he attempted to blackmail prominent doctors by accusing them of causing his victims' deaths. One target was Dr William Broadbent, a renowned neurologist and physician to Queen Victoria. Using an alias, Cream sent letters demanding money in exchange for his silence about Broadbent's alleged involvement in the murders. Naturally, Broadbent reported the incident to the police, which led to an investigation into the author of the letters.

Cream's recklessness increased. He began openly boasting about the murders to acquaintances, unaware that one of these new "friends" was an undercover detective. Cream's detailed knowledge of the murders, especially those not publicly known, ultimately sealed his fate. When two previously unsuspected deaths were investigated and confirmed to be caused by strychnine poisoning, Cream was arrested on 3 June 1892 at Lambeth Palace Road. Initially charged with attempted extortion, he faced murder charges after a search of his lodgings uncovered substantial evidence, including seven bottles of strychnine.

The trial at the Old Bailey in 1892 concluded within days. He was charged and convicted of murdering four women in London (1891–1892). He was strongly suspected of, but not tried for, the deaths of several other women in London, who died suddenly from convulsions after contact with him. The jury took only 12 minutes to convict him of killing Matilda Clover. On 16 November 1892, outside Newgate Prison, thousands gathered to witness his execution. As the executioner prepared the noose, Cream reportedly began to say, "I am Jack...," before the trapdoor opened. Whether he was about to admit to being Jack the Ripper remains one of London's enduring criminal mysteries. However, he could not have been Jack the Ripper, as he was in jail in Canada during the period when the Ripper was most active.

Cream was the first serial killer to be hanged in Britain.

Historians and criminologists identify three overlapping motives behind Cream's murders: the first is sexual and personal control. Many of his victims were women in vulnerable positions (often seeking abortions or treatment for venereal disease). Cream appears to have derived gratification from poisoning and from wielding life-and-death power over women. He contracted syphilis as a young man whilst in London, UK, so revenge against women might also have been a motive.

There was also the motive of financial gain and blackmail. Cream habitually wrote anonymous letters accusing innocent people (doctors, pharmacists, businessmen) of poisoning his victims, then demanded money to suppress the "evidence." Murder thus became a tool for extortion as well as gratification.

Finally, arrogance and the thrill of cleverness took control. He could not resist involving himself in investigations, sending letters to coroners, police, or acquaintances. His behaviour indicates he killed not only for gain but also for the narcissistic pleasure of outwitting authority and flaunting his medical knowledge.

In short, Cream killed for a mix of lust, greed, and egotism, with poisoning giving him both secrecy and control (Mclaren, 1995).

LINDA BURFIELD HAZZARD (1867–1938): *THE STARVATION DOCTOR*

Linda Laura Hazzard, the only woman in this chapter and one of the few in this book, employed a more sinister method of killing: hunger itself. She did not stab, shoot, or poison; she simply starved her victims to death, all the while claiming it was for their health. Some regard her as Washington's first female serial killer, whilst others see her as a pioneering healer.

Born in Minnesota in 1867, she studied alternative healing with a fasting pioneer, a doctor who started the fasting movement before moving to Washington in 1907, where she became licensed to practise medicine through a loophole in licensing laws that grandfathered practitioners of alternative medicine. She called herself a "Fasting Specialist." She published books extolling the benefits of extreme fasting and established a remote clinic, Wilderness Heights, in Olalla, Washington, which locals later nicknamed "Starvation Heights." Her "cure" was brutal: weeks, sometimes months, of almost complete fasting. Patients, believing they were detoxing their bodies, gradually turned into skeletal shadows. Many never survived.

Nevertheless, hundreds of Linda Hazzard's followers, including socially and politically prominent Washingtonians, swore by her methods, praising her as an intelligent and gifted healer. Yet closer inspection of her practice reveals a darker story. Between 1907 and 1913, at least fourteen patients in Washington alone died of starvation whilst under her direct care. This figure does not include earlier deaths linked to her work in Minnesota. Many of these patients had, before their deaths, signed over their land, inheritances, or power of attorney to Hazzard.

The most notable patient was Claire Williamson, a wealthy young British woman who came to Wilderness Heights seeking a wellness retreat. In 1910, she and her sister Dora saw an advertisement for treatment by Linda Hazzard in the *Seattle Times*. Wealthy heiresses from England, both in their thirties, the sisters suffered from various health complaints and sought a natural cure. Because their family and friends disapproved of such pursuits, they kept their plans secret. In February 1911, the sisters began their treatment. It was severe. Each day, they were given just two cups of broth, subjected to long, vigorous walks, hours-long enemas, and punishing massage sessions. By April, both sisters were too weak to stand. They were carried on stretchers into an ambulance, ferried by boat, and transported to Hazzard's own home, where they were installed in her attic. Seventeen days later, Claire Williamson was dead, her body weighing less than fifty pounds. Linda Hazzard performed the post-mortem herself and, unsurprisingly, failed to attribute the death to starvation. The family discovered that Hazzard had forged Claire's will, making herself the primary beneficiary, and had stolen her jewellery and clothing.

When the case went to trial in 1912, the courtroom heard evidence of systematic fraud, abuse, and death inflicted by the Starvation Doctor. Hazzard was convicted of manslaughter and sentenced to between 2 and 20 years in prison. She served only two. Remarkably, she was granted a full pardon in 1916 on the condition that she leave the United States. She moved to New Zealand, where she continued practising covertly, referring to her patients as "students." She also published a best-selling book on using starvation as a remedy.

By 1920, she was back in Washington, her licence revoked, her reputation damaged, yet she still attracted patients. She reopened her health school and continued supervising fasts that proved fatal. The fatalities continued, but enforcement was weak, and Hazzard's followers remained loyal.

Her career finally came to an end in 1935 when her sanatorium was destroyed in a fire. However, fate, it seems, enjoys irony: in 1938, Linda Hazzard herself died of starvation whilst undergoing one of her own fasting "cures."

MARCEL PETIOT (1897–1946): *THE BUTCHER OF PARIS*

War is chaos, and in chaos, predators thrive. For Dr Marcel André Henri Félix Petiot, World War II provided an unmatched hunting ground. Paris was under Nazi control, its streets patrolled by soldiers, and its residents gripped by fear. People longed to escape, and Petiot offered them a way out.

Born in 1897 in the French town of Auxerre, Petiot had a troubled childhood. He was expelled from school multiple times, arrested for theft as a teenager, and considered mentally unfit to stand trial. During the First World War, he served in the army, but after suffering a mental breakdown and another incident involving military theft, he was discharged. None of this stopped him from enrolling in medical school, where he graduated in 1921 and established a reputable practice in Villeneuve-sur-Yonne.

Beneath the respectable veneer was a man with a penchant for fraud and manipulation. Dr Petiot's first victim was likely Louise Delaveau, the daughter of one of his patients, with whom he had an affair. She disappeared in 1926, and witnesses recalled seeing the town's doctor loading a large trunk into his car at the time of her disappearance. The authorities investigated but ultimately concluded that Mademoiselle Delaveau had run away.

He became mayor of this town in 1926 but was suspended due to corruption. Patients died under suspicious circumstances, and a man who accused Petiot of murder was found dead shortly after. Rumours swirled, but Petiot's charm and the absence of concrete evidence kept him in office.

Soon after being compelled to resign as mayor of Villeneuve-sur-Yonne, Dr Petiot appears to have taken out his frustration by killing one of his patients. Not long afterwards, another patient, who had accused the disgraced mayor of various offences, also died under suspicious circumstances. Despite a record that now included corruption charges, a conviction, and increasing indications of criminality, Petiot maintained a surprising level of popularity. When he was suspended from office, the entire town council resigned in protest.

In the autumn of 1931, he was elected Councillor of the Yonne Department. However, within a few months, Councilman Petiot was convicted of stealing electricity from his town. Forced once again to resign, he abandoned provincial politics and sought a fresh start in Paris, where he established a new medical practice in the capital.

When the Nazis occupied Paris, Petiot saw his opportunity. He claimed he could smuggle people out of France: Jews, resistance fighters, anyone with enough cash. His clients were advised to bring valuables for their "new life" abroad. Instead, Petiot took them to his house at 21 Rue Le Sueur. There, he injected them with a deadly cocktail of drugs, telling them it was an inoculation to protect them for their upcoming journey to safety. The victims died within minutes. Their bodies were burned in a makeshift crematorium in his basement. The ash and bone fragments began to accumulate. Neighbours complained about the smell, but during wartime Paris, foul odours were common.

It wasn't until March 1944, when black smoke billowed from the chimney for days, that the police investigated. What they discovered was horrifying: human remains scattered among the ash, personal belongings from missing persons, and evidence of numerous killings.

Petiot, always the opportunist, initially claimed he had been killing Nazis and collaborators for the Resistance. It was a clever lie in a city where the lines between hero and villain were blurred. However, the truth was far more straightforward and brutal. His victims had been desperate refugees, and he had taken everything from them before ending their lives.

By the time he was arrested later that year, Petiot was suspected of killing at least 60 people. During his trial in 1946, he sat in the dock with a sardonic smile, mocking witnesses, engaging in verbal sparring with the judge, and insisting on his innocence. The jury did not believe him. He was convicted on 26 counts of murder and sentenced to death. On 2 May 1946, in the courtyard of La Santé Prison, Petiot faced the guillotine. Moments before the blade fell, he reportedly said, "Gentlemen, I am ready."

Like many medical serial killers, Petiot used the trust people placed in doctors as his shield. However, his murders were not motivated by mercy, ideology, or even a perverse sense of medical experimentation. They were driven by greed and the realisation that, in a city overwhelmed by fear, people would believe almost anything if it offered an escape.

Marcel Petiot is considered the most infamous serial killer in French history. The estimated number of victims attributed to him ranges from 100 to 200.

RONALD E CLARK

Ronald E Clark was an American doctor whose career was tarnished by abuse and neglect of his patients. From the mid-1950s to the late 1960s, Clark sexually assaulted and murdered patients in his consulting room. His medical licence was revoked on no fewer than four occasions, once for "gross misconduct," twice for "moral turpitude," and once without any specific charge. Astonishingly, each time he was reinstated.

By the time authorities finally intervened, at least 25 serious complaints had been lodged, including deaths from drug overdoses, accusations of illegal abortion, sexual assault, reckless prescribing, and even practising medicine without a licence. The end came when Clark killed his secretary, and the post-mortem revealed traces of sodium pentothal in her body. Clark was charged with manslaughter. Investigators examined nine other deaths, vaguely attributed to "therapeutic misadventure" or unexplained cardiac arrest. However, none of these investigations led to any action. Ultimately, Clark was convicted of only two manslaughter charges, related to the deaths of his assistants. He was sentenced to between three and 15 years in prison. On 23 March 1972, in prison, Ronald E. Clark died from a fall.

In the forthcoming chapters, we will be looking at doctors who used poison to kill. This chapter has focused on the doctors of a different era who murdered their patients and were able to use their positions to do so.

REFERENCES

Mclaren, A. (1995). *A Prescription for Murder: The Victorian Serial Killings of Dr. Thomas Neill Cream* (The Chicago Series on Sexuality, History, and Society). 1st Ed. Chicago: University of Chicago Press.

Murder by Gaslight. (2010, August). *The Lambeth Poisoner.* https://www.murderbygaslight.com/2010/08/lambeth-poisoner.html

7

When medicine becomes murder

CLARE GERADA

INTRODUCTION

The cases of Harold Shipman and Michael Swango, both of whom used poisons to kill, may seem chillingly modern, but they belong to a tradition reaching back centuries. Long before their crimes, the figure of the murderous doctor using poisons to do the deed haunted the public.

As the English poet Letitia Elizabeth Landon noted in her 1839 poem The Venetian Bracelet, there are "those subtle poisons which made science crime,/ And knowledge a temptation."

Even the pursuit of healing could be corrupted, with medicine itself turned into a source of death.

Nowhere was this more evident than in the eighteenth and nineteenth centuries, when poisoning became the weapon of choice. It was subtle, hard to detect, and could be easily concealed within ordinary medical practice. A dose might disguise itself as a remedy, a powder dissolved in a glass of sherry for a temperature or headache, or, after the invention of the hypodermic syringe in 1856, injected directly beneath the skin. In an era when toxicology was still in its early stages, the physician-poisoner operated almost perfectly disguised by their professional respectability.

This chapter examines that dark tradition: from the morphine-laced Parisian salons of Edme Castaing to William Palmer's strychnine, Edward Pritchard's antimony, and George Lamson's aconitine capsule. These men were not anomalies, but part of a recurring pattern: doctors whose authority concealed their crimes and whose betrayals of their Hippocratic Oath shocked the Victorian public. In an era when toxicology was still a young science, a clever poisoner could operate undetected for years.

In mid-Victorian Britain, fears of poisoning escalated into a moral panic. Newspapers highlighted sensational trials, penny dreadfuls published melodramatic

 DOI: 10.1201/9781003781066-7

stories, and novels fuelled the public's fascination with the macabre. Across Britain, Western Europe, and the United States, "poison panic" became a widespread cultural phenomenon. The fear was that anyone could be a poisoner: the spouse serving your tea, the servant bringing your supper, or, most disturbingly, the trusted doctor at your bedside. Writers frequently explored this theme. Robert Louis Stevenson's *The Strange Case of Dr Jekyll and Mr Hyde* (1886) examined the unsettling idea that a respectable doctor could turn monstrous through his potions. Wilkie Collins, in *The Moonstone* (1868), incorporated opium and medical ethics into the character of Dr Ezra Jennings. Charles Dickens, ever the social critic, was among the first novelists to voice concern about the unchecked power of the medical profession. In his fiction, doctors often appear not as purely benevolent figures but as ambiguous, sometimes menacing presences. In Bleak House (1853), for example, the medical profession is embodied in the figure of the coroner, who conducts his inquest with chilling detachment, more interested in procedure than in humanity. The physician in *Our Mutual Friend* (1865), Dr Sloppy, is depicted as mechanical and impersonal, a man of "science" who appears to have lost sight of compassion. Even more revealing is Dickens's satire of so-called "quacks," opportunists who exploited the public's faith in new cures while enriching themselves at their patients' expense.

Conan Doyle's *Sherlock Holmes*, in *The Adventure of the Speckled Band* (1892), issues a warning:

> When a doctor does go wrong, he is the first of criminals. He has nerve, and he has knowledge.

Conan Doyle was working under the shadow of real-life doctors whose trials captivated the nation: William Palmer, Edward Pritchard, Thomas Neill Cream, names that, at the time, became shorthand for death by prescription. These cases were the Victorian equivalent of today's binge-worthy true crime documentaries: lurid, detail-rich, impossible to look away from.

By the middle of the nineteenth century, The Illustrated Times had declared poison to be the "Crime of the Age." Whispered warnings suggested that undetected poisonings were far more common than anyone dared to believe.

Not all authors exploring the theme of medical poisoners were from the United Kingdom. In 1905, the Swedish writer Hjalmar Söderberg published Doctor Glas, a novel that captured the enduring cultural unease around doctors and poison. Written as the private diary of a general practitioner, the book follows Dr Glas as he wrestles with the morality of killing one of his patients, the clergyman Gregorius.

Glas is both repelled by Gregorius and drawn to his young wife Helga, who is also his patient. When Gregorius comes seeking treatment for his heart, Glas decides to act. He hands him a pill, claiming it will help. Within minutes, Gregorius is dead, poisoned by cyanide. Glas records the event with chilling composure:

> I heard the clergyman's tumbler fall over on the tray. I did not want to look, yet I saw his arm fall limply down and his head nod on his breast... I myself wrote out the death certificate.

The fictional Glas got away with murder.

In reality, to "get away with murder," the nineteenth-century poisoner needed a certain level of scientific knowledge. The ideal poison was believed to be colourless, odourless, and tasteless, but even then, a basic understanding of chemistry was necessary to select the right substance and conceal its presence. For example, prussic acid would reveal itself with a bitter taste; an experienced poisoner would hide it in a strong drink such as coffee. Medical knowledge was equally crucial. The most effective way to avoid detection was to administer poison in doses that mimicked the progression of a natural illness. Arsenic, given in small amounts over several days, could produce symptoms resembling cholera or other infectious diseases, easily overlooked by busy or inattentive doctors. A single large dose, on the other hand, caused violent and unmistakable reactions that clearly indicated foul play.

As chemical testing became more reliable, poisoners adjusted their tactics. They sought substances that dissolved quickly or left minimal traces in the body, a trend reflected by the increasing use of strychnine in the later decades of the century. The science of detection would eventually keep pace. But before that, the era produced its share of medical men who were as inventive in their methods as they were unscrupulous in their motives.

Let us look at some of the cases that stole the headlines.

EDME CASTAING (1796–1823): *THE FIRST TO USE MORPHINE AS A MURDER WEAPON*

Paris, 1823. The young Dr Edme Castaing displayed all the sophistication of an emerging medical luminary, with a composed demeanour, a gentle voice, and polished courtesy that could soothe any patient. But behind his carefully pressed cravat was a man in trouble. Gambling debts depleted his income, and he had both a family and a mistress to support. Into this despair, Hippolyte Ballet, a wealthy friend and his patient, stepped in, whose fortune, along with that of his brother Auguste, provided Castaing a way out of his misery.

Hippolyte's sudden death initially caused no concern. People died young, even among the wealthy. However, when Auguste collapsed shortly after a hunting trip with Castaing, suspicion grew. Investigators traced the doctor's recent purchase of morphine, a substance so new to medicine that few physicians had used it.

The suspicion was that Castaing had used the drug to kill.

Castaing was arrested and charged with murdering the two men and forging Hippolyte's will to make himself the beneficiary of his extensive estate. Suspicion grew as it came to light that Castaing had even dared to consult a lawyer before Hippolyte's death to enquire whether a doctor could inherit money left in a patient's will.

The trial at the Paris Assize Court in November 1823 became a media sensation, with the public captivated by the idea that a doctor could be responsible for such cold-blooded murders. Instead of the typical bloodstained clothes or murder weapons, the evidence table "The Bar" gleamed with decanters, bottles, and delicate glass phials. Each one, the prosecution argued, might have been the vessel of death. Sixty-five witnesses testified for the prosecution: twenty-six for the defence. Castaing's explanation for purchasing large quantities of morphine was absurd, claiming it was needed to kill stray cats and dogs near his hotel. The staff quickly pointed out that there were no such animals in the area. After 2 hours of deliberation, the jury acquitted him of Hippolyte's murder but found him guilty of destroying the man's will and of killing Auguste. By a narrow majority, only seven jurors in favour, the court sentenced him to death and ordered him to pay the Ballet family 100,000 francs.

He faced the guillotine on 6 December 1823, never admitting guilt. His final words were a cautious dance around blame.

> *I am not guilty of the crime which is imputed to me. I can look you in the face... and say I have not committed it.*

Castaing's notoriety extended beyond the murders to his choice of weapon. Morphine was then celebrated as a medical miracle, a painkiller unlike any physician had previously known. The fact that such a renowned remedy could also act as a silent killer struck a nerve. Detecting it in the body was impossible. Toxicology was still in its infancy, forcing scientists to rely on experiments with mice and then assume the same in humans. Experts testified at trial with confidence, yet much of what they claimed was based on limited evidence and untested theories. Some witnesses strayed well outside their areas of expertise, one muddying the effects of morphine on the pupils; morphine, as with other opiates, causes pin-prick pupils. This witness claimed the opposite. Others spoke of the post-mortem findings as being suggestive of poisoning with morphia even though there are no typical post-mortem changes of acute morphine poisoning.

During his trial, the courtroom was not merely a seat of justice; it was an arena where competing theories, egos, and the boundaries of human knowledge clashed, with a man's life hanging in the balance. It was also a place where the limitations of so-called experts were tested; this theme of experts working beyond their level of competence persists today.

WILLIAM PALMER (1824–1856): *THE RUGELEY POISONER*

Moving now to Rugeley, Staffordshire, England, in 1855, a shared passion for horse racing cemented Dr William Palmer's friendship with John Parsons Cook. Cook, younger and flush with winnings, had just seen his horse, Polestar, claim victory at Shrewsbury Races in November 1855, earning him nearly £3,000, a small fortune. The celebrations were as lavish as they were fateful.

At dinner, Cook freely drank wine before switching to brandy and water, only to complain that the drink had burned his throat. By nightfall, he was violently ill. Curiously, he voiced his fears the very next day, entrusting money to a friend and confiding that he believed Palmer had "dosed" him. Despite his suspicion, he returned to Rugeley with Palmer and continued to accept his medical care. Over the following days, Cook's condition worsened.

Meanwhile, Palmer purchased strychnine from a local chemist. That evening, Cook suffered terrible convulsions, shrieking in agony before dying. Palmer pressed the elderly attending doctor to declare apoplexy (stroke) as the cause of death. The same doctor had certified many of Palmer's relatives, who had also died in suspicious ways.

Given the circumstances of Cook's death, a post-mortem was ordered, and in a twist as chilling as it was bizarre, Palmer himself assisted with the procedure. From the very beginning, his behaviour was unsettling, and full of deception. When the stomach contents of the deceased were carefully sealed in a jar, bound with parchment, and set aside for analysis, the jar briefly vanished. Palmer had taken it and was seen clutching it, making his way to the door, with the parchment already slashed with two cuts. When confronted, Palmer claimed he was merely moving it and insisted he had done nothing to compromise the evidence. However, he later told the court that any subsequent analysis would now be useless because of possible contamination due to the cuts in the seal. His schemes to tamper with the evidence did not end there. Palmer brazenly tried to bribe the driver, whose job was to deliver the sample jar to London, to destroy it en route. When that failed, he resorted to further corruption, offering money to the coroner in a desperate attempt to hide the toxicology results forever. The coroner did not accept the bribe, regarding it as improper and suspicious. The attempted bribe became a significant piece of circumstantial evidence against Palmer.

He was arrested and accused of murdering Cook with strychnine and antimony. The trial, which occurred in 1856, was delayed because a special Act of Parliament was needed to transfer it from Staffordshire to the Old Bailey in London. This was because it was believed that, due to Palmer's notoriety in his home county, he would not receive a fair trial. From the very beginning, it became a nationwide obsession. The press dubbed him "The Rugeley Poisoner." The courtroom was packed every day, with the public queuing from early morning to gain entry, and even the corridors outside the court were crowded. Crowds gathered in the streets.

Strychnine was still a relatively new substance, and its terrifying nature fascinated as much as it repelled. Like Edme Castaing before him, Palmer's respectable façade masked financial ruin. Gambling debts had him in ruins.

The science of toxicology had advanced since Castaing's era, but proving strychnine poisoning remained difficult. The substance leaves no trace in the body. No chemical test can detect it; only its distinctive symptoms reveal the cause. The most convincing evidence for the prosecution did not come from the laboratory, but from a book found in Palmer's possession. On its first page, in his handwriting:

> Strychnine kills by causing tetanic fixing of the respiratory muscles.

As with Castaing's trial, it depended on experts from the highest levels of the medical profession, all with distinguished careers and extensive experience. Seventeen medical experts testified for the prosecution, while fifteen supported the defence. The court again became a battleground of scientific opinions. Some argued that Cook's death was due to idiopathic tetanus, a disease with no identifiable cause. Others attributed it to a fanciful "traumatic tetanus" caused by syphilitic ulcers... which Cook did not have.

Dr Alfred Taylor, a Fellow of the College of Physicians and a consultant at Guy's Hospital, and the country's leading expert in the emerging speciality of toxicology, took the stand. He had never encountered a case of strychnine poisoning in a human, but the effects on animals closely resembled the description of Cook's death. His evidence lasted a whole day, and although he admitted that no strychnine was found in the deceased's stomach, his expert opinion was that this was the cause of Cook's death and that the amount in the stomach would have been too small to detect in tests.

The trial revealed the uncomfortable truth about Victorian science: in court, expertise was often partly knowledge, partly educated guess, and partly performance. In the summing-up, the judge instructed the jury to consider "moral evidence" that Palmer had misused the deceased's money and tried to conceal his crimes, relying on circumstantial evidence to connect the events, which led to Palmer's undeniable poisoning of his friend.

The jury, uninfluenced by scientific uncertainty and guided by the judge's summing-up, found Palmer guilty of "Willful Murder by Poison."

Although he was never charged, he was considered responsible for the deaths of his wife, mother-in-law, brother, and nearly all of his 14 children, with the motive again being financial gain, as Palmer had initially taken out life insurance on these individuals and altered their wills.

On 14 June 1856, over 50,000 people gathered to witness the execution of this notorious doctor. His actions made him a symbol in Victorian Britain. Due to Palmer's notoriety, a wax figure of him remained in Madame Tussaud's Chamber of Horrors for over a century.

The ease with which he could commit murder exposed flaws in medical oversight, pharmacy regulation, and forensic practices. His trial ignited debates on medical ethics and poison regulation, eventually resulting in the enactment of the 1857 Poisons Act. Before this legislation, doctors could repeatedly obtain and administer poisons such as strychnine, arsenic, prussic acid, antimony, and opium without oversight. There was no national poison register nor any requirement to verify the purchaser. These drugs were easily available without prescriptions and sold in poorly labelled bottles, if labelled at all. If someone bought poison, there was no legal obligation to record who had purchased it or their reasons for doing so.

The 1857 Poisons Act represented a significant step in modernising poison regulation. In Britain, the Act required a legal obligation to maintain a poisons register, where sellers had to record the buyer's name, address, and signature, alongside the intended use of the poison. Containers had to be clearly labelled with the word "Poison" and the seller's name. Restrictions were introduced for selling certain poisons, such as strychnine, prussic acid, and arsenic. These substances could only be sold to individuals with a legitimate reason, such as for healthcare, and only under the supervision of a qualified pharmacist. Palmer's case also prompted the development of forensic toxicology and more detailed chemical testing during post-mortem examinations. Ultimately, his actions also played a significant role in later professional reforms, including the Medical Act of 1858, which established the General Medical Council to regulate doctors.

EDWARD PRITCHARD (1825–1865): *THE LAST PUBLIC EXECUTION IN SCOTLAND*

Glasgow, 1865. Two women in the same household died within weeks of each other: Mary Pritchard, the doctor's wife, and her mother, Mrs Taylor. Both had wasted away gradually, their bodies weakened by an illness that puzzled some and increased the suspicions of others.

At the heart of the tragedy was Dr Edward William Pritchard. Tall, attractive, and socially refined, he appeared the perfect Victorian gentleman-physician. Yet beneath his politeness lay a cunning killer. His weapon of choice: antimony. This compound has one of the most peculiar histories in medicine. For centuries, doctors thought that if a medicine could induce vomiting, sweating, or purging, it must be removing disease. Antimony, a shiny grey metalloid, seemed ideal for this purpose. In the seventeenth century, patients would even swallow the same solid antimony pill repeatedly; it would pass straight through the gut, be retrieved from the chamber pot, washed off, and reused, sometimes for years. Access to the drug was easy. Antimony compounds were widely available, sold as remedies for digestive issues, fevers, and as tonics. As a practising doctor, Pritchard had straightforward access to them. He could obtain preparations like tartar emetic (antimony potassium tartrate), which was still used as a purgative and expectorant. He administered it gradually, slipping small doses into food and drink. Antimony's effects work gradually. It's not a sudden dagger thrust or a single fatal swallow. Instead, it slowly weakens the body over days and weeks, with symptoms like nausea, vomiting, exhaustion, until the victim becomes too weak to resist inevitable death. The symptoms resembled those of natural disease, making it an ideal cover for murder.

Mary Pritchard's decline was long, painful, and overseen by her husband himself, acting as her physician. Other doctors voiced concern that her illness seemed unusual, but no action was taken, even after she had died. Shortly afterwards, her mother, Mrs Taylor, fell ill in the same house. When she died in March, just weeks after Mary, suspicion could no longer be ignored.

The investigation uncovered Pritchard's complicity in their deaths. Records showed that in the months before the deaths, he had bought large amounts of poisons, including strychnine, laudanum, aconite, and more antimony than all the other doctors in Glasgow combined. His motive was painfully clear: Mrs Taylor's will leave her fortune to Mary, and if Mary died, to her husband.

In court, Pritchard attempted to shift the blame onto the housemaid, a girl of sixteen. The Solicitor-General's rebuttal was scathing:

> Was it possible that gradual poisoning could have been carried out by a girl of sixteen? The hand of the doctor was very plainly indicated.

The jury delivered a verdict. Pritchard was found guilty and received a death sentence. On the morning of 28 July 1866, around 100,000 people gathered in Glasgow's streets to watch his execution. It would be the last public hanging in Scotland.

Pritchard stood on the scaffold, calm and composed, maintaining the same polished exterior he had throughout the trial. However, his name was now etched into Scottish history, not as a physician but as a murderer.

Like many scandals involving doctors, Pritchard's actions prompted reforms, especially in the process of death certification. Pritchard issued death certificates for both his wife and mother-in-law, claiming they had died of natural causes (gastric fever and apoplexy). There was no requirement for independent verification, despite Pritchard's apparent conflict of interest; he was related to them and stood to inherit their money upon their deaths. A doctor could, therefore, treat a relative, certify their death, conceal a murder, and benefit financially without an automatic inquest or second opinion being necessary. After several cases involving doctor-murder, reforms to death certification now meant that doctors could not certify the deaths of close relatives without oversight. The Births and Deaths Registration Act 1874 (UK) marked a significant tightening of death registration requirements and mandated that suspicious deaths, or those without clear medical attendance, required an inquest. The lengthy process from Pritchard in 1865 to 2025 (when the Medical Examiner system was introduced as the final recommendation following the Shipman Inquiry) now ensures that no death can be certified solely on one doctor's authority without scrutiny.

GEORGE LAMSON (1852–1882): *THE WIMBLEDON POISONER*

Wimbledon, December 1881. Percy John was only twenty, a gentle young man born with a curvature of the spine that caused paralysis of his lower limbs. He was the only surviving male of the five John children. He attended and boarded at Blenheim House School. His half-brother-in-law, Dr George Henry Lamson, arrived one winter evening bearing gifts: a Dundee cake, a cordial visit, and death in a gelatine capsule, an innovative method of administering medicines he had brought back from his recent trip to America.

Lamson's life was falling apart. Having qualified from St Thomas's Hospital and been decorated as a war hero (he served as a surgeon in the British Army during the Serbo-Turkish and Russo-Turkish wars), he was now addicted to morphine, drowning in debt, and eyeing his brother-in-law's inheritance. Percy's death would allow him to claim the estate. The method: aconitine, a lethal alkaloid distilled from monkshood, so rare that little was known about it, and extremely difficult to detect with Victorian forensic science. Lamson had purchased multiple quantities of aconitine from different chemists, claiming he needed it for research and medical purposes. Despite changes to tighten up the sale of poisons, they could still be easily obtained by doctors who only needed to say that the drugs were required for medical or research purposes.

Within hours of swallowing the capsule that Lamson had given Percy, together with a slice of Dundee cake and sweets, Percy was in agony. Convulsions ravaged his frail body. His muscles seized so violently that two visiting doctors had to restrain him. His face distorted, his hands clenched, and his body arched in a tetanic spasm. By nightfall, he was dead. Lamson by this time had left London for the night train to Paris.

The doctors attending him had the presence of mind to preserve the contents of Percy's stomach, along with the cake and the remaining capsules, for analysis. At the post-mortem, no natural cause of death was identified. The symptoms indicated a plant-based alkaloid. But which one?

A few days after Percy's death, Lamson returned from Paris and voluntarily went to Scotland Yard, saying that as his name had been related to the death, he thought it best to call and see what was to be done. He was arrested and formally charged with the death, with aconitine still in his possession. The Wimbledon Poisoner believed his choice of a little-known toxin would keep him hidden from detection.

The trial was memorable for the conclusive nature of the scientific evidence.

One of the key experts at his trial was Sir Thomas Stevenson, a pioneer in forensic toxicology and the Home Office Analyst. He suspected aconitine as the cause of death, but lacked a specific test for it. So, he and a colleague devised one. First, they tasted aconitine themselves, recognising its distinctive, numbing effect on the lips. Then, they sampled small portions of Percy's vomit and experienced the same numbing burn. They also injected extracts from the vomit into mice, which quickly died in spasms identical to those caused by pure aconitine. The conclusion was unmistakable: Percy had been poisoned. Sir Thomas had set new standards for forensic work, preserving specimens, demonstrating causation through physiological testing, and presenting scientific evidence to a jury. The case led to the professionalisation of forensic pathology.

Lamson was found guilty and sentenced to death. On hearing the verdict, Lamson stood with his arms folded and in a loud voice proclaimed his innocence before God.

He then claimed insanity because of being under the influence of morphine and sedatives, which, he asserted, "had rendered him almost incapable of knowing what he was really doing."

The judge was unmoved. On 28 April 1882, at only 30 years old, Lamson was hanged at Wandsworth Prison (The Execution of Lamson, 1882).

In the opinion of Montagu Williams, who defended Lamson at his trial, there was little doubt that he had previously murdered his brother-in-law, Herbert, in the same manner, without arousing any suspicion (Mitchell, 1911/1980).

ALFRED WILLIAM WARDER (1823–1866): *THREE WIVES, THREE GRAVES*

In the summer of 1866, less than a year after the execution of Dr Edward Pritchard for poisoning his wife, another doctor was accused of the same offence. The press quickly drew the parallel, dubbing Alfred Warder "The Second Pritchard."

Warder's origins were unremarkable. He was the youngest son of an innkeeper, with no family ties to medicine. But ambition motivated him. He qualified in 1840 and soon married into influence, taking Alicia Gunning, a member of a distinguished medical family, as his wife. Through marriage, he gained what birth had denied him: connections. Together, they had four children.

The veneer of respectability did not last. Warder's practice soured through disputes with his partner. Lawsuits followed, debts increased, and the marriage broke apart. He separated from Alicia, taking the children with him. When the couple briefly reunited, tragedy struck. Alicia died in 1863. Her death certificate listed three conflicting causes: an ovarian abscess, fatty degeneration of the heart, or "unknown causes" after a short illness. Whatever the truth, her fortune was locked away in a trust for the children, leaving Warder with little to gain.

Within months, he remarried. His second wife, Jane Anne De Valerie, was the daughter of a Scottish naval officer. Their marriage was short-lived. By the summer of 1865, Jane had passed away. Among the witnesses at the wedding was her close friend Ellen Branwell. Soon after, Ellen herself became Mrs Warder.

Ellen was wealthy, well-connected, and, importantly, in excellent health. She was a third cousin of the Brontë sisters. However, almost immediately after her marriage in 1866, she began to fall ill. The Warders relocated to Brighton, where Alfred became not only her husband but also her doctor and sole carer.

Her brother grew uneasy about his sister's declining health and asked a Brighton physician to give a second opinion. What this doctor heard worried him. Warder admitted to dosing his wife daily with twenty drops of Fleming's tincture of aconite, one of the deadliest poisons known, ostensibly for "bladder problems." The Brighton doctor ordered him to stop immediately and replaced the medication with a safer opiate mixture.

It was too late. Ellen's condition worsened. On 1 July 1866, she died at the hotel where they had been staying.

At her brother's insistence, a post-mortem was carried out. No natural cause of death could be identified. Samples were sent to Dr Alfred Taylor at Guy's Hospital, the same expert instructed as in Cream's case. However, Taylor's tests failed to confirm aconite. It mattered little. The jury at Ellen's inquest delivered their verdict in clear, ringing tones:

> Ellen Vivian Warder died from aconite poisoning, delivered wilfully and of malice aforethought by her late husband, Alfred William Warder.

Rumours spread quickly. Alicia in 1863, Jane in 1865, and now Ellen in 1866, each woman had entered Warder's household in good health and left in coffins. Few doubted that he was responsible for each one.

Alfred Warder followed his wives to the grave, swallowing prussic acid in the same hotel room as Ellen. Staff found him naked in bed, a gruesome end to a once-promising physician.

At Alfred Warder's inquest, the jury deliberated only briefly. The verdict was felo de se – suicide, a crime under English law. The Crown seized his estate, and he was refused Christian burial. Around a hundred spectators gathered to watch as he was lowered into an unmarked grave, denied even the dignity of consecrated ground.

These cases – Palmer, Pritchard, and now Warder – heightened the moral panic. The image of the murderous doctor dominated Victorian imagination. However, in reality, such cases were rare. Between 1840 and 1890, only eighteen British practitioners were suspected of deliberate killing or attempted murder. Two-thirds of them used poison. Most of their victims, 70%, were wives, in-laws, or other close relatives. The rest were servants, neighbours, policemen, or strangers who had crossed their path. But in the public mind, the pattern was set: doctors who healed by day and poisoned by night.

MODERN-DAY POISONERS

From Victorian parlours to modern hospitals, poisoning remains a doctor's most sinister weapon; only the tools have changed.

Paul Vickers (1934): *The surgeon and the perfect poison*

In November 1981, Newcastle orthopaedic surgeon Paul Richard Jarvis Vickers stood trial for the murder of his wife, Margaret. On paper, he was a respectable man: consultant, chairman of the British Medical Association's Ethical Committee, with political ambitions that might one day have taken him to Westminster or Brussels. Yet behind this professional façade lay a story of deception, ambition, and ultimately, lethal betrayal.

The weapon he selected was the cytotoxic drug Chloroethyl-Cyclohexyl-Nitrosourea CCNU (lomustine), a newly introduced chemotherapy agent. Tasteless and bitter only when chewed, it metabolises within hours and remains invisible to the pathologist's knife. CCNU was almost the perfect contemporary poison.

Margaret Vickers was a brilliant mathematician, a Cambridge graduate, who suffered from schizophrenia. Her illness, treated with the drugs Stelazine and Disipal, left her vulnerable and dependent. Vickers had tired of the marriage, taking lovers during it, but divorce threatened to damage his professional and political ambitions. By 1977, he had begun a passionate affair with a glamorous former beauty queen and political aide. The two plotted a future together. The obstacle was Margaret.

When CCNU became available in Britain in late 1977, Vickers saw an opportunity. Prescribed in carefully measured doses, it could slow the growth of brain tumours. In larger, repeated doses, it silently destroyed the bone marrow, leaving the victim anaemic, prone to infection, bleeding, and ultimately unable to survive without transfusion.

Between 1978 and 1979, Vickers wrote a series of prescriptions for CCNU, not in his wife's name but in those of acquaintances and patients. He collected more than 2,000 milligrams of the drug, ten times the amount any legitimate treatment would require. By early 1979, Margaret was gravely ill with aplastic anaemia. She became breathless, bruised, and very weak. Admitted to hospital in Newcastle, she underwent repeated transfusions. But neither she nor her husband ever mentioned CCNU to her doctors.

On 14 June 1979, after a collapse on the ward, Margaret died. The post-mortem revealed no obvious cause beyond bone marrow failure. Aplastic anaemia can arise spontaneously or from viral infection; no one suspected foul play. The death certificate passed without question (Richard, 1994).

Vickers might have escaped justice had his affair endured. But when he broke off the relationship, his lover went first to a government minister she knew socially, and then to the police. She told them she had collected prescriptions from John Bell & Croyden, the exclusive Wigmore Street pharmacy, on Vickers's behalf. The drug she said had been for Margaret.

At trial, the evidence presented painted a damning picture for Vickers. All the medical experts agreed CCNU had caused Margaret's death. The defence argued Vickers had acted recklessly, perhaps even negligently, but without intent to kill, claiming he believed she had a brain tumour. The jury did not accept it. They saw a man who had used his medical knowledge to administer a modern, sophisticated poison, exploiting both his wife's vulnerability and the trust of the medical system to pursue his affair and his ambitions.

Paul Vickers was convicted of murder.

This case was remarkable not just for its drama but for its method. Poison has always been the weapon of the subtle killer. Still, Vickers's choice of CCNU marked a shift into the modern era: a doctor reaching into the armoury of contemporary pharmacology to find a substance almost undetectable, devastatingly effective, and available only to those within the profession. In the history of medical murder, it was one of the first examples of a contemporary poison, not the arsenic of the nineteenth century, nor the barbiturates of the early twentieth century, but a drug born of cutting-edge cancer treatment, turned to lethal use by a man who should have known better.

Raynaldo Rivera Ortiz: *The "medical terrorist"*

We move on to another century and another country. Dallas, Texas, 2022. In a busy private surgical centre, patients began experiencing unexplained cardiac arrests during minor procedures. These were not fragile patients on intensive care; they were healthy individuals undergoing routine operations. One by one, they collapsed. At first, it seemed to be a cruel coincidence. However, the emergencies followed a pattern: all occurred shortly after a new intravenous (IV) bag was connected to them.

The poisoner was neither an intruder nor a resentful ex-employee sneaking in after hours. He was there openly, dressed in scrubs. Dr Raynaldo Rivera Ortiz, a 60-year-old anaesthetist, had turned the simplest instrument of patient care, an intravenous saline infusion, into a weapon.

Surveillance footage revealed the story. Ortiz would fetch an IV bag from a warming bin outside the operating theatre, inject it with a cocktail of drugs, and then return it. Minutes later, the bag would be used during surgery. Inside was a deadly mix: bupivacaine, a nerve-blocker that can stop the heart; epinephrine, a potent stimulant; and lidocaine, another anaesthetic that can disturb the heart's rhythm.

The first of his victims to die was a fellow doctor, Melanie Kaspar, who had taken a bag home to treat herself for dehydration. She collapsed and died almost immediately. Others, including an 18-year-old undergoing sinus surgery, survived only because of frantic, high-level emergency intervention.

Ortiz's motive was as petty as it was chilling. He was facing disciplinary action for a separate medical error, and prosecutors argued that he was lashing out, creating chaos that might deflect scrutiny from himself.

The trial was a spectacle of disbelief. Colleagues described the chaos in the theatre as patients' blood pressures rose sharply, and their hearts faltered. Survivors recalled waking in intensive care, intubated, terrified, and unable to understand what had occurred. After the 8-day trial, the jury took just 7 hours to convict him on ten counts, including intentional adulteration of a drug and tampering with consumer products that caused serious bodily harm. His sentence: 190 years in federal prison.

The US Attorney described Ortiz as *no better than an armed assailant spraying bullets into a crowd*, except his weapon was invisible, a clear plastic bag meant to heal. His crimes shattered the unspoken pact between patient and doctor, the quiet faith that the hands putting up your IV are there to keep you alive, not to bring you down.

Dr Thomas Kwan: *The "booster" shot*

Sunderland, England, January 2024. The letter looked official, displaying an NHS logo, medical terminology, and a friendly invitation for a home visit to receive a COVID-19 booster. It was addressed to Patrick O'Hara, a man in his seventies, the partner of the mother of local GP Dr Thomas Kwan. Like many patients in general practice, he was being targeted to protect him from any future covid infection, ensuring that the vulnerable and elderly received the booster. When Kwan arrived at the house, he was in disguise, dressed as a community nurse and fully equipped with personal protective equipment (PPE). He administered the "vaccine" with practised ease. Hours later, O'Hara was in hospital fighting for his life, the injection site inflamed, his body battling necrotising fasciitis, a rare, flesh-eating infection. Surgeons worked through the night to save him.

The motive, prosecutors argued, was as old as many in this book: greed. O'Hara was the life tenant of Kwan's family home, and his continued presence was an obstacle to Kwan's inheritance. Removing him would open the way for the doctor's financial gain.

The investigation quickly revealed Kwan's façade. CCTV tracked his movements before and after the attack. A search of his home uncovered not only the tools of his medical practice but also a hidden stockpile of toxins: arsenic, liquid mercury, and instructions on manufacturing ricin.

Confronted with compelling evidence, Kwan ultimately admitted guilt to attempted murder. The judge called it an "audacious plan to murder a man in plain sight." His sentence: over 31 years in prison.

CLOSING REFLECTION: KNOWLEDGE AS CURE, KNOWLEDGE AS WEAPON

The archetype of the poisoner-doctor did not disappear with the Victorians. Whether using aconitine in a cake, strychnine in a cordial, morphine in a flask, or a hypodermic syringe filled with lies, the core danger remains the same: mixing medical skill with malicious intent.

These doctors caused harm, not in spite of their profession, but because of it. Their medical authority acted as their disguise, and their technical skill as their weapon.

However, the methods have progressed. The poisons of the Victorian era, such as morphine, strychnine, antimony, and aconitine, have been replaced by modern pharmaceuticals, anaesthetic agents, and even the distorted imitation of public health measures. The opportunities remain essentially unchanged: the doctor still enters the sickroom, the operating theatre, or the home.

REFERENCES

Mitchell, C. A. (1911). *Science and the Criminal.* Boston: Little Brown and Company.

The Execution of Lamson. (1882, June 17). *South Australian Weekly Chronicle (Adelaide, SA: 1881–1889),* p. 6. Retrieved November 6, 2025, from https://trove.nla.gov.au/newspaper/article/91469480

Richard, R. V. P. (1994). EWHC J0329-8. Retrieved July 2026, from https://vlex.co.uk/vid/r-v-paul-richard-792829501

8

Gross negligence manslaughter: A dangerous intersection

ZAID AL-NAJJAR

When I was a young doctor in Southampton in the early 2000s, whispers began circulating through the hospital corridors. From fragments of conversations, we learnt that two doctors had been arrested and charged with manslaughter. The details were initially unclear, but the atmosphere was unforgettable: the staff appeared somewhat frightened, defensive, and on edge. Of course, we understood that any mistakes we made could be fatal, and if it was proven that our error resulted from poor practice, we could face the regulator. But a criminal charge? That was entirely different; in my experience, it was the first time law itself had entered the wards.

The patient, Sean Phillips, who was at the centre of the case, underwent routine surgery on 23 June 2000, to repair his patellar tendon. At the time of the surgery, he was a healthy man. Unfortunately, postoperatively, he contracted Staphylococcus aureus; the infection was left untreated, leading to the development of toxic shock syndrome, which caused his death on 27 June. Two senior house officers were involved in his postoperative care from the evening of 23 June until the afternoon of 25 June. Both would be convicted of manslaughter by gross negligence (Fitzpatrick, 2005).

The prosecution's case against the doctors was not that they failed to diagnose Sean Phillips's exact condition. Given its rarity, this alone might not have been enough to prove negligence. Instead, it was their failure to recognise that the patient was seriously ill at all. During the time they were both caring for him, he displayed clear signs of infection, including a raised temperature and pulse, and lowered blood pressure. These persistent signs should have been obvious, even from a glance at the relevant charts hanging at the end of his bed. Blood results, available from the hospital computer on Saturday evening, were not checked, and

 DOI: 10.1201/9781003781066-8

certainly not before it was too late. Had the doctors done so, they would have seen that the patient had developed acute renal failure and probable sepsis. His illness progressed beyond the point where treatment could have saved him.

In 2003, both doctors appeared before Winchester Crown Court.

During the trial, the four legal tests for gross negligence manslaughter (GNM) were outlined in turn:

- Duty of care.
- Breach of duty.
- Causation.
- The breach had to be so severe that it demonstrated a disregard for life and safety.

The court determined that ignoring the blood results and failing to act on them surpassed the threshold for GNM. Both doctors were convicted and received an 18-month prison sentence, suspended for 2 years. They were both erased from the medical register. The hospital was also fined £100,000 for inadequate supervision of these junior doctors, given that the defence argued that if a senior specialist had been present, the patient's deterioration might have been identified in time.

The repercussions were severe. A family lost their loved one. The hospital's reputation was damaged. The doctors' careers were ended barely months after they had qualified. Every staff member involved in the man's care bore some responsibility.

A culture of fear grew, fuelled by concerns about being involved in the next tragedy and facing legal action. This led to defensive behaviours, such as ordering unnecessary blood tests, conducting routine checks on stable patients, or nurses filing incident reports if they believed the doctor had not responded promptly, along with widespread mistrust amongst team members.

We worried that any of us could be the next to face charges of GNM if a patient died whilst in our care.

The truth, of course, is that prosecutions for GNM are rare, and successful convictions are even more uncommon. Between 1795 and 2005, 85 doctors faced this charge. Sixty were acquitted, 22 convicted, and 3 pleaded guilty. Although prosecutions have increased since 1990, the conviction success rate remains very low. Between 2007 and 2019, only 12 doctors in the United Kingdom were charged (Ferner & McDowell, 2006).

EARLY CASES OF MANSLAUGHTER IN MEDICINE

Most of the early cases of GNM originated in obstetrics; the first recorded prosecution occurred in 1831, when Dr Raeburn was charged after a woman died in childbirth at the Lent Assizes, York. *The Times*, 31 March 1831: 4.

In the 1920s, a doctor from New Cross in South London became involved in a tragedy that led to his prosecution for manslaughter and provoked an outcry amongst fellow doctors (https://transpont.blogspot.com/2013/08/history-corner-medical-negligence-in.html). A midwife asked Dr Percy Bateman in July 1924 to assist with a difficult labour. The mother, Mary Ann Harding, was the wife of a labourer and lived in Deptford in a two-room flat at the top of four flights of stairs. She was 33 years old and had previously given birth to four children. The baby died, and Mary Ann Harding became seriously ill. Over the following week, her condition worsened, and Bateman visited her twice daily. He refused requests from Mary's husband and the midwife to admit her to the hospital. When she was finally admitted, she was considered unfit for an operation, and she died on July 30. A post-mortem revealed that the doctor had mistakenly removed most of her uterus along with the placenta during childbirth. He was charged with manslaughter, found guilty, and sentenced to 6 months' imprisonment in December 1924. What impressed the jury was the callous neglect he showed. He did not call in another doctor; he took the uterus home with him and he concealed the facts of the matter from everybody who might be able to give help or advice.

However, Bateman received backing from the medical profession, which was worried about the implications of doctors being imprisoned for negligence. On appeal, the Lord Chief Justice, Lord Hewart, overturned the conviction in February 1925, leading to his release. The appeal judgment in Rex v Bateman (1925) is still referenced today, as it helped define the boundaries of manslaughter in similar cases. The court ruled that simply causing someone's death was not enough to establish manslaughter; instead, it was necessary to demonstrate that the accused exhibited such disregard for the safety and life of others that it constituted a crime against the State and conduct deserving punishment, and in this case, the threshold was not met (R v Bateman, 19 Cr App R 8 (C.C.A. 1925))

This threshold would be reconsidered in a landmark case involving Dr John Adomako. In 1987, 33-year-old Alan Loveland underwent routine eye surgery at St Bartholomew's Hospital under general anaesthetic. Midway through, the oxygen supply to his endotracheal tube became disconnected. The alarm on the monitor sounded 4 and a half minutes later. By then, his pulse was collapsing, and he was turning cyanotic. The surgeon had to halt the operation to attempt resuscitation, and it was only then that the ventilator was found to be disconnected.

Although Alan Loveland was briefly revived, the damage had already been done. He never regained consciousness and died months later. The details that emerged in court painted a troubling picture. Adomako had qualified overseas but had no formal postgraduate training in anaesthetics. He had worked for 15 years in Britain, mainly as a locum. The hospital had not even sought references before employing him, explaining that it was "only a short-term attachment."

Adomako was found guilty of GNM. His appeal was rejected. The trial judge determined that his failings went far beyond mere error; they crossed the line into criminal conduct. He was sentenced to 6 months' imprisonment, suspended for 12 months.

The case marked a turning point. The Court of Appeal upheld the four-part legal test that would later be used in cases like Misra and Srivastava: duty of care, breach of duty, causation, and negligence so severe that it became a crime. The final question, how severe "gross" is, would be decided by the jury.

THE HIGH BAR FOR CONVICTION

In the early 1990s, the distinction between human error and criminal acts was once again challenged. In 1991, two junior doctors, Dr Michael Prentice and Dr Barry Sullman, were tasked with administering chemotherapy into the spine of a 16-year-old patient with leukaemia. They were instructed to do this without supervision, despite hospital policies indicating otherwise. Initially, they refused. However, with no senior doctor available for assistance and being told to "get on with it," they proceeded. What followed was disastrous. Vincristine, a drug that must never be injected into the spine, was mistakenly administered via this route, instead of methotrexate, a standard chemotherapy drug. The mistake resulted in death. Both men were convicted of manslaughter, but the Court of Appeal later overturned their convictions. The judges recognised the seriousness of the doctors' mistake but also acknowledged they were placed in an impossible situation. The ruling highlighted that context was crucial: a lack of proper training, insufficient supervision, and systemic failures all contributed to their actions.

What made this case even more troubling was that it was not an isolated incident. At that time, vincristine was supplied in small syringes that closely resembled those prepared for intrathecal chemotherapy, such as methotrexate or cytarabine. This created a high risk of picking up the wrong syringe. Before the convictions of Sullman and Prentice, there had already been five other incidents where vincristine was wrongly injected into patients' spines. Three of these patients died, and one was left severely paralysed.

Until the packaging was finally changed, more cases occurred.

In 1997, at Great Ormond Street children's hospital in London, a 12-year-old boy, Richie William, who was undergoing treatment for non-Hodgkin's lymphoma, died after vincristine was again mistakenly given via spinal injection. The registrar in anaesthesia, Dr John Lee, and the registrar in haematology, Dr Dermot Murphy, were charged with manslaughter, and their cases were heard at the Old Bailey. During the trial, prosecutors accepted that the death resulted not from gross negligence but from a series of "chance events and failings" at the hospital. The judge concurred, describing it as a "chapter of accidents and misunderstandings." Both doctors were acquitted.

Lee and Murphy were fortunate: their tragedies were seen as a result of systemic failure rather than criminal intent.

Sullman and Prentice ended up with criminal records, whilst Lee and Murphy were spared conviction for what was essentially the same mistake.

Overall, these cases show how the line between error and crime in medicine was quite blurry during this period and how outcomes depended not only on the "crime" but also on the legal climate, prosecutorial discretion, and public perception.

Dr Prabhaker Gadgil, an anaesthetist, was a doctor whose actions were viewed through a criminal lens. In 1997, he served a 6-month prison sentence after the death of his 14-year-old patient, whom he had mistakenly given nitrous oxide instead of oxygen during a dental procedure.

Dr Gadgil was charged with and admitted manslaughter.

The trial judge stated: "*This offence was one of the most gross negligence. I have concluded that I would be failing in my public duty if I did not pass a custodial sentence.*"

The case revealed serious safety failures in dental anaesthesia and prompted new guidance from the General Dental Council, restricting the use of general anaesthetics in dental surgeries.

Another case in 2008 involved Dr Sudhanshu Garg, a 44-year-old consultant urologist working in Bradford, who was found guilty of GNM. His patient, 37-year-old Lisa Quinn, was a mother of two. On the morning of 22 August 2008, a Friday marking the start of a bank holiday weekend, she was admitted to the hospital's Accident and Emergency Department. She had been complaining of abdominal pain and pain when passing urine, with strongly smelling urine.

The admitting doctor ordered an X-ray and, upon review, concluded that Lisa was suffering from a kidney stone and prescribed an antibiotic. An ultrasound was ordered to confirm the diagnosis, but due to the bank holiday, it was not performed until considerably later after admission. During this period, her care was transferred to the urologist, Dr Sudhanshu Garg. By Monday afternoon, Lisa had developed pulmonary oedema and suffered a fatal cardiac arrest.

In late September 2008, Garg was arrested on suspicion of GNM. The case against him can be summarised as four main breaches of duty: (1) failing to ensure that Lisa Quinn's clinical condition was correctly identified; (2) failing to detect or diagnose the possibility of a renal infection and the development of sepsis; (3) failing to arrange urgent interventional treatment for a renal infection, which showed early signs in the A&E X-ray and the patient's clinical condition; (4) failing to organise a transfer to an appropriate hospital after 8.00 am on the morning of Sunday, 24 August.

Expert evidence demonstrated that if active intervention had been initiated, even as late as Sunday evening, she probably would have survived. Her chances of ultimate survival only became very unlikely by Monday, which was 48 hours after her condition was first brought to the Garg's attention. Medical experts instructed by the prosecution stated that these breaches of duty represented a significant departure from usual professional standards and that no reasonably competent consultant in this discipline would have acted as he did. The Crown argued that these breaches of duty caused Lisa Quinn's death, and that collectively they painted a disturbing picture of neglect in treating a healthy 37-year-old woman who could have survived if proper action had been taken. Garg was found guilty and sentenced to 2 years in prison. His appeal was unsuccessful.

However, it was not just the delay in care that led to Garg's conviction. After Lisa Quinn's death, Garg tampered with her medical records by falsifying blood pressure readings, altering fluid charts, removing notes, and creating an impression that he had conducted investigations he had not. He also removed the original history sheet and replaced it with a fake one, attempting to copy another doctor's handwriting.

Finally, he made false statements on her death certificate, which meant the Coroner's Office was not informed of the possibility that her death resulted from negligence; as a result, the body was cremated, and no post-mortem examination was carried out.

His deception became a crucial part of the prosecution's case. This was not only a professional failure but also a dishonest response in the face of tragedy (Garg v R., [2012] EWCA Crim 2520 (Eng.)).

THE CASES THAT SHOOK THE PROFESSION

In February 2010, James Hughes, a 66-year-old man recovering from knee replacement surgery at a private hospital in London, experienced sudden abdominal pain. An X-ray revealed free air beneath the diaphragm, indicating a bowel perforation. He was referred to Mr David Sellu, a highly regarded colorectal surgeon with an impeccable 40-year career, who became the centre of national attention following Hughes's death.

Hughes was admitted with abdominal pain. Mr Sellu examined him, ordered a CT scan, and advised starting antibiotics, although the timing and appropriateness of this decision were later questioned. The following morning, the CT scan confirmed a bowel perforation. Surgery, however, was delayed until late that evening because no anaesthetist was available. Despite the eventual operation, Hughes died 2 days later.

Given the circumstances, the hospital launched an investigation into Hughes's death and also reviewed Mr Sellu's previous cases. The report following the investigation criticised aspects of his management. He was referred to the General Medical Council (GMC) for providing care that was significantly below the standard expected of a doctor of his seniority. Initially, the GMC concluded there was no case to answer but deferred a final decision pending the outcome of other inquiries, including the coroner's inquest.

At the inquest in October 2010, concerns about Mr Sellu's care were raised, which led to the initiation of a criminal investigation. In July 2012, he was arrested and charged with two offences:

1. GNM of James Hughes.
2. Perjury, relating to the answers he gave in the coroner's court when first reviewing the CT scan report.

During the trial, the prosecution alleged multiple failings, including:

- A delay after the initial X-ray.
- Failure to prescribe antibiotics promptly.
- Slow responses to nurses' concerns.
- A lengthy delay between confirmation of perforation on the CT scan and surgical intervention.

The jury found Mr Sellu guilty of GNM but cleared him of perjury. He received a sentence of two and a half years. He served 8 months at Belmarsh before being released on licence.

His conviction was appealed, and in November 2016, the Court of Appeal quashed it. It found that the trial judge had misdirected the jury on the key legal test of "gross negligence." As said earlier in this chapter, whilst experts can judge clinical standards, it is solely for the jury to decide whether the actions of a doctor are so deplorable as to be considered criminal, rather than a matter of civil negligence.

Mr Sellu was reinstated to the medical register, although the case had already caused significant personal and professional harm. His conviction and imprisonment sparked broader debate within the medical community about the fairness of prosecuting doctors for errors in complex, resource-limited systems.

The case was cited as an example of how systemic issues, such as shortages of theatre and anaesthetic supplies, can be unfairly attributed to individual clinicians. In 2019, Mr Sellu published his memoir *Did He Save Lives?*, reflecting on his ordeal and broader implications for patient safety, medical accountability, and justice. He later considered not only the personal devastation caused by imprisonment but also the suspicion that racial bias may have influenced the case. Many doctors prosecuted for GNM come from minority ethnic backgrounds.

If Sellu's conviction caused tremors in medicine, the case of Dr Hadiza Bawa-Garba triggered an earthquake.

On 18 February 2011, 6-year-old Jack Adcock was admitted to Leicester Royal Infirmary with diarrhoea, vomiting, and difficulty breathing. Jack had Down syndrome and a congenital heart defect, which placed him at higher risk of complications. Dr Hadiza Bawa-Garba, a paediatric registrar who had only that day returned from maternity leave, was covering multiple wards without immediate consultant supervision. Conditions were challenging:

- The hospital's IT system was failing, causing delays in receiving blood results.
- A crucial chest X-ray was not reviewed in a timely manner.
- Other critically unwell children needed her urgent attention, further stretching her capacity.

Although sepsis was recognised and treatment was started, a series of delays led to Jack's condition worsening. By evening, he was in septic shock. During resuscitation, Dr Bawa-Garba briefly confused Jack with another patient who had a "Do Not Resuscitate" order, but she quickly corrected herself and continued full resuscitation efforts. Jack died later that day.

In 2015, after a lengthy investigation, Bawa-Garba was convicted of GNM. She received a 2-year suspended prison sentence. She was initially suspended from the medical register by the GMC. However, the GMC's decision to allow her to return to practice after the suspension was challenged by the Professional Standards Authority (PSA). Following the PSA's appeal, the High Court in 2017 ruled that she should instead be erased from the register, effectively ending her medical career.

Systemic failures were widely recognised: understaffing, IT breakdowns, delayed investigations, and a lack of senior support. Yet, the entire legal burden fell on a single doctor. Many feared that if a trainee working under such pressure could be convicted of manslaughter, no clinician would be safe from prosecution. Outrage amongst the profession grew when it was revealed that her educational reflective notes, written for training and appraisal purposes, had been used as evidence against her. Reflection was supposed to be a safe and confidential space for learning, not self-incrimination.

In 2018, after widespread campaigning, the Court of Appeal overturned the striking-off order and reinstated the original GMC decision only to suspend. This eventually enabled Dr Bawa-Garba to return to practice. She resumed work in the NHS in 2019 under close supervision. The official investigation into Jack's death concluded that there was no single cause but a series of failings on a day when "everything went wrong."

In 2012, Frances Cappuccini was admitted to Tunbridge Wells Hospital to give birth to her second child. She was only 30 years old. Her son Giacomo was safely delivered by caesarean section. However, in the hours that followed, complications arose. Frances began to bleed heavily and was taken back to the theatre for further surgery. During this second operation, she suffered a cardiac arrest. The focus of the tragedy soon shifted to the anaesthetic care she received from Dr Nadeem Azeez. He was held responsible for her death due to errors on his part, including not physically examining her before surgery, failing to call a consultant anaesthetist to assist with intubation after judging it would be difficult, and delaying reintubation even though Frances was struggling to breathe. He displayed poor record-keeping throughout.

Dr Azeez, who trained in Pakistan, was not actually qualified for the role of speciality doctor grade anaesthetist when he was appointed in 2008 and undertook very little additional training thereafter. By the time the case reached court, he had fled to Pakistan, evading trial.

Another doctor was involved in the case, consultant Dr Errol Cornish. He was a locum who arrived to assist Dr Azeez at a time when the situation was "recoverable."

The prosecution argued that both men failed in what it called "the elementary task of protecting her airway." If either was guilty of gross negligence, it was contended, then the Trust itself was responsible for employing a doctor who was not adequately trained.

But the case faltered almost as soon as it began. The trial judge, Mr Justice Coulson, found that Cornish had followed the hospital's guidelines, called for help when it was needed, and that his decisions, whether right or wrong, were far from the level of "reprehensible or atrocious" behaviour required for a conviction. The arguments against the Trust, he added, were "perverse." He instructed the jury to acquit.

In his closing remarks, Coulson praised the family's dignity throughout, whilst bluntly acknowledging the loss: "There is no question that Frances Cappuccini should not have died at the hospital on October 9."

The case had repercussions that extended far beyond the courtroom. The Right Honourable Jeremy Hunt, then health secretary, was heavily criticised for posting what the judge described as a "highly inappropriate" tweet during the trial, in which he speculated that lessons should be learned from the tragedy. He was instructed to delete it. The case was historic for another reason: it was the first time an NHS Trust faced a charge of corporate manslaughter. Those charges, like the ones against the doctors, eventually fell apart. However, the questions raised by Frances's death about responsibility, accountability, and how the law should respond when tragedy occurs in a hospital continued to influence policy, regulation, and professional practice. The NHS trust expressed its sympathy to the family, admitted that aspects of Frances's care had fallen short of expected standards, and apologised. Yet, it also argued that the prosecution should never have taken place.

Some are concerning because of their sheer avoidability.

In 2018, Dr Isyaka Mamman-Aka'Aba, a haematologist at the Royal Oldham Hospital, attempted a routine bone marrow biopsy on Shahida Parveen, a 48-year-old mother. Instead of using the standard hip approach, he opted for the rare and perilous sternal route. Using the wrong needle, he punctured her pericardium. She bled to death almost instantly, as her husband cried out, "He killed her. I told him to stop three times, and he did not listen."

Mamman was believed to be 85 years old at the time. He had a long history of poor performance, including previous suspensions and dismissal for dishonesty regarding his age. Despite this, the trust had re-employed him, brushing aside concerns with vague promises of "light duties."

This time, there was no ambiguity. Mamman pleaded guilty to GNM and was sentenced to 3 years in prison.

THE LEGACY OF TRAGEDY

Every case of GNM begins with the loss of human life, often very unexpectedly. This leaves families facing irreplaceable grief and pain, which is worsened by the complex process of investigations, court proceedings, and media coverage that follows.

The death of Frances Cappuccini and other high-profile prosecutions, including that of Hadiza Bawa-Garba, prompted the government to commission, in 2018, a review of GNM. Led by Sir Norman Williams, a former president of the Royal College of Surgeons, the task was to examine how GNM was applied to healthcare professionals, whether doctors were being unfairly criminalised for honest mistakes, and how to promote both patient safety and a culture of transparency within the NHS.

The main conclusions of the *Williams Review* (UK Parliament, 2018) were that prosecutions are infrequent, convictions are notably rare, and the legal threshold for GNM is set high.

CONCLUSION

Those of us who have never gone through the sudden death of a family member or friend in healthcare cannot fully grasp the deep sense of loss and grief that will inevitably arise in such circumstances. This must never be underestimated.

Families and loved ones require transparency, a thorough investigation, an explanation of what went wrong, and reassurance that measures are in place to prevent similar tragedies from occurring.

Many bereaved families have emphasised that their goal is not just justice or punishment but learning and growth, so that others do not suffer the same pain. However, a culture of fear and retribution often stifles the reflection and openness needed for genuine learning.

Nicola Adcock, mother of Jack Adcock, has spoken publicly about her family's suffering following Jack's death and her hope that his death was not in vain. Whilst she condemned Dr Bawa-Garba for her role in Jack's death, she also criticised the medical profession for what she saw as closing ranks during the criminal and regulatory proceedings. The Adcock family's experience has been widely cited by patient safety campaigners and in official reviews examining accountability and learning.

The relatives of Lisa Quinn also emphasised the importance of honesty and transparency, calling for accurate medical records and openness during investigations. Similarly, the family of Frances Cappuccini advocated for more robust protocols in obstetric emergencies and maternal care. The outcomes of the investigation and the subsequent Coroner's Regulation 28 report, which addressed systemic risks, led to significant reforms within Maidstone and Tunbridge Wells NHS Trust.

The problem often resides with the system, which remains confrontational despite policymakers' efforts to prioritise compassionate engagement and transparency. Only by genuinely listening to families and fostering a culture of openness can healthcare shift from fear to learning, ensuring tragedies lead to safety improvements rather than blame.

REFERENCES

Bateman, V, 19 Cr App R 8 (C.C.A. 1925). https://www.e-lawresources.co.uk/r-v-bateman#google_vignette

Ferner, R. E and McDowell, S. E. (2006). Doctors charged with manslaughter in the course of medical practice, 1795–2005: A literature review. *Journal of the Royal Society of Medicine, 99*(6), 309–14.

Fitzpatrick, B. (2005). Gross negligence manslaughter: Compatibility with European convention on human rights, Article 7: R v Misra and Srivastava [2004] EWCA Crim 2375. *The Journal of Criminal Law, 69*(2), 126–131. https://doi.org/10.1350/jcla.69.2.126.63514 (Original work published 2005)

Garg, V. R. (2012). EWCA Crim 2520 (Eng.). https://www.bailii.org/ew/cases/EWCA/Crim/2012/2520.html

UK Parliament. (2018, June 11). *Gross negligence manslaughter in healthcare: Review* (Vol. 642, Commons debate). Hansard. Retrieved from https://hansard.parliament.uk/commons/2018-06-11/debates/1806114000018/GrossNegligenceManslaughterInHealthcareReview?utm_source=chatgpt.com

9

Assault in medicine

CLARE GERADA

This chapter examines cases where doctors have deliberately harmed their patients. These are not merely errors or slips in judgement, but purposeful acts of abuse.

Many examples in this chapter involve surgeons, but this does not mean that surgery attracts more violent doctors than other specialities. Instead, surgeons have a unique advantage: immediate access to vital body systems and the authority to act often without challenge. This combination of surgical power, patient vulnerability, and the cultural deference surgeons command can be intoxicating for those with certain personality traits who wish to cause harm. When skill becomes a platform for ego, and the patient a prop in the performance, motives can vary, ranging from greed and sadism to a desire for prestige or the thrill of breaking taboos. Some doctors who assault patients also seem to derive satisfaction from the transgression itself – the act of crossing the most sacred professional boundaries and "getting away with it." For them, the assault becomes a means of asserting dominance, demonstrating their exceptionalism not just through skill but also through impunity. Whatever the reason, the patient's body becomes an object, a tool to achieve a purpose.

Institutions often enable this abuse, not through complicity, but by default. Hospitals may shield high-profile or well-paid doctors, dismiss complaints, ignore whistleblowers, or delay investigations to avoid reputational or financial damage. In such environments, misconduct can worsen unchecked.

Professional culture can act as an extra shield for the perpetrator. As demonstrated in many cases in this chapter, hierarchical and paternalistic systems mean that challenging a senior colleague might be seen as career suicide. Silence, driven by fear, loyalty, or learned helplessness, can sustain harm over many years. When whistleblowers are nurses, they are often ignored, with gender imbalance adding to the professional disparity.

Although the doctors in this chapter differ in backgrounds, specialities, countries, and ways of harming their patients, they share several traits: grandiosity,

 DOI: 10.1201/9781003781066-9

exploitation, institutional complicity, and the abuse of medical authority. Without addressing all these issues together, medicine will remain vulnerable to those willing to exploit its power.

DR CHRISTOPHER DUNTSCH: *THE "DR DEATH" OF DALLAS*

The idea that a doctor might commit assault is disturbing enough when we imagine physical abuse or exploitation in the consulting room. But what happens when the assault is carried out under the guise of surgery itself? When a knife, wielded in the name of healing, is used to cause harm?

In the early 2010s, Dallas neurosurgeon Christopher Duntsch was a rising star. He graduated in 1998 amongst the top students in America. He was inducted into the prestigious Alpha Omega Alpha Medical Honor Society. This honour signifies a lasting commitment to professionalism, leadership, scholarship, research, and community service, and recognises a physician's dedication to the profession and the art of healing.

After graduating, he entered a neurosurgery residency programme. Alongside his clinical work, he also completed a PhD, conducting research into stem cell treatments for neurological conditions. He excelled, securing millions of dollars in grants, filing patents for innovative stem cell therapies, and managing two laboratories. His future could have been very different if he had remained in research. Instead, he chose the clinical path and became a board-certified neurosurgeon in 2010, gaining the legal authority to operate in the State of Texas. During his neurosurgery residency, Duntsch reportedly participated in fewer than 200 operations, far below the more than 1,000 typically performed by neurosurgical trainees. Much of his time was spent on research, and concerns about his competence and possible substance abuse further limited his operative experience; at one point, he was suspected of operating under the influence of cocaine, referred to a programme for impaired physicians, and restricted from performing surgery without direct supervision. Much later, he was to use the lack of supervised "cutting" time as part of his defence, claiming incompetence rather than deliberate assault.

Nevertheless, at the time, this lack of experience did not deter Duntsch. He had the confidence, academic qualifications, and persuasive charisma that reassured patients and impressed colleagues. Trained in both surgery and stem cell research, he claimed to be an established academic at the forefront of spinal procedures. He was lauded as a man capable of changing lives and healing patients where others could not.

What followed, however, was a trail of destruction unlike anything seen in Texas. The operating theatre became a stage for recklessness. Red flags emerged quickly. Colleagues described him arriving late, appearing disoriented, or working in ways that breached the most basic surgical principles. During his training years, there were suggestions that he was under the influence of drugs and alcohol. He appeared dishevelled as if he had slept in his operating scrubs; he would be unshaven and act oddly. One scrub nurse recalled him muttering that he was "ready to leave the love and kindness and become a cold-blooded killer." Senior surgeons refused to operate with him. Nurses raised concerns. Patients complained of increasing pain and new disabilities after their operations.

Over 2 years, Duntsch operated on 38 patients and caused considerable harm to most of them. Arteries were severed, nerves cut, and surgical screws inserted into muscle instead of bone. Instruments were left inside the patients. In one operation, a patient's vocal cords and oesophagus were injured during a spinal fusion attempt. Another patient was left brain-dead. Others experienced permanent bladder and urinary issues, or ended up requiring parenteral (tube) feeding, lost control of hand movements, and many suffered severe psychological problems.

One particular incident involved his childhood friend, whom Duntsch operated on for a routine spinal procedure. The outcome was catastrophic: the patient became quadriplegic. Instead of addressing the complications immediately, Duntsch left his friend in limbo to operate on another patient. When he returned to his friend's care, the damage was beyond repair.

Overall, of the thirty-eight patients he had operated on, two died. Thirty-one were left with life-changing, irreversible injuries: paralysis, chronic pain, loss of mobility.

The system surrounding him, although aware of the harm he caused, failed to intervene; instead, it allowed him to continue without raising concerns, as if an arsonist was aided or abetted by firefighters. The reluctance to share damaging information, partly to avoid legal action and protect reputations, permitted him to operate on unsuspecting patients. Instead of suspending him or revoking his privileges, hospitals repeatedly allowed him to transfer to new facilities. In the United States, this practice is called "pass the trash."

Duntsch's operating skills were so poor that one department head suspected he might be an imposter, an untrained person who had stolen the identity of a legitimate surgeon. The implication was that the surgeon lacked even basic knowledge of human anatomy. This prompted him to fax a photograph of Duntsch to his training university for verification. Duntsch was not an imposter.

The tipping point occurred after Kellie Martin, an otherwise healthy woman aside from back pain, bled to death following what should have been a straightforward spinal operation. Her death and reports of other severely injured patients prompted a criminal investigation.

In 2015, Duntsch was arrested and charged with five counts of aggravated assault with a deadly weapon, his scalpel, and the deaths of at least two individuals, as well as elder abuse. Prosecutors faced a rare challenge: proving that a surgeon's actions in the operating theatre were not just incompetent but intentionally harmful.

Throughout the 2-week trial, former patients testified, sharing their experiences of seeking Duntsch's care. The jury was able to witness patients, either remotely or in the court, who were paralysed, tetraplegic, unable to speak, swallow, or care for themselves. Colleagues also gave evidence, describing Duntsch as one of the most reckless and dangerous spinal surgeons they had ever encountered. In his defence, Duntsch's legal team argued that he was merely an incompetent surgeon, not malicious or criminal. However, the prosecution highlighted

Duntsch's training and experience, implying his actions were deliberate. They pointed to his erratic behaviour, including self-identifying as a "stone-cold killer" in emails to colleagues. One expert witness described Duntsch as someone with a licence to operate on people legally as if he were a butcher.

In February 2017, after just over an hour of deliberation, jurors unanimously found Duntsch guilty of a first-degree felony for deliberately injuring an elderly patient. He was sentenced to life imprisonment and will be in his seventies before he becomes eligible for parole.

Duntsch's case was unusual in American legal terms because it was the first time a physician was criminally prosecuted for acts committed in the operating theatre. In the United States, medical errors, even when they result in severe injury or death, are almost always dealt with through civil malpractice lawsuits or professional disciplinary actions. Criminal prosecutions of doctors for surgical errors were virtually unheard of, as the law typically considers these failures as negligence rather than crimes.

What made Duntsch's situation exceptional was the extent and consistency of the harm he caused. Prosecutors argued that this pattern demonstrated more than incompetence; it revealed a reckless disregard for patient safety.

Duntsch's life sentence set a legal precedent in America. His case demonstrated that the justice system can intervene in extreme situations where professional regulation and malpractice laws fail to protect patients. However, it also raised difficult questions about where to draw the line between incompetence and criminal behaviour, and whether similar prosecutions might happen in future cases of grossly negligent medical care.

Following the trial and subsequent investigations, three main factors were identified as enabling him to evade accountability for so long. Whilst specific to the American healthcare and legal systems, these themes reflect failures seen in other jurisdictions where doctors have been able to practise harmfully without early intervention.

Firstly, the University of Tennessee allowed Duntsch to keep working despite a documented history of persistent drug and alcohol misuse. Colleagues reported that he kept vodka in his office, stored white powder in his bathrobe, and often arrived at work in the same torn and dishevelled scrubs, seeming as if he had not changed for days. He was also observed to be intoxicated both before and during medical procedures. Although these concerns were raised with hospital authorities, no action was taken. The institution's financial interests may have influenced this leniency, as by the end of his specialist training, he had acquired a valuable medical patent and co-founded a company with his supervisors.

Secondly, several hospitals failed to report Duntsch's adverse outcomes to the National Practitioner Data Bank (NPDB). The NPDB was established as a confidential database containing information on physicians' malpractice payments, disciplinary actions, and restrictions on their clinical privileges. Hospitals and other healthcare entities were legally obliged to submit reports when a doctor's clinical privileges were reduced, suspended, or revoked for more than 30 days, specifically to prevent unsafe practitioners from moving between institutions undetected. In Duntsch's case, however, hospitals where he had caused catastrophic harm either negotiated discreet resignations or allowed him to leave without formally documenting the incidents. Because no reports were filed, his history of dangerous conduct could not be tracked or compared across institutions, and subsequent hospitals that employed him had no access to his prior record of harm. This failure in the reporting system enabled him to continue practising despite repeated red flags.

Finally, the state regulator, the Texas Medical Board (TMB), was slow to act despite increasing complaints. The TMB is the state agency responsible for licensing physicians (similar to the UK GMC), investigating complaints, and enforcing professional standards to safeguard patient safety. It has the authority to restrict, suspend, or revoke medical licences when doctors are found to be practising incompetently or dangerously. In Duntsch's case, multiple complaints had been submitted to the TMB as early as 10 months before his final operation. Yet, no disciplinary action was taken during that period. This regulatory delay proved crucial: whilst the Board's review process was ongoing, Duntsch continued operating, and more than 20 additional patients suffered devastating injuries. The case demonstrated longstanding criticisms of the TMB for being overly cautious and slow in disciplinary matters, often prioritising due process for doctors over urgent patient safety concerns.

The case became a national scandal, inspiring documentaries, podcasts, and even a television drama that brought his story to a global audience. Yet beyond the sensational headlines lay a sobering truth: the safeguards designed to protect patients from dangerous practitioners can break down when self-interest, fear of litigation, or institutional reputation take precedence over transparency and accountability.

DR PAOLO MACCHIARINI: *THE CELEBRITY SURGEON WHO PLAYED GOD*

If Duntsch had a God complex, then Dr Paolo Macchiarini, our next surgeon, suffered from something even darker: the delusion of being a saviour, a false God who truly believed his own lies. Macchiarini, the charismatic Italian surgeon once lauded as a miracle worker, was later exposed as a fraudster, a pathological liar, and ultimately a criminal convicted of aggravated assault.

His story has inspired television programmes, including *Dr Death* and the Netflix docuseries *Bad Surgeon: Love Under the Knife*. The fascination is apparent: Macchiarini promised nothing less than a revolution in regenerative medicine. For a time, he seemed to achieve this. But beneath the glamorous exterior lay deception, recklessness, and the systematic exploitation of vulnerable patients, whose suffering became the price of his fame.

For several years, Macchiarini was the darling of international surgery. Journalists portrayed him as a pioneering scientist, a superstar, and a miracle worker. With his broad, handsome face, easy charm, and impeccable tailoring, whether in a crisp white coat or surgical scrubs, he undeniably looked the part. He created the impression of a saviour. Patients, colleagues, and institutions wanted to believe in him. And for a time, almost everyone did.

Macchiarini's curriculum vitae, submitted when he was recruited to the prestigious Karolinska Institute in Sweden in 2010, extended to more than 80 pages. It listed roles across Florence, Stockholm, London, France, Spain, Italy, Germany, and the United States. He also spoke several languages, endearing himself to a global scientific and general audience. He positioned himself at the forefront of thoracic surgery, particularly in repairing and replacing damaged windpipes, an obscure yet high-stakes field where innovation seemed urgently needed. His career trajectory suggested brilliance, mobility, and a man in constant demand.

The truth, as later investigations revealed, was more ambiguous. References were inconsistent, achievements exaggerated, and claims unsubstantiated. Nevertheless, institutions were captivated by his charisma and the prospect of remarkable breakthroughs. Karolinska, home of the Nobel Prize in Medicine, sought a scientific star, and they believed they had found one.

Macchiarini first gained international prominence in 2008 when he operated on Claudia Castillo, a 30-year-old woman from Barcelona with severe airway damage caused by tuberculosis. The surgery was quite daring. He took a trachea from a deceased donor, chemically stripped it of its cells, then seeded the scaffold with stem cells taken from Castillo's own bone marrow. The idea was that her cells would grow, colonise the structure, and transform it into a living organ indistinguishable from her own tissue.

The operation was hailed as a global breakthrough. Castillo soon returned home, reportedly able to chase after her children. Since the graft contained only her own cells, she did not require any immunosuppressant drugs. For the media, it was a triumph: the first real step towards a future where organs could be grown in laboratories and transplanted without rejection.

Just weeks later, in 2011, the case was published in *The Lancet* medical journal. Macchiarini's reputation soared. The tone in many reports, both in *The Lancet* publications and media responses, was optimistic; the idea of a "miracle" tracheal transplant elevated Macchiarini's standing in the medical world. The paper was eventually retracted, but at the time, it was regarded as a breakthrough in clinical practice (Macchiarini et al., 2008).

Speaking about himself, he stated in an interview with *The Lancet*, "I'm just a surgeon; I need action," "I'm like a wild animal that does not need to be in a cage; I need to express my convictions that I can help a patient with innovative things."

Even after his "breakthrough," concerns were raised. Critics pointed out the lack of comprehensive pre-clinical studies, the absence of animal testing, and the rushed way in which the procedure was publicised. The Lancet, many years later, acknowledged these criticisms. However, at the time, the world was in search of heroes, and Claudia Castillo's story offered one. For Macchiarini, this was merely the start.

In 2010, after he was recruited by the Karolinska Institute, he thrived.

His operations were filmed, his research widely promoted, and his charisma showcased to journalists and visiting dignitaries. He was portrayed as a visionary, a genius. Patients travelled from around the world to consult him, eager for cures.

At Karolinska, he moved from donor windpipes to synthetic ones, employing plastic scaffolds seeded with bone marrow stem cells, which were believed to be capable of transforming into living airways. In 2011, he carried out his first synthetic trachea transplant on Andemariam Beyene, an Eritrean doctoral student in Iceland. His story was prominently featured including on the front page of *The New York Times* and in a TV documentary, "*A Leap of Faith*."

The reality, however, was devastating. The synthetic trachea failed to turn into living tissue; it deteriorated and the patient suffered infection, bleeding, and organ failure.

Andemariam Beyene died two and a half years after his operation, having endured intractable pain and multiple revisions. Other patients experienced similar outcomes, with some dying within months. Overall, at least 17 patients worldwide received Macchiarini's "regenerative trachea" implant surgeries. Most of them are now deceased. The few survivors suffer from severe complications, living not because of the transplants but despite them.

Within Karolinska, colleagues noticed that the outcomes reported by Macchiarini bore little resemblance to what they observed. Patients he described as thriving were, in reality, severely ill. The data appeared to be manipulated. Ethical approval was bypassed. Consent was insufficient. In some cases, patients were not terminally ill but were persuaded into experimental procedures that drastically shortened their lives.

One critic, Professor Pierre Delaere of KU Leuven, raised the alarm early. He described Macchiarini's artificial tracheas as "hot air," scientifically unsound and destined to fail. Later, with harsh bluntness, he said: "If I had the choice between a synthetic trachea or a firing squad, I would choose the latter, as it would be the least painful way of execution."

By 2014, four Karolinska doctors openly challenged Macchiarini. They accused him of grossly misrepresenting his results and endangering patient safety. An independent investigator agreed. However, the Institute's leadership, led by Vice-Chancellor Anders Hamsten, dismissed the findings. They argued that, at most, he had acted "without due care."

The whistleblowers paid a heavy price, as they often do. One, Karl-Henrik Grinnemo, was accused by Macchiarini of stealing his work. The allegation stuck, ruining his chances of securing research grants and collaborations. His career was nearly wrecked. "We were doing good research," he later recalled, "but it didn't matter … I thought I was going to lose my lab, my staff – everything."

This atmosphere of intimidation, combined with the allure of linking with a supposed genius, created what investigators later called the "bandwagon effect." Staff sought to associate themselves with success. Criticism was met with punishment. Silence proved to be safer.

If Macchiarini deceived patients and colleagues in his professional life, he was equally manipulative in his personal life. In 2016, Vanity Fair published an exposé of his affair with Benita Alexander, an award-winning NBC producer who had covered his work. Alexander broke one of journalism's most fundamental rules: she fell in love with her subject. By mid-2014, they were engaged and planning a fairy-tale wedding.

Macchiarini claimed that the guest list would include friends such as Barack and Michelle Obama, Bill and Hillary Clinton, Nicolas Sarkozy, Vladimir Putin, and other world leaders. Andrea Bocelli and Elton John were expected to sing. None other than Pope Francis himself was to officiate at his papal palace in Castel Gandolfo. He also fabricated numerous stories, including one where he claimed he had been called to operate on Princes Diana after her car crash in Paris but failed to arrive in time.

It was all lies. As the wedding date drew near, Alexander realised the truth: Macchiarini was still married to his wife of 30 years, and none of the so-called wedding plans were genuine. The illusion was shattered, leaving her humiliated. Vanity Fair transformed the story into a psychological case study, quoting Harvard psychiatrist Ronald Schouten: "Macchiarini is the extreme form of a con man with a Walter Mitty-like persona. He's clearly bright and has achieved a great deal, but he struggles to contain himself. There's a void in his personality that he seems to want to fill by conning more and more people."

The obvious question then came to mind: if he lied so openly in his personal life, what about his science?

That year, Swedish television broadcast *Experimenten* ("The Experiments"), a three-part documentary exposing the disastrous results of Macchiarini's surgeries. It showed evidence that patients were not on the brink of death, as he claimed, but had been persuaded into operations that robbed them of years of life. It depicted how the tracheas failed, how patients endured agony, and how Karolinska had ignored the reality of the situation.

Within weeks, Karolinska announced that Macchiarini's contract would not be renewed. Senior leaders, including the Vice-Chancellor and the Secretary-General of the Nobel Committee, resigned. The Swedish government dismissed the entire Board of the Karolinska. The scandal not only shook the institute but also damaged Sweden's international reputation for medical integrity.

By 2016, Macchiarini had been dismissed from Karolinska. Swedish prosecutors initiated an investigation. In 2017, he faced charges of manslaughter regarding three patients who died following his operations. The charges were later upgraded to aggravated assault, a significant legal recognition that his procedures were not simply medical errors but acts of violence disguised as care.

In 2022, he received a suspended sentence after being convicted of aggravated assault in one of the cases. On appeal by the prosecution, in 2023, the sentence was increased to 2 years and 6 months in prison for three counts of aggravated assault. His final appeal to Sweden's Supreme Court was rejected later that year.

As with the charges against Duntsch, the language of assault is crucial here. Their actions and the harm caused were not accidents or unforeseen complications. Instead, they were deliberate acts of harm inflicted on vulnerable individuals without sufficient justification. Under the pretence of healing, Macchiarini used his scalpel as a weapon.

The Macchiarini case is not merely about a rogue surgeon; it again reveals systemic problems in modern healthcare.

First, the culture of celebrity science. Institutions chase after stars. The Nobel Prize itself fuels the myth of the solitary genius. Karolinska sought a messiah and overlooked red flags to secure one. Once established, Macchiarini was seen as exceptional, above rules, beyond scrutiny.

Second, the hype surrounding stem cell research. Stem cells show genuine potential but have long been associated with exaggerated claims and fraud. Articles in this field are retracted at disproportionately high rates. The desire for breakthroughs, combined with media enthusiasm, creates a fertile environment for charlatans. Patients, desperate for hope, become easy targets.

Third, the failure of oversight. Ethical review boards were bypassed. Compassionate use exemptions, which allowed companies or physicians to administer unproven treatments without proper testing in controlled studies, were misused. Whistleblowers were silenced. Regulators acted too late. In the race for innovation, core principles of patient safety and informed consent were neglected.

Finally, the psychology of deception. Macchiarini's pathological lying, from his fantasy wedding to his fabricated medical stories, reveals a void he sought to fill with increasingly grander deceptions. His attacks were not only physical but also psychological, manipulating patients, colleagues, lovers, and institutions alike.

DR JAYANT PATEL: *DR DEATH*

Moving on to another surgeon, this time one whose career spanned both America and Australia, Mr Jayant Patel. He was given the nickname "Dr Death," a title, as we have seen, that has been attributed to more than one doctor in this book. During his brief tenure at Bundaberg Base Hospital in Australia in the early 2000s, Patel was linked to the deaths of dozens of patients and accused of numerous failed or unnecessary procedures. Nurses reported hiding patients from him when they knew he was on duty, and colleagues later described his surgical techniques as outdated, careless, and hazardous.

What shocked many was not only the extent of harm in Bundaberg but also the history that preceded it. Patel had practised in the United States for 20 years, where his career was affected by disciplinary restrictions, malpractice claims, and ongoing concerns about his competence. In New York, he was fined and put on probation for failing to examine patients before operating. In Oregon, his licence was restricted after multiple deaths and serious complications were linked to his procedures. Despite this record, Patel received glowing references from colleagues and was able to secure a senior surgical role in Australia through an "area of need" scheme that fast-tracked overseas-trained doctors into understaffed hospitals.

The consequences were devastating. Between 2003 and 2005, Patel cared for over 1,000 patients in Bundaberg. Official investigations linked him to at least 87 deaths, with many more patients suffering severe injuries. In 2010, he was found guilty of manslaughter in relation to three deaths and received a sentence of 7 years' imprisonment.

Patel's convictions were not the final chapter. In 2012, the High Court of Australia overturned his manslaughter convictions, ruling that the jury had been exposed to highly prejudicial evidence that should never have been admitted. Six weeks into the trial, the prosecutors could not prove Patel's incompetence as a surgeon, but the damage had already been done: the jury had heard repeated testimony about his conduct and character. The convictions were quashed, and a new trial was ordered.

A retrial the following year resulted in Patel being acquitted of one manslaughter charge. This outcome increased pressure to drop the remaining cases. Ultimately, the prosecution agreed to a plea bargain: Patel pleaded guilty to fraud charges related to dishonestly obtaining medical registration and employment in Queensland. In exchange, the outstanding manslaughter and grievous bodily harm charges were withdrawn. He received a 2-year suspended sentence, not for the deaths or injuries of his patients but for the deception that had facilitated his appointment in the first place.

The Patel case drew international concern. In 2010, the American news channel CNN aired a documentary titled *They Called Him "Dr. Death,"* in which several of his colleagues in Bundaberg testified that they had repeatedly tried to raise concerns about his behaviour, only to be ignored by superiors and regulators. Questions were raised about the lack of due diligence in his appointment, given his long history of disciplinary issues abroad. He was not an isolated figure who went unnoticed. His pattern of negligence and harm was recorded across two continents. Yet, he still managed to move between institutions, sometimes protected by professional loyalty, regulatory inertia, and the persistent belief that a doctor's authority should not be questioned.

The fallout extended into the political arena. In Queensland, the scandal led to the removal of the state's Director-General of Health. It prompted reforms to the Medical Board. However, for many patients and families, these changes arrived too late.

In 2015, Patel was ultimately and permanently barred from practising medicine in Australia. His ban marked the end of a medical career defined not by healing but by harm.

MR IAN PATERSON: *THE BUTCHER SURGEON*

A similar case in England involved Mr Ian Paterson, a highly regarded breast surgeon in the Midlands, known for his skill and attentiveness. Patients described him as charming and reassuring, a doctor who genuinely appeared to care about their well-being. His clinics were busy, with long waiting lists, and he held senior positions in both the NHS and the private sector.

Behind this façade lay a pattern of abuse that would eventually be recognised as one of the worst medical scandals in modern British history. Over more than a decade, Paterson subjected hundreds of women to unnecessary and sometimes dangerous operations. Some had no cancer at all but were told they did. Others had small, treatable lesions exaggerated into urgent surgical problems. He performed what he called "cleavage-sparing" mastectomies, leaving breast tissue behind against accepted guidelines, significantly increasing the risk of cancer returning.

The harm experienced was physical, psychological, and financial. Women underwent life-altering surgery, sometimes losing one or both breasts, without any medical necessity. Some received unnecessary chemotherapy and radiotherapy. Many paid privately for their procedures, unaware that the surgeon profiting from them was also their deceiver.

Concerns about Paterson's work were consistently raised by colleagues as early as 2003. Fellow surgeons noticed unusually high rates of post-operative complications. Pathology reports sometimes showed no evidence of the cancers he claimed to have removed. Nurses and junior doctors questioned his techniques. However, internal investigations were slow and indecisive, hampered by hospital managers who feared reputational damage and the costs of compensation, a recurring theme in this book.

It was not until 2011 that Paterson was suspended from practice. By then, hundreds of women had already been affected. A criminal investigation was initiated, examining whether his actions amounted to assault and fraud. In 2017, he was convicted of 17 counts of wounding with intent and three counts of unlawful wounding.

He was sentenced to 20 years in prison.

An independent investigation later discovered that at least 1,000 patients might have received unnecessary or harmful treatment. The report, chaired by Bishop Graham James, spans nearly 200 pages and includes testimonies from Paterson's victims and their families. It described a "culture of avoidance and denial" where warnings were ignored, whistleblowers were marginalised, and patient safety was considered less important than protecting the institution.

Paterson's motives remain unclear. Although financial gain has been suggested, since many of his surgeries were performed privately, his conduct within the NHS (where no money changes hands) indicates a more complex psychological motivation. He described himself as a saviour, offering hope and reassurance to women facing a cancer diagnosis, whilst secretly exploiting their fear (Independent Inquiry into the Issues Raised by Paterson, 2020).

Paterson was labelled a rogue surgeon who, according to the trial judge, let his arrogance persuade him he was untouchable and that no one would dare challenge his authority. Whilst there may be some truth to this regarding his motives, we will never know, as he has never publicly explained his actions.

HARRY BAILEY (1922–1985): *THE SLEEP CURE*

Like many doctors in this book, it wasn't easy to decide in which chapter to include Dr Harry Bailey in. Charged with manslaughter but also guilty of subjecting many patients to gruesome assaults and committing fraud, Bailey could have been placed in several different sections.

Bailey concealed his criminal deeds behind a treatment he asserted was revolutionary, as depicted in this fictional vignette.

She arrived at Chelmsford Private Hospital exhausted, depressed, and desperate for help. Dr. Bailey told her family that his "deep sleep therapy" would give her brain a chance to heal. They imagined rest, recovery, renewal. Instead, she was injected with heavy sedatives and slipped into a coma that lasted for days. Nurses fed her through tubes, cleaned her, and restrained her when she thrashed in confusion. Electroconvulsive shocks were administered while she was still unconscious. She woke, if she woke at all, disoriented, incontinent, and broken. The promise of healing had been a mask for something closer to destruction.

Harry Bailey was born in New South Wales, Australia. His family had a modest background; his father was a stationmaster. Due to financial constraints, he was unable to complete his science studies at the University of Sydney and worked as a pharmacy assistant. He later returned to university to study medicine, qualifying in 1951, and specialising in psychiatry in 1954. He received awards in psychiatry and paediatrics (Garton, 2007).

After his internship, Bailey worked at a military hospital that treated returned servicemen with psychological trauma. There, he administered full-coma insulin therapy for schizophrenia, injecting patients with 2,000 units of insulin daily to induce a deep coma, which was later reversed with glucose.

He was to spend 15 months on a World Health Organization fellowship closely observing sedation techniques, psychosurgery, and electroconvulsive therapy methods employed by specialists across the world. Armed with this experience, and on his recommendation, the Cerebral Surgery and Research Unit was established at Callan Park Mental Hospital, Australia, in 1957. Bailey was appointed its director and began offering patients what he considered to be cutting-edge physical treatments, such as ECT and psychosurgery.

With his reputation riding high, Bailey then moved to private practice. He became a psychiatric consultant. He was a member of several esteemed psychiatric institutions, including the Australian Medical Association, the Australasian Association of Psychiatrists (later Royal Australian and New Zealand College of Psychiatrists), the American Electroshock Research Association, and the Pan-Pacific Surgical Association. He served as president of the Sydney Biophysics and Medical Electronics Society.

Bailey openly disliked the dominant treatment approach in psychiatry at that time, which was psychoanalytical psychotherapy. Instead, influenced by his background as a research chemist and pharmacist, as well as his overseas experience, he focused on drug and ECT treatments.

During an inquiry into a patient's death, he recounted, as evidence for the appropriateness of his treatment, his first experiment in 1951. He told the coroner that he had kept a young psychotic woman in a coma with sodium pentothal for 2 weeks; when she awoke, he claimed she was "completely cured".

From 1962 to 1979, he was the chief psychiatrist at Chelmsford Private Hospital in Pennant Hills, Sydney. It was at this small private hospital that Bailey administered drug-induced comas to patients that lasted for days or even weeks. He called this process *deep sleep therapy.*

Bailey's deep sleep therapy (DST) was based on his observations during his training abroad. Sleep therapy, at this time, was defined as pharmacologically induced sleep lasting about 20 hours a day over an extended period, such as 2 weeks, and was first introduced in the early 1900s but became more prominent in the 1930s. At the Maudsley Hospital in London, Professor William Sargant used intermittent narcosis to treat soldiers during World War II, waking them daily and providing close medical supervision.

Between the 1930s and 1960s, "sleep therapy" was used to treat conditions ranging from manic and catatonic excitement to severe anxiety and depression, as well as various forms of schizophrenia.

Various drug combinations were used to induce and maintain sleep, mainly relying on a mixture of barbiturates and chloral hydrate. Sleep therapy provided only marginal benefits but carried significant risks, with a fatality rate exceeding 5% due to pneumonia and circulatory collapse. Nevertheless, "sleep therapy" persisted even after the introduction of new psychotropic drugs, with some medications like chlorpromazine incorporated into certain "sleep mixtures" before this narcosis treatment gradually fell out of favour during the 1960s. However, under Bailey's care, its use was increasing whilst worldwide it was being phased out. At Chelmsford Hospital, it was the primary treatment for various conditions, including depression, anxiety, addiction, and even as a "cure" for homosexuality.

Bailey's approach to therapy involved flooding patients with barbiturates and antipsychotics until they lost consciousness, keeping them in this state, immobile, for up to 39 days, with a median of 14. Whilst in a coma, they were subjected to ECT, often without muscle relaxants. Bailey compared the treatment to switching off a television; his self-developed theory was that the brain, by shutting down for an extended period, would "unlearn" habits that caused depression, addiction, and other psychiatric issues.

Complications such as pneumonia, infections, dehydration, vomiting, and respiratory issues were common. Within 2 years, five patients had died as a result of this treatment. More deaths occurred, although a coroner's inquest was not held until 1967. Impressed by Bailey's medical reputation and his justification for his therapeutic regime, the coroner did not consider him culpable. Aside from private murmurs within psychiatric circles and occasional published criticisms of Bailey's research, there were few attempts by the profession to regulate his methods. He continued to publish research papers on psychosurgery alongside reputable psychiatrists.

Bailey and his colleague treated over 1,000 DST patients in Chelmsford between 1963 and 1979. By the time it closed in 1979, at least 24 patients had died; others had taken their own lives, and many survivors endured physical and mental complications from their treatment, including weight loss, paralysis, respiratory and bowel issues, loss of self-confidence, personality changes, drug dependence, and alcohol problems.

The typical Bailey patients were young men or women, mostly in their twenties and thirties, suffering from depression or addiction. Once admitted, they were stripped naked, shackled, and left sedated, supposedly to prevent them from falling out of bed or thrashing in delirium. Nurses' incident books, later smuggled out and shown to the later Royal Commission, documented a list of neglect and brutality: patients biting through their tongues during ECT; others tumbling from beds and sustaining fractures; incorrect medications administered; sedation extended far beyond prescribed doses; escape attempts prevented by force.

Written consent for ECT, as required by law, was never obtained. Death certificates were falsified or left incomplete.

As the death toll rose, Bailey dismissed fatalities as inevitable side effects of his treatment, assuring families that their loved ones had been "too ill to save."

In 1970, the NSW Department of Health received an anonymous letter about Bailey's DST. The letter was written by Rosa Nicholson, a nurse who had worked at Chelmsford for a while. She spent 18 months attempting to secure a position at the hospital, specifically to gather evidence of what was happening there. She smuggled out nursing records and incident sheets. Besides the potentially lethal drug combination prescribed during DST, she also highlighted that Bailey often left pre-signed drug forms at the hospital for staff to admit patients to the "Zombie" (DST) room, causing them to fall into a drugged coma. She exposed the dangerous nature of his treatment and the serious side effects patients suffered. Rosa Nicholson managed to stay undercover for 10 years, leaking damaging evidence against Bailey to those willing to listen.

The Department of Health chose not to act on the information they received from Rosa, arguing that, since the clinic was already under police investigation (following a patient's death), it would be inappropriate for them to carry out a separate inquiry. Consequently, Bailey was allowed to proceed with his treatments. They were later heavily criticised for their inaction. Although inspections occurred in 1978–79, the historical record, and later the Royal Commission, confirmed that there had been no thorough assessment of the clinical appropriateness or safety of deep-sleep therapy.

In 1973, a patient named Barry Hart was admitted to Chelmsford for treatment. According to his account, he was given a glass of water and a tablet, after which he was in a coma for 14 days. When he woke, he was confused, hallucinating, in pain, and very angry. He also suffered from pleurisy, deep vein thrombosis, and a pulmonary embolism. He was transferred to a nearby acute hospital where he remained, recovering, for over 2 weeks. As a result of his experience, he became an advocate against one of the doctors who administered the treatment. Before his admission to Chelmsford, he had explicitly refused to consent to ECT. Nonetheless, it was administered during his barbiturate-induced coma. By the end of 1973, he began legal proceedings. However, for several years, he failed to persuade anyone to take his story seriously. Eventually, he succeeded, and his case reached court in 1980. This resulted in him being awarded $60,000 (Aust.) in damages.

The first group to genuinely listen to Rosa's concerns and act was not psychiatrists or their professional bodies (although they were aware, as she and others had already written to raise the alarm), nor the health officials responsible for safeguarding patients' lives. It was the Citizens Committee on Human Rights, an organisation connected to the controversial Church of Scientology, that stepped in, specifically by launching a campaign exposing the practices at the hospital.

In the 1980s, the Church of Scientology launched a public campaign, and the television programme *60 Minutes* exposed the scandal in its documentary *The Chelmsford File,* which included details of a death, that of Miriam Podio in 1977. Miriam was in her mid-twenties when she became a patient under Bailey's care at

Chelmsford. Diagnosed with schizoaffective disorder, she was treated with deep sedation and psychotropic drugs, including the sedative Tuinal. Her story is used in historical accounts of Chelmsford to illustrate the personal suffering under Bailey's so-called "treatments," especially his use of sedatives and DST, and the lack of strict oversight regarding whether those treatments were safe or medically justified (Eastgate, 2020).

Ultimately, the death of another young woman, Sharon Hamilton, in 1978 led to what many had hoped for years, the closure of the clinic. Sharon was a young dancer who, in 1976, during a performance at a concert held in a prison, was violently assaulted by a notorious convicted murderer. She was awarded nearly $100,000 (Aus dollars) in damages for the assault, but her fragile health and emotional well-being never fully recovered. The attack left her with physical and emotional scars, and she later received treatment at Chelmsford Private Hospital.

What started as a therapeutic relationship soon crossed ethical boundaries; Hamilton became both Bailey's patient and his lover. In 1976, Sharon Hamilton died from a barbiturate overdose. An inquest recorded her death as a suicide. However, the revelations that followed shocked colleagues and the public alike: Bailey had been named the principal beneficiary of her estate.

For Bailey, Hamilton's death marked a pivotal turning point. Allegations of malpractice at Chelmsford had already been emerging, but this was the story of a vulnerable patient who ended her life, leaving everything to the doctor who had treated her and seduced her. It captured public attention in a way that official reports and whistleblower letters had not. It permanently damaged his reputation and increased suspicion that Bailey's professional authority was driven by self-interest and abuse of power.

Like many of the doctors in this book, it was the press that finally blew the whistle, making it heard. This was true for Bailey. Janet Fife-Yeomans, a journalist from the Daily Telegraph, frequently covered the story and co-authored *Deep Sleep: Harry Bailey and the Scandal of Chelmsford.*

In 1983, Bailey was charged with manslaughter. Although the charge was dropped in 1985, media scrutiny continued to be intense. Once a flamboyant, well-dressed, handsome, and cherub-faced charmer, he was now overweight, a heavy drinker, and broken. Sick, exhausted, dispirited, and facing years of litigation, he drove to Mount White on 8 September 1985 and parked on a remote track. The next day, police found him dead; the cause of death was Tuinal, the same drug he had used to sedate his patients.

During his years in practice, he amassed a considerable fortune. He charged high fees, inflated his income with fraudulent Medicare claims, and made a fortune as an expert witness. He was also a sexual predator: notorious for propositioning female patients with "What you need is a good fuck." Staff at Chelmsford said Bailey had sex with his female patients, often sending them by taxi to his office or home late at night. In his early career, as a lecturer to medical students, he coerced female patients into demonstrating masturbation in front of them.

In 1988, the Australian government set up a Royal Commission to examine DST. The Commissioner concluded that the events at Chelmsford were horrific and uncovered evidence of fraud, obstruction of justice, and serious medical negligence. He condemned all the doctors involved but identified Bailey as central, asserting that without him, there would have been no DST. The New South Wales parliament banned the treatment and introduced stricter regulations for admitting and treating patients with mental health issues.

The Chelmsford Royal Commission Report spans 14 volumes, but its details have mostly faded from public memory. Its lessons, however, remain vital: that patients are highly vulnerable; that institutional protection of doctors can be risky; and that without transparency and accountability, medicine itself can cause harm (Wyndham, 2021).

DR FARID FATA (1965–): *CANCER CREATING CASH*

The following case could easily be included in the chapter on fraud. However, his crimes were so heinous that it feels like an understatement. His offences caused death and lifelong illnesses for hundreds of patients. Farid Fata was not a surgeon, but an oncologist, a cancer specialist responsible for highly skilled tasks, including diagnosing life-threatening conditions and guiding patients through treatment. In the Detroit suburbs, he built one of the largest private cancer practices in the United States.

He had seven offices in Eastern Michigan and owned an in-house chemotherapy pharmacy, a radiation oncology practice, and a diagnostic testing company equipped with radiographic devices, including a positron emission tomography scanner. He also managed his own cancer charity, Swan for Life. He owned the whole care pathway.

His clinics were modern and welcoming. He was admired by patients, referred to simply as "Dr Fata," and regarded as a man who could save lives.

Yet, behind the polished veneer lay one of the most shocking frauds in American medical history, as described by US Attorney Barbara McQuade, who called his actions "the most egregious" her office had ever encountered. Fata pleaded guilty in September 2014 to 16 federal charges: thirteen counts of health care fraud, two counts of money laundering, and one count of conspiring to pay and receive kickbacks and cash payments for referring patients to a specific hospice and home health care company. The court found that Fata's crimes resulted in at least $17.6 million in payments for fraudulently ordered treatments. Between 2007 and 2013, he submitted $225 million in claims to Medicare, receiving at least $91 million in reimbursements, with additional funds from private insurers. The basis for these fraud charges was Fata's chemotherapy treatment of patients who either did not have cancer or did not need treatment, as well as the excessive use of costly supportive care medications, including haematopoietic growth factors, intravenous iron salts, and intravenous gamma globulin (IVIG). Additionally, at sentencing, the court found that Fata also mistreated patients with inappropriate parenteral vitamins, octreotide, and potent antiemetics. The charges against Fata involved patients covered under Medicare, Blue Cross Blue Shield, Health Alliance Plan, and Aetna.

Fata initially trained in Lebanon before relocating to America, where he became one of Michigan's most respected oncologists. His empire eventually expanded to seven cities, serving over 16,000 patients. At his peak, he was regarded as a leader in oncology, with clinics offering state-of-the-art treatments and comprehensive services under one roof. However, this integrated model, seemingly beneficial on the surface, was actually a tool for his fraud, shielding him from scrutiny and making it very difficult for external providers to challenge his decisions.

What makes Fata's case particularly unsettling is not just the fraud but also the way he exploited his patients' deepest vulnerabilities.

He created a hierarchy of deception:

- Informing healthy patients that they have cancer.
- Giving cancer patients with indolent disease the impression that their illness was aggressive.
- Persuading terminal patients that "one more dose" of chemotherapy could save them.

Patients were promised a 70% chance of remission if they followed his regimen. Many sold their homes, depleted their savings, and endured unnecessary chemotherapy. Some were left disfigured and injured due to toxic drugs. Others, already terminal, died not only in agony but also financially ruined. His "treatment" often turned into a prolonged form of torture.

Whistleblowers attempted to raise the alarm. In 2010, a nurse voiced concerns, but as is often the case when a junior staff member challenges a powerful doctor, her warnings were ignored. Staff across his clinics felt uncomfortable: some resigned, others quietly disagreed, but many obeyed. The culture of reverence towards doctors, coupled with fear of career repercussions, resulted in widespread silence.

The whistle was finally blown in 2013 when Dr Soe Maunglay, a doctor working with Fata, examined a patient who had fractured her leg shortly after starting chemotherapy. Whilst reviewing her records, he realised she probably did not have cancer at all. Concerned, he investigated further and uncovered a troubling pattern: many of his patients also did not have cancer. His bravery in contacting hospital management ultimately led to an FBI investigation and Fata's arrest.

Fata's dishonesty was both personal and systemic. He excelled in a healthcare setting where fee-for-service medicine prioritises the quantity of treatment over its quality. Insurers, including Medicare, are set up not to question physician claims without questioning them. Oversight agencies lack the resources or the will to scrutinise someone with Fata's reputation. The very traits that made him admired, charisma, authority, and apparent benevolence, created a mask that hid his crimes.

Why would a doctor sworn to heal deliberately cause harm?

Fata himself, in court, spoke of "power and greed" and admitted his quest was "self-destructive." Yet his actions suggest more than mere greed. His empire and the admiration it garnered may have fostered narcissistic traits: a desire to be seen as indispensable, powerful, and admired. Some analysts have compared his behaviour to that of a cult leader, encouraging dependence and exploiting fear. Psychologically, Fata demonstrates how moral disengagement enables a professional to override their conscience, redefining harm as a benefit, blaming patients' desperation, or framing wealth as a deserved reward. Unlike many doctors who "slide" into overprescribing or billing fraud, Fata crossed into outright cruelty. His patients were not simply defrauded; they were poisoned.

For the victims, the impact was devastating. Some suffered permanent disability, whilst others spent years undergoing unnecessary treatment. Families faced financial ruin. Perhaps the most damaging was the betrayal of trust: patients who believed their doctor was their protector discovered he was their exploiter. One survivor described the experience as "a death sentence of another kind," enduring both physical suffering and the loss of faith in the very institution of medicine. The emotional trauma extended beyond individuals, affecting the wider community and eroding confidence in oncology itself.

At the trial, the extent of Fata's deception shocked even seasoned prosecutors. A medical ethicist described it as "one of the most extensive cases of fraud I've heard of." Prosecutors argued that "rather than use his medical degree to save lives, Dr Fata instead destroyed them in pursuit of profit." In court, Fata wept and apologised, claiming shame and remorse. "I misused my talents because of power and greed. My pursuit of power is self-destructive," he said. He forfeited $17.6 million and was sentenced to 45 years in federal prison.

The Fata case prompted calls for reform in the US healthcare system. Insurers improved their oversight mechanisms for oncology billing, and professional bodies re-evaluated the need for external review of unusual treatment patterns. It also emphasised the importance of protecting whistleblowers, ensuring that those who raise concerns are not silenced by hierarchy or fear (Steensma, 2016).

Fata also highlighted some potentially concerning aspects of medical oncology practice in the United States. In a fee-for-service model where evaluation and management codes alone often do not suffice to keep clinics financially viable, there may be an incentive for cancer specialists to prescribe, image, and treat even when observation would be the more appropriate choice.

SIGNING THEIR WORK

Mr Simon Bramhall was a respected surgeon specialising in liver, spleen, and pancreas transplants in Birmingham. His technical skill was exceptional, and he dealt with some of the most complex procedures in British medicine. Colleagues described him as calm under pressure, decisive, and highly respected by both patients and peers.

That is why it was so disconcerting when, in 2013, a colleague noticed something unusual whilst operating on one of Bramhall's former transplant patients. Etched into the surface of the liver were the initials "SB," visible under the theatre lights. The marks had not been made with a scalpel but with an argon beam coagulator, a device designed to stop bleeding by cauterising tissue. When used skilfully, it can seal vessels precisely. In this instance, however, it had been employed as a surgical pen.

The incident was not isolated. Investigations revealed that Bramhall had "signed" at least two patients' livers during transplant operations, and when a nurse saw him mark his initials on the liver, he told her, "I do this." When Bramhall realised that she was watching, he said nothing more.

The markings did not cause any physical harm, but the symbolic breach was significant. In surgery, each incision is meant to serve a medical purpose, not as a personal expression of the operator.

When the story became public, reactions were sharply divided. Some argued it was a harmless, if somewhat arrogant, flourish, a surgeon leaving his mark like an artist on a canvas. Others saw it as a troubling abuse of power: an unconscious patient, an open body, and a surgeon engaging in an act that was utterly self-centred.

Bramhall resigned from his hospital post in 2014 and was later charged with assault by beating. This charge under English law can apply even if no injury occurs. In 2017, he pleaded guilty to two counts of assault at Birmingham Crown Court, and the following year, he was fined £10,000 and given a 12-month community order.

The General Medical Council suspended him from practice. He was eventually to lose his medical licence, with the GMC stating that his actions were "borne out of a degree of professional arrogance" and that they "undermined" public trust in the medical profession.

Bramhall's case stands out from many others in this chapter. His actions were not physically harmful, and his patients recovered from their transplants. Nevertheless, it remains a key example of the same pattern: a doctor abusing their extraordinary access and authority for personal gain, whether motivated by greed, sadism, or, as in this case, vanity. The fundamental breach remains unchanged.

In the United States, **Dr Allan Zarkin** pleaded guilty to carving his initials, "AZ," into a patient's abdomen following a caesarean section because he believed he had performed a work of art worthy of signing.

He avoided prison through a plea deal, which his victim, a 32-year-old dentist, approved. Instead, at age 62, he received 5 years' probation and was barred from applying for a medical licence for 5 years. He could have faced up to 25 years in prison if convicted of the most serious charge, first-degree assault. The hospital where the incident occurred was fined $14,000 and ordered to improve oversight of its doctors. His victim was awarded $1.75 million in compensation. It later emerged that several hospital staff had complained about Dr Zarkin's erratic behaviour and inappropriate comments, which the defence lawyers attributed to his having Pick's disease, an Alzheimer's-like illness.

In 2002, another case surfaced again in America. A gynaecologist, Dr James M. Guiler, was accused of using a cautery instrument to inscribe the letters "UK," shorthand for his alma mater, the University of Kentucky, on the uteri of women undergoing hysterectomy.

The discovery occurred when a patient, Stephanie Means, experienced post-operative haemorrhage and reviewed the videotape of her surgery, which Guiler had provided. On the recording, she saw the unmistakable initials seared into her uterus. She and her husband filed a lawsuit in January 2003.

Within weeks, nine more women came forward, each discovering the same markings on their uteri. Amongst them was Dana Kelly, a nurse who had worked in Guiler's office. She admitted that she saw the branded initials immediately after her operation, but felt too ashamed and intimidated to confront her employer. For more than 3 years, she continued to work alongside him in silence.

The women's accounts revealed shared themes: anger, humiliation, and a deep sense of betrayal. Some described the branding as chauvinistic and disrespectful, whilst others saw it as a blatant violation of the doctor–patient relationship. For them, the uterus was not just tissue to be discarded, but an organ that had carried their children. Marking it without consent was, in their view, an assault on their dignity.

The medical community's response showed a split between technical justifications and ethical limits. Some surgeons supported marking tissue to maintain orientation during surgery. However, experienced gynaecologists and pathologists emphasised that such initials went well beyond any reasonable navigational need. One professor of obstetrics and gynaecology noted that "I'm not aware of any pathologists who require the marking of the uterus before removal." "It's not a technique that we teach."

Importantly, the Kentucky medical licensure board reported no prior complaints against Guiler in the past decade. However, the absence of regulatory action did not reduce the patients' sense of violation.

This case demonstrates a key issue in medical ethics: the difference between what a surgeon might consider benign or routine and what patients see as a serious breach of autonomy. Consent is not merely a formality; it is the basis of the doctor–patient relationship. By marking women's reproductive organs with his initials, Guiler moved from surgery into assault.

In medicine, the patient's body is not a canvas, a stage, or a personal notebook. It is entrusted solely to the doctor for care.

POWER, TRUST, AND THE THIN LINE

The doctors in this chapter come from different nationalities, specialities, and approaches. Some cut too much or too deeply; some deliberately poisoned; some lied about diagnoses; and some used the patient's body as a canvas. What unites them is not their technique but betrayal. Each case demonstrates how medical authority, when misused, can cause harm that is personal, long-lasting, and often invisible until it is too late.

These were not fleeting lapses or errors in judgement. They were calculated actions, carried out by individuals who recognised the power they held and used it for profit, pleasure, or self-expression. In each case, the patients believed the doctor was there to help. That belief made them vulnerable, and it was exploited against them.

Institutions also played a part. Warning signs were ignored. Whistleblowers were dismissed. In some cases, hospitals quietly removed a problematic doctor without informing future employers, favouring reputations and finances over safety. This type of complicity allows abuse to flourish in the shadows.

REFERENCES

Eastgate J. (2020, September 16). *Tribute to whistleblower nurse who exposed deadly drug and shock practice: Deep sleep therapy.* TruthAboutECT.org. https://truthaboutect.org/tribute-to-whistleblower-nurse-who-exposed-deadly-drug-and-shock-practice-deep-sleep-therapy/#_ednref2

Garton, S. (2007). *Bailey, Harry Richard (1922–1985).* In *Australian Dictionary of Biography.* National Centre of Biography, Australian National University. https://adb.anu.edu.au/biography/bailey-harry-richard-12162

Independent Inquiry into the Issues Raised by Paterson. (2020, February). *Report of the Independent Inquiry into the Issues Raised by Paterson* (HC 31). Department of Health and Social Care. https://assets.publishing.service.gov.uk/media/5e3947ed40f0b6090e0b446b/issues-raised-by-paterson-independent-inquiry-report-web-accessible.pdf

Macchiarini, P., Jungebluth, P., Go, T., Asnaghi, M. A., Rees, L. E. N., Cogan, T. A., Dodson, A. L., Martorell, J., Bellini, S., Parnigotto, P. P., Dickinson, S. C., Hollander, A. P., Mantero, S., Conconi, M. T., & Birchall, M. A. (2008). Clinical transplantation of a tissue-engineered airway. *The Lancet, 372*(9655), 2023–2030. https://doi.org/10.1016/S0140-6736(08)61598-6

Steensma, D. P. (2016). The Farid Fata Medicare fraud case and misplaced incentives in oncology care. *Journal of Oncology Practice, 12*(1), 51–54. https://doi.org/10.1200/JOP.2015.008557

Wyndham, D. (2021). *Chelmsford Private Hospital Royal Commission 1988–90.* In *The Dictionary of Sydney.* https://dictionaryofsydney.org/entry/chelmsford_private_hospital_royal_commission_1988_90

10

Doctors, drugs, and crime

CLARE GERADA AND ZAID AL-NAJJAR

When doctors come before the courts, it is most often because of addiction. Alcohol is the leading cause. Drink-driving cases occur far more frequently than fraud, assault, or sexual offences. These are not crimes of the consulting room but of everyday life: a party that ran too late, a poor decision to drive, the intervention of the police. For that reason, they fall outside the focus of this book.

The more serious concerns arise when professional practice intersects with crime, and this almost always involves drugs. Doctors work in constant proximity to them, prescribing, administering, and monitoring their effects, and this closeness carries risk. What begins as self-medication, perhaps a tablet for sleep or a prescription in one's own name, can evolve into dependency. The boundary between legitimate use and criminal conduct is narrow: writing false prescriptions, retaining unused vials, or sourcing drugs outside the system all constitute offences.

In rarer cases, the pattern extends beyond self-use. Some doctors supply colleagues, an even smaller number progress to organised dealing. These transgressions, though uncommon, represent the most troubling convergence of medical authority and criminal behaviour.

This chapter explores that uneasy intersection of medicine, crime, and drugs: how professional lives unravel under the weight of dependency, and how society's view of the addicted doctor has shifted, from sympathy to suspicion, from compassion to stigma.

THE SLOW CREEP OF ADDICTION

Addiction is not simply a matter of weak willpower. It is a chronic and recurring condition that rewires the brain's reward systems, penalises absence with withdrawal symptoms, and encourages repetition through increasing tolerance.

DOI: 10.1201/9781003781066-10

Addiction is regarded as a treatable medical condition, and interventions may involve counselling, therapy, medications, and support groups. As this chapter will demonstrate, the addicted doctor is often met with condemnation rather than understanding. Fear of career-ending consequences causes many sufferers to remain silent. Some never seek help at all, instead relying on secrecy and self-management until a crisis forces the truth to come to light. This crisis might be a drink-drive offence, or, for some, the first indication that the doctor has a problem is a failed or in some sad cases, a successful suicide attempt.

Dependency often begins in the most ordinary of ways: a glass of wine after a brutal shift, a pint in the pub across on the way home from the hospital, codeine bought over the counter to help sleep after the night shift. What started as a way of unwinding could, for some, slip quietly into something far more insidious.

Take Dr A, a surgical registrar, ambitious, hardworking, admired by colleagues. After a back injury during training, her GP prescribed oxycodone. At first, she took it only when the pain flared. But as the pressures of on-call shifts and exams mounted, the pills became less about easing pain and more about coping. Soon she was writing prescriptions in her own name, persuading herself it was temporary, under control. It wasn't. Dependency crept in. When the hospital pharmacy flagged irregularities, she panicked and stopped attending work.

Her story was far from unique. Dr B, a GP partner, had slipped into dependency on benzodiazepines. Reliable, steady, never missing a clinic, he was the kind of doctor colleagues leaned on. But years of 12-hour days, endless paperwork, and caring for an elderly parent left him sleepless. A colleague gave him a few tablets "to help." They worked. Soon he was prescribing for himself, first occasionally, then nightly, and eventually during the day "just to get through." His behaviour shifted: irritable with staff, missing meetings, cutting corners. When prescription discrepancies came to light, he sought help in despair.

Then there was Dr C, a medical registrar running on empty. Ward rounds, exams, research deadlines, nights on call, the pace was relentless. He discovered stimulants whilst revising for finals and later relied on them to get through consecutive shifts. At first, they seemed a secret weapon: energy, focus, stamina. But dependence came swiftly. The drugs kept him awake but left him paranoid, volatile, and short-tempered. Colleagues began to notice. One night, after a double shift, he collapsed from an arrhythmia triggered by stimulant use. Only then did the extent of his dependency become clear.

Each story is different, opioids, benzodiazepines, stimulants, but the threads are strikingly similar: proximity, pressure, silence. Dependency grows quietly, entangling not just the body but the career, until shame and fear force a reckoning.

Factors contributing to addiction in doctors

Addiction in doctors arises from the intersection of personal vulnerability, professional culture, and occupational environment.

Addiction can become the hidden outlet for distress that cannot be safely expressed within medicine. On the personal side, risk may come from genetic predisposition, impulsive temperament, early trauma, or a family history of substance misuse. What makes them excellent clinicians, education, high standards, and resilience, also makes them reluctant patients (Brooks et al., 2011).

Being senior, celebrated, or powerful offers no immunity. Dr Clive Froggatt, once a health adviser to Margaret Thatcher, began prescribing diamorphine under false names, including those of deceased patients. At his peak, he presented nearly 5,000 prescriptions in a single month, visiting multiple pharmacies daily. When exposed, he admitted guilt and was given a suspended sentence. He never practised again, though he later retrained as a counsellor.

The pattern repeats elsewhere. In Boston, USA, Dr Peter Grinspoon, a respected family physician, concealed an oxycodone addiction for over a decade. He wrote fraudulent prescriptions until 2005, when his practice was raided by police and the Drug Enforcement Administration. He served probation, entered rehab, and later became a leading advocate for reform in how medicine responds to addicted doctors.

Environment adds to the risk. Proximity and easy access to prescription drugs make temptation immediate. A young anaesthetist, finishing a night shift, slips a small vial of fentanyl into her pocket. She tells herself it's curiosity, that she wants to understand what her patients feel. Later, she insists it's just for the occasional night when sleep won't come. No one notices, not at first. Easy access helps explain why the incidence of drug abuse amongst anaesthetists is three times higher than in other groups (Mayall, 2016). Unlike other specialities, anaesthetists handle the medications directly, administering rather than prescribing, and the closeness to drugs creates both opportunity and risk. The culture of medicine amplifies this: perfectionism, long hours, and emotional strain normalise the idea of "taking something" just to keep going. Fashion plays a role too; drug choices are shaped as much by culture as by pharmacology. Today's trend of so-called "chem-sex," where substances are used to heighten sexual experience, is one example of that shifting landscape.

Occupational pressures complete the picture. Doctors are expected to perform flawlessly, to hide fatigue, to never fail. In that environment, chemical shortcuts can seem almost rational. Some fall into what's called iatrogenic addiction, not through recklessness, but because another doctor prescribes a powerful drug and fails to review it. Peer-to-peer prescribing is often dangerously casual, especially when one doctor assumes another doctor "knows what they're doing."

Others experiment deliberately, using themselves as "human guinea pigs." Sigmund Freud famously tested, and became dependent on, cocaine. He described it as a "magical drug." Harold Shipman claimed his own pethidine addiction began at medical school, when he was told to try it during training.

From the solitary theft of codeine by a young anaesthetist to the large-scale deception of a political insider, the pathways differ. Yet the threads are the same: access, pressure, opportunity, and a culture slow to confront its own vulnerabilities.

When the bar was in the hospital: The 1970s and 1980s

For those trained in the 1970s or 1980s, the hospital culture of that time is nearly unrecognisable today. In many doctors' messes, alcohol was a common feature.

Wine was served with lunch in hospital dining halls. Senior consultants might pour a glass of sherry before afternoon ward rounds. Some pubs had direct telephone lines to the on-call rooms, allowing the hospital to summon the doctor if needed. This was mainly a male workforce, bonded by traditions of stoicism and gallows humour, where alcohol was not only a social bonding tool but also an unspoken way of coping. Celebrations, condolences, and the relief from tension after complex cases all found expression over drinks.

Drug misuse had equally open channels.

Until the early years of this century, it was common for doctors to prescribe for themselves or their family members. Strong opioids, benzodiazepines, and sleeping tablets could be obtained with little or no difficulty. Many GPs kept spare prescription pads in desk drawers at home, and hospital doctors could sign out controlled drugs with minimal oversight. The old saying "physician, heal thyself" was more than a proverb; it was a daily practice. Unsurprisingly, benzodiazepine and painkiller addictions were widespread.

This changed in the United Kingdom following the Shipman Inquiry. The recommendations tightened prescribing regulations, introduced closer monitoring of controlled drugs, and granted pharmacists greater authority to challenge unusual patterns. In the United Kingdom, self-prescribing or prescribing to close family members became a disciplinary offence. Whilst access to drugs is never fully restricted, it has certainly been severely curtailed over the last two decades.

A nineteenth-century normality

Step further back, to the late nineteenth century, and the moral landscape is almost unrecognisable.

Imagine a small-town family doctor in 1876. The day has been long, with house calls along muddy streets, a waiting room full of patients suffering from winter coughs, and one difficult delivery that has left him exhausted. He sits at his desk in the fading light, takes a small glass vial of morphine from the drawer, and injects himself. Within minutes, the headache lifts, his body relaxes, and his mind sharpens. The warmth comes quickly, easing the edge of fatigue and dulling the headache that started somewhere between his fifth patient with rheumatism and his third house call to a child with scarlet fever. He will feel clearer now, more precise. In another hour, he'll walk down to the public lecture hall to speak on "Advances in Surgical Asepsis," a subject he can approach with renewed vigour, thanks, in no small part, to the contents of that vial. There is nothing covert about this. In his world, addiction is regarded as an occupational hazard, a result of long hours, emotional strain, and constant contact with the very drugs he prescribes.

Opium, morphine, and later cocaine were central tools of the profession. In 1817, morphine was derived from opium by the German pharmacist Friedrich W Serturner after a series of experiments on himself. This breakthrough heralded the availability of a substance, named after Morpheus, the Greek God of dreams, which was of a predictable form, meaning it could be used in medical practice. The invention of the hypodermic syringe in the mid-nineteenth century made these drugs and others more potent and immediate. Some of the most renowned doctors of the era were dependent. Self-medication amongst doctors with the drug was rife and unique to this profession, given their access to the drug and knowledge of how to use it and the tradition of doctors using their bodies to test drugs. Dr Thomas Beddoes who discovered the medicinal use for nitrous oxide and Dr William Stewart Halsted, a pioneering surgeon and founder of Johns Hopkins Hospital, both worked for decades whilst addicted to both cocaine and morphine (Imber, 2011). Dr Wilkie Collins, the novelist and physician, fought a long battle with laudanum, a mixture of opium and alcohol. Even Sherlock Holmes's fictional cocaine habit mirrored the reality of many of Conan Doyle's contemporaries. By the turn of the century, the issue was openly acknowledged. Sir James Paget, a British surgeon and pathologist, studied why students failed their exams. He found that out of the 56 of the 1,000 who failed, ten (17.8%) did so because of drug or alcohol problems, writing "through the continuance in habits of intemperance or dissipation as had made us, even when they were students, anticipate their failure" (Paget, 1875). The American doctor, JB Mattison made the surprising claim in 1883 that "most morphine habitues were doctors" citing rates of addiction as high as 30%–40%. His work was one of the earliest to be done on doctors' vulnerability to addiction (Mattison, 1883). The British physician Oscar Jennings, himself addicted to morphine, estimated that in 1909, one in five medical practitioners' deaths were linked to morphine addiction and that the proportion of medical addicts amongst total cases was as high as 90% (Jennings, 1909; Milligan, 2005). In 1924, the German psychopathologist, Louis Lewin suggested that it was not just 40% of doctors who were addicted to morphine but that 10% of their wives were as well (Lewin, 1924; Milligan, 2005). Official government figures in 1935 suggested that there were 700 morphine addicts in Britain, with a sixth of them being medical practitioners (Rolleston Committee, 1936).

Of course, all this data is somewhat questionable since reliable measures would have been difficult. Still, we can reasonably conclude that medical professionals remained the most prominent group amongst morphine addicts in the Western world after the mid-nineteenth century. And this was primarily accepted as not interfering with their ability to practise. These doctors, of course, were not (for the most part) involved in criminal behaviour to obtain their drugs but sourced them through colleagues or by self-prescription. Whilst some at the time advocated restricting access to the drug, especially to the public, the question of prohibition was rarely explicitly linked to doctors' addiction. The tone used when discussing doctors' addiction was sympathetic, and medical addicts were viewed differently from those outside the profession. It was widely believed that morphine was needed to help doctors cope with their work, and it was thought to be a stimulant and necessary to meet the intellectual demands of the job required by "superior" people (Milligan, 2005).

It wasn't only opium or its derivatives that doctors turned to. Another favourite was prussic acid, better known as hydrocyanic acid or cyanide. Swift and deadly, it was nevertheless prescribed in the eighteenth and nineteenth centuries for everything from convulsive fits in children to headaches, indigestion, chest complaints, and general bodily pains. It was even promoted as a quick "sobering" agent for those who had drunk too much.

Though not addictive, its danger lay in its lethality. Doctors who used it themselves, or prescribed it liberally, were at particular risk of fatal accidents. One such case was Dr Charles Porter, long troubled by alcoholism, who regularly relied on prussic acid for himself and his patients. One evening, intoxicated, he mistook a vial of the poison in his surgery for the ginger beer his wife had left for him, with fatal results.

Another fatal incident involved Dr James Cockburn Belaney, who was also in the habit of self-dosing. When his bottle of prussic acid shattered, he poured the remainder into a tumbler, intending to find another container. Distracted by his work, he left it unattended. His wife, believing the glass was empty, filled it with water and Epsom salts, drank it, and died within 20 minutes. Belaney was charged with murder. Although acquitted, the scandal destroyed his career. On returning home, he faced public fury: he was stoned in the street, an effigy of him was burned by a mob, and his house was eventually set ablaze.

FROM OPEN SECRET TO STIGMA

A century later, the picture is very different. The prevalence of addiction amongst doctors is far lower than it was in the Victorian era. Yet, as noted in the introduction, substance misuse remains the leading cause of doctors acquiring a criminal record.

A national survey of a sample of American doctors registered with the American Medical Association was conducted in 2015. It surveyed more than 20,000 doctors from all specialities (Oreskovich et al., 2015). Rates of drug misuse in this survey were very low (less than 1%). These results found that 13% of male doctors met the diagnostic criteria for alcohol dependence, compared to 21% of female doctors. That the rates for women were higher is surprising given that, in most national surveys (of the general population), the prevalence rates for alcohol use disorder in women are usually lower than for men, and usually hover between 4% and 7%, depending on age and methodology. Several possible explanations could account for this discrepancy. It may reflect a factual finding, suggesting that female physicians face unique stressors, such as increased work, family conflict, gender bias, and often disproportionate caregiving responsibilities. These stressors can lead to maladaptive coping mechanisms, including heightened alcohol consumption, even amongst those who are otherwise highly functioning. However, the elevated rate is more likely a reflection of sampling or response bias: the study had a 26.7% response rate, and it is also possible that women were more willing than men to disclose substance use in anonymous surveys. Most treatment samples show a male bias; for example, those attending the NHS Practitioner Health service seeking addiction treatment are predominantly male. This is in keeping with other treatment samples (Sathanandan et al., 2019).

Drug addiction is not randomly distributed amongst the medical population. Unsurprisingly, clinicians who have better access to potent drugs exhibit higher rates of addiction, particularly anaesthetists. For instance, they can (and do) reuse partially used ampoules for personal use rather than disposing of them properly (Boulis et al., 2015).

The cases that follow have been anonymised and some details changed to maintain confidentiality as the individuals were patients of NHS Practitioner Health.

Alex: An anaesthetist

It is 7:15 a.m. on a Tuesday. The operating theatre lies silent, the team not yet assembled. In the sluice room, Alex, a seasoned anaesthetist, draws a syringe of fentanyl from the controlled drugs cupboard. What began years earlier as "experimentation" had spiralled into dependency. Soon he was injecting daily combinations of fentanyl, morphine, tramadol, and more. Cyclizine was added to blunt the nausea and heighten the euphoria; a local anaesthetic to ease injections as his veins collapsed.

The ritual became routine: the sting, the spreading warmth, the fleeting calm. Over time, he was using from morning to night, before surgical lists, in his car during breaks, and again after work to stave off withdrawal. Eventually, his body gave way: he developed septicaemia, endocarditis, a stroke, epilepsy, and required a heart valve replacement.

When a foul smell from his locker prompted a search, colleagues discovered blood-stained clothes, used syringes, and stolen ampoules. Alex was convicted of theft and given a suspended prison sentence. The judge called it a profound betrayal of trust towards his patients, employer, and family, sustained over years and revealed only when illness forced it into the open. His licence to practise was revoked.

Peter: A GP

Peter worked in a rural village practice. Unlike Alex, his licence was not removed immediately. His deception first came to light when a pharmacist, suspicious of repeated prescriptions for large amounts of oxycodone, delayed dispensing and called the police. The prescription, supposedly for a patient the pharmacist knew, made no clinical sense. The fraud unravelled.

Peter's dependency had begun with back pain, relieved by oxycodone taken from a deceased patient's home. The drug did more than dull pain; it soothed his anxiety and made him feel confident. Soon he was self-prescribing, presenting prescriptions under his own name to multiple pharmacies, sometimes dozens in a day. Later he fabricated patients, or used the details of real ones, with no intention of supplying them.

Charged with theft and fraud, he was given a suspended 8-month prison sentence and 200 hours of unpaid work. Surprisingly, he was allowed to continue practising under strict conditions: no prescribing, no administration, no unsupervised responsibility for drugs.

But within a year, he relapsed. He attempted to obtain oxycodone again, this time with a prescription written in his own name and fraudulently signed by a colleague. It was the end. He was struck off the medical register and left unemployed.

Together, these stories illustrate the spectrum of medical addiction, from the hospital anaesthetist with ready access to controlled drugs, to the village GP manipulating prescriptions. Different contexts, same trajectory: secrecy, escalation, collapse, and the ultimate loss of their jobs.

Where the Victorian doctor might once have been pitied, or even quietly admired, for enduring the strain of practice with chemical assistance, today's addicted doctor meets almost universal condemnation. This change began in the mid-twentieth century, when sympathy had given way to stigma.

A psychiatric textbook from 1939 declared that "rarely does a well-integrated person become a morphine addict," reflecting the growing view that dependency signalled poor character rather than misfortune (Noyes, 1939). This perception lingers. Addiction is now regarded as evidence of bad judgement or self-indulgence, and the consequences are severe: loss of job, licence, income, and reputation. Investigations by employers and the regulator can drag on for years, leaving doctors in limbo.

Small wonder secrecy becomes the norm and issues related to addiction remain the most common reason why doctors obtain a criminal record.

It would be unwise to end this chapter without talking about some of the advances which have been put in place to support the addicted health professional.

In 1973, the American Medical Association published a landmark report titled *The Sick Physician*. This formally recognised that doctors can suffer from psychiatric illness and addiction, and that such impairments threaten both physician health and patient safety. It was pivotal in shaping the development of physician health services in the United States and abroad (American Medical Association, 1973). The report described the challenges doctors faced regarding their health and called for dedicated systems to treat and monitor physicians impaired by illness, whether through addiction, depression, or other serious conditions. In the years that followed, physician health programmes emerged. Now present in nearly every American state and all Canadian provinces, these services assess doctors in difficulty, develop treatment plans, and monitor progress, with a particular focus on stress, burnout, and substance misuse (McLellan et al., 2008).

The conversation about addicted doctors in Britain began, at least publicly, in 1975. It was the psychiatrist Dr Max Glatt, a Holocaust survivor, who first spoke out about the hidden struggles of alcoholic doctors. He observed how many "shy away from asking a doctor for help," paralysed by fears of exposure, professional ruin, and personal shame. He established what was to become the British Doctors and Dentists Group, a form of Alcoholics Anonymous for doctors and dentists. Specialist private (fee-paying) services that provided confidential help for doctors also existed, but these were few and far between and expensive to access.

Nationwide services for doctors in the United Kingdom were not put in place for decades. As a result of government recommendations in response to the Shipman Inquiry, in 2008, NHS Practitioner Health, a national, confidential service for doctors in distress, was established. Practitioner Health was different by design. It was not the regulator. It was not a probationary scheme intended to police or punish. Its purpose was therapeutic, not disciplinary: to offer a safe space where doctors could seek help without the automatic fear of referral, where addiction and mental illness could be treated as health problems rather than moral failings. Within the necessary limits of law and professional standards, it carried the flexibility to support recovery rather than enforce compliance (Brooks et al., 2011).

In its first 15 years, NHS Practitioner Health, has treated more than two thousand doctors with drug or alcohol problems, and smaller numbers with gambling or other behavioural addictions. Of those treated for substance use, as many as 80% remained abstinent after 5 years. The impact on careers is equally striking. At the start of treatment, fewer than half were working. By the end, 85% were back in practice (Sathanandan et al., 2019).

Behind those statistics are stories of lives being restored to almost normality: doctors who walked into the clinic broken, fearful of losing everything, and who walked out with sobriety, stability, and the chance to rebuild not only their lives but the trust of their patients.

In the next chapter, we move from the personal to the commercial, the pill mills, where prescribing becomes an organised business, and the casualties can be counted in hundreds of thousands.

REFERENCES

American Medical Association. (1973). The sick physician: Impairment by psychiatric disorders, including alccholism and drug dependence. *JAMA, 223*(6), 684–687. doi:10.1001/jama.1973.03220060058020

Boulis, S., Khanduja, P. K., Downey, K., & Friedman, Z. (2015). Substance abuse: A national survey of Canadian residency program directors and site chiefs at university-affiliated anesthesia departments. *Canadian Journal of Anaesthesia = Journal Canadien D'anesthesie, 62*(9), 964–971. https://doi.org/10.1007/s12630-015-0404-1

Brooks, S. K., Chalder, T., & Gerada, C. (2011). Doctors vulnerable to psychological distress and addictions: Treatment from the Practitioner Health Programme. *Journal of Mental Health, 20*(2), 157–164. https://doi.org/10.3109/09638237.2011.556168

Imber, G. (2011). *Genius on the Edge: The Bizzare Double Life of Dr William Stewart Halsted*. Kaplan Publishing.

Jennings, O. (1909). *On Morphinism and Other Drug Habits*. Baillière, Tindall and Cox.

Lewin, L. (1924). *Phantastica: Narcotic and Stimulating Drugs, Their Use and Abuse*. Kegan Paul, Trench, Trubner & Co.

Mattison, J. (1883). *Morphia Habituation: Its Etiology and Treatment*. E.B Treat.

Mayall, R. (2016). Substance abuse in anaesthetists. *BJA Education, 16*(7), 236–241. https://doi.org/10.1093/bjaed/mkv054

McLellan, A. T., Skipper, G. S., Campbell, M., & DuPont, R. L. (2008). Five year outcomes in a cohort study of physicians treated for substance use disorders in the United States. *BMJ, 337*(nov04 1), a2038. https://doi.org/10.1136/bmj.a2038

Milligan, B. (2005). Morphine-addicted doctors, the English opium-eater, and embattled medical authority. *Victorian Literature and Culture, 33*(2), 541–553. https://doi.org/10.1017/S1060150305050977

Noyes, A. (1939). *Modern Clinical Psychiatrist*. W. B Saunders Company.

Oreskovich, M. R., Shanafelt, T., Dyrbye, L. N., Tan, L., Sotile, W., Satele, D., West, C. P., Sloan, J., & Boone, S. (2015). The prevalence of substance use disorders in American physicians. *The American Journal on Addictions, 24*(1), 30–38. https://doi.org/10.1111/ajad.12173

Paget. (1875). *Studies of Old Case-Books*. Longmans, Green and Co.

Rolleston Committee (1936). Report of the Departmental Committee on Morphine and Heroin Addiction. HMSO.

Sathanandan, S., Abrol, E., Aref-Adib, G., Keen, J., & Gerada, C. (2019). The UK Practitioner Health Programme: 8 year outcomes in Doctors with addiction disorders. *Research and Advances in Psychiatry, 6*(2), 43–49.

11

From victim to vector: Doctors and pills

CLARE GERADA AND ZAID AL-NAJJAR

So far, in discussions about addiction, we have considered doctors as patients vulnerable to the same biological, circumstantial, and opportunistic factors as anyone else. However, there is a darker, more troubling aspect to this narrative. Sometimes, the doctor is not the one fighting their addiction but the one enabling it in others. Whether through negligence, misplaced compassion, or deliberate exploitation, these doctors become part of the supply chain, linking pharmaceutical manufacturing to the illegal drug trade. Here, professional trust can turn into professional betrayal.

DRUGS AND MONEY

Where potent drugs such as opioids, psychostimulants, and tranquillisers intersect with direct payments, the profit potential for the doctor as prescriber and patient as payer increases the risk of abuse. In legitimate private practice, prescribing is an essential part of patient care; however, the blurry line between clinical judgement and commercial interests can tempt some to misuse their position. This is where *pill mills* come in: doctors working in situations where drugs are prescribed to nearly anyone who requests them, often without an apparent medical reason. In the most serious cases, especially in the United States, where direct-to-consumer pharmaceutical advertising has long encouraged patients to demand specific, potent opioids, doctors have fully adopted the role of high-status drug dealers. In exchange for money, they ensure prescriptions continue without interruption, sometimes with fatal consequences. These doctors' business models depend on volume: the more patients, the more prescriptions, the more income. The victims are counted in lives lost, communities devastated, and an epidemic of dependency driven not by street dealers but by those with medical degrees.

DOI: 10.1201/9781003781066-11

FROM THE BRITISH SYSTEM TO PILL MILLS

London, 1962. A young man in a leather jacket pushes open the frosted-glass door of a Harley Street clinic. He is shown into a consultation room where the doctor, impeccably dressed, with a silver pen in hand, barely lifts his eyes from his desk. There is no examination, no questions. A few quiet words are exchanged. The prescription is signed, and the man leaves with enough pharmaceutical heroin to last a week. Outside on the pavement, he lights a cigarette and begins calculating how much he will use and how much he can sell on, using the money to pay for another visit to this private doctor.

When people think of pill mills nowadays, they usually refer to those in the United States, where clinics line up with patients waiting for prescriptions of potent opioids after only a brief (if any) consultation, rather than to those, as in the vignette above, in 1960s London.

However, Britain, especially London, was the "pill mill" hub from the 1960s to the mid-1990s. Starting in the 1930s, and almost unique amongst other countries, doctors in Britain were allowed to prescribe controlled drugs, including cocaine, pharmaceutical heroin (diamorphine), amphetamines, and barbiturates, to patients suffering from addiction. This approach, later known as the British System, was based on the belief that addiction was a medical issue rather than a criminal one. It stood in stark contrast to how addicts were treated in other parts of the world (Strang & Gossop, 2005).

In the United Kingdom, doctors were allowed to prescribe medication to:

- Patients for whom all efforts at cure had failed and withdrawal caused severe symptoms that could not be safely managed in private practice, or
- Those who can sustain a stable, relatively normal life on a limited, non-progressive supply of the drug, but whose condition worsens if that supply is stopped.

In practice, this gave doctors considerable clinical discretion. For many, prescribing was motivated by genuine compassion and a desire to keep patients stable, and for decades, the system seemed effective, especially considering the type of patients receiving treatment. Many of those treated from the 1930s to the late 1950s were "professional addicts," meaning they were doctors, dentists, and pharmacists who, like their Victorian predecessors, had become addicted through easy access to morphine.

Others were "therapeutic addicts," individuals who developed dependency after treatment with morphine, now called iatrogenic addiction. Although early data on the proportion of therapeutic addicts is unavailable, it is believed that before World War I, most cases of addiction were therapeutic in origin, making up between one-fifth and one-quarter of all instances. The number of known addicts receiving treatment was as low as 290 in 1952, so few that the Home Office could monitor each of their personal lives.

In the UK, recreational (meaning not prescribed) use of morphine and cocaine was limited to a small "artistic" circle and isolated Chinese communities.

There was little or no black-market trade in heroin, so before the 1960s, only small quantities of heroin entered the United Kingdom illegally, mainly through sailors, travellers, and smuggling routes from the Far East (especially from China and later Hong Kong) or through thefts from pharmacies or wholesalers.

In the late 1940s, the first signs of change appeared through raids on London nightclubs, where opioids were seized, confirming a shift in addiction patterns in Britain. Younger, non-professional, or non-therapeutic addicts were emerging, and recreational use was beginning to increase.

Between 1961 and 1965, further changes occurred in the British drug scene. Once again, there was an increase in young, non-medical users, especially in London. By 1962, for the first time, the number of heroin addicts overtook those addicted to morphine. The rise in heroin use was mainly driven by smuggling from Hong Kong and later from the "Golden Triangle" (Burma, Laos, Thailand), which made heroin more accessible and affordable. Additionally, a few private practitioners began prescribing large quantities of heroin to hundreds (if not thousands) of addicts in London, many of whom sold part of their prescriptions, creating a "grey market" (illegal supply of pharmaceutical drugs stemming from doctors' prescriptions) in pharmaceutical heroin.

The flaws in the British system became evident. A new type of patient appeared: North Americans with criminal pasts, attracted to Britain by reports that doctors were openly prescribing heroin. For career addicts familiar with illegal street markets in their home countries, Britain's medicalised system offered something invaluable: a legal and dependable source. This influx exposed the weaknesses of a system based on trust between doctor and patient. What had worked for the professional or therapeutic addict was much less effective with a more criminally inclined group.

New restrictions were introduced, requiring doctors to hold a Home Office licence to prescribe heroin and several other Class A drugs.

This did not stop a few doctors, through reckless prescribing, fuelling a vicious cycle: more addicts seeking help, more prescriptions, more diversion, and ultimately, even more addiction (Strang et al., 2005).

At the same time, the rise of 24-hour pharmacies transformed London into both the prescription hub of the United Kingdom and the centre of its emerging drug subculture. Boots opened its Piccadilly branch in the mid-1920s, followed shortly after in the 1930s by John Bell & Croyden on Wigmore Street, near Harley Street, and Allen & Hanbury's. These all-night chemists quickly became more than just dispensaries; they served as meeting points, communication hubs, and unofficial centres of the drug trade (Mars, 2003).

Four doctors stand out at this time: Lady Frankau, John Petro, Ann Dally, and Christopher Swan, each pushing the boundaries of medical ethics (Stimson & Oppenheimer, 1982).

Of these doctors, Lady Frankau set the tone. She was one of only twelve doctors in England legally permitted to prescribe heroin; she stood at the centre of a controversy that would influence the country's drug policy for years to come.

A psychiatrist trained at the Maudsley Hospital, Lady Frankau specialised in treating drug and alcohol dependence. However, her methods were far from conventional. She became notorious for liberally issuing prescriptions for controlled substances, her clinic attracting patients from all over Britain and as far as North America. Rumours about Frankau's approach spread widely, and like bees to a honeypot, addicts travelled great distances to obtain the drugs they sought. Between 1958 and 1964, she claimed to have treated just over 500 patients. Her influence extended well beyond London. After a lecture tour in Canada, addicts there began making pilgrimages to England, enticed by stories of easily prescribed heroin and a system with loopholes large enough to exploit. Some arrived by ship to Liverpool, then took the train straight to London. Others remembered more direct journeys; one patient described stepping off a plane, hailing a taxi to Holloway Road, and leaving a doctor's surgery with immediate prescriptions for heroin and cocaine.

Drugs were dispensed from the back of her Bentley; prescriptions written in quantities far exceeding what her peers would dare recommend, sometimes fifty times more. The excess did not stay confined to her patients; it spilt onto London's streets, fuelling an illegal trade that thrived on her "generosity." The figures speak volumes. In 1962 alone, Lady Frankau prescribed six kilograms, 600,000 tablets of heroin to about 2,000 registered addicts. On one occasion, she handed a patient 900 tablets, only to issue 600 more 3 days later to replace a batch allegedly "lost in an accident." Yet, despite growing concerns within the Home Office, she avoided prosecution. Many believed that her marriage to a knighted surgeon, along with her connections to London's glamorous social elite (jazz legends and embassy officials were amongst her patients), provided her with a shield from legal action, a shield strong enough to withstand the controversy caused by her prescriptions.

When Lady Frankau died in 1967, her list of patients, which included hundreds reliant on her supplies of diamorphine and cocaine, was handed to Dr John Petro. A Polish-born GP who emigrated to Britain in 1916, Petro was once regarded as a respectable doctor. During the Second World War, he worked alongside Alexander Fleming, administering life-saving penicillin to wounded soldiers. However, by the mid-1960s, his career had taken a darker turn. Inheriting Frankau's patients, a clientele of complex addicts, drew him into a world that blurred the line between medicine and vice. Then came the crash, literally in this sense. In 1966, Petro suffered serious injuries in a car accident. Unable to work and overwhelmed by debts, he declared bankruptcy in March 1967. Without a clinic or the means to rent space from landlords who refused to lease to a doctor "treating junkies," Petro moved to the fringes of medical practice. He saw patients wherever he could, from London hotels to Baker Street tube station to dingy cafés and even in the back seat of his Vauxhall Viva.

The prescriptions revealed his desperation. Large doses of heroin and cocaine, far beyond medical necessity, changed hands; some users consumed the drugs, whilst many sold them illegally on the streets, fuelling the grey market and creating new addicts who would become Petro's next generation of patients. The press dubbed him "the junkie's friend," a doctor who, for the right fee, supplied addicts with staggering amounts of any drug they demanded. Petro defended himself fervently, claiming he was doing what the Government refused to do, providing a clean, pharmaceutical alternative to the deadly black market. But to the authorities, he was not a hero. He was a supplier, feeding chaos. His downfall unfolded in the spotlight. Invited onto David Frost's prime-time TV show on 1 January 1968, Petro, perhaps carried away by fame, admitted live on air to overprescribing. Minutes after the cameras stopped rolling, Scotland Yard's Drug Squad arrested him outside the studio. The 60-year-old doctor was taken to Paddington Police Station and accused of offences against the Misuse of Drugs Act. He was refused bail and held in a cell until he appeared in court the following month (Alamy, n.d.).

By February 1968, Petro was standing in the dock at Marylebone Magistrates' Court, admitting guilt to seventeen offences, mainly for failing to keep proper records of his controlled drug prescriptions. The court fined him £1,700, a considerable amount at the time. On 31 May, that same year, the General Medical Council struck him off, citing reckless prescribing and neglect of professional protocols.

Lady Frankau had avoided punishment in her lifetime, but Petro faced the consequences, losing his career, reputation, and freedom to a system that ultimately drew the line.

Both became central figures in a national debate about the limits of medical freedom. Some viewed them as representing a compassionate, pragmatic approach by assisting those with addictions through providing a known, pharmaceutical-grade drug to prevent crime. Others saw them as symbolising a dangerous permissiveness that had flooded Britain's streets with heroin and cocaine. Their cases did more than dominate tabloid headlines; they influenced policy. The sight of prescriptions being issued from Bentleys or hotel lobbies made it politically impossible to defend the "British System" in its most liberal form.

Yet not everyone understood the message.

Dr Ann Dally's career demonstrated that some doctors still supported a liberal approach. Raised in a reformist household, her father, a pioneer in marriage guidance and family planning, believed in a progressive approach to medicine. As a psychiatrist, she based her practice on the idea that prescribing drugs like morphine, Diconol, amphetamines, and methadone was safer than leaving addicts to street dealers. Her patient numbers grew from just a few to over 500, with around 200 patients under treatment at any given time. However, her methods, similar to those of Frankau and Petro before her, brought her into direct conflict with the General Medical Council. In 1983, she was convicted of overprescribing. Four years later, more charges followed. Although Dally defended herself, the GMC remained resolute, emphasising the dangers her prescribing posed and the comfortable lifestyle it provided her. A 14-month ban on prescribing controlled drugs marked a turning point, ushering in a newer, stricter era of regulation. The Home Office and police would no longer tolerate doctors who blurred the boundaries between treatment and supply.

Dr Christopher Michael Swan pushed boundaries more than most. Within London's addiction scene, he was notorious for his willingness to prescribe powerful stimulants. His reckless overprescribing eventually drew police attention, and it wasn't limited to stimulants alone. In January 1969, Swan appeared at the Central Criminal Court and pleaded guilty to multiple offences, mainly related to his dangerous trade in prescription drugs. He had issued prescriptions for large quantities of Drinamyl and Durophet, both powerful stimulants. Most of the names on the prescriptions he signed were false. Swan claimed they were for genuine patients, but the drugs were for fictitious ones and then diverted for sale on the streets. The scale was substantial. In less than 9 months, Swan and his assistant, Stephen Hartford, had prescribed half a million Drinamyl and over 40,000 Methedrine (also called methamphetamine) tablets. Many prescriptions were pre-signed by Swan with patient details and drugs to be prescribed left blank, allowing Hartford, who was not a doctor, to fill in the details and pass himself off as one. Prescriptions were issued not based on medical need, but on how much money the "patient" offered. Both addicts and dealers queued at his surgery. The profits were significant. One estimate suggested that over 3 months, the trade earned Swan £15,000, a fortune at that time. The figures tell the story: 168 prescriptions in September 1967, rising to 23,000 by January, 44,000 by April, and an astonishing 64,000 by June 1968.

But Swan's downfall was not solely caused by the scale of the drug scandal. The court also uncovered more about the darker world he was involved in. Amongst the addicts and dealers frequenting his practice was a petty West End drug dealer called Wall, one of many drawn into the orbit of Swan.

Wall's mistake was simple: he disclosed too much about what actually occurred inside Swan's practice. Loose tongues were dangerous, and Swan decided to silence him.

On 7 June 1968, in the basement of Swan's surgery, a man named Gordon obeyed the doctor's orders. Armed with a knife, he stabbed Wall in the back and neck before fleeing. Upstairs, Swan heard what had happened. He came downstairs, saw the bleeding man on the floor, and did nothing. It was Hartford, Swan's assistant, who finally called an ambulance. Against the odds, Wall survived.

The payment for the attack was not in money but in drugs. Gordon's agreed fee was 1,600 Drinamyl tablets, supplied through eight prescriptions written by Hartford. Violence, like everything else in Swan's world, could be bought with pills.

Once arrested and remanded, Swan took a further step by approaching a fellow prisoner with a request that seemed more fitting for the underworld than a medical professional. He asked for witnesses against him, including Hartford, to be eliminated. Swan offered his cellmate thousands of pounds if he could organise the killings and even discussed how the bodies should be disposed of. Unbeknownst to him, the so-called "hitman" he arranged for the murder, whom Swan met in prison to discuss the details, was in fact an undercover detective, and the conversation was secretly recorded. When the police presented him with the tapes, Swan's career and his freedom were over. He was not just a doctor who had lost control of his prescribing; he had crossed into something darker, a doctor willing to deal in drugs, money, and murder. Swan did not attend his GMC hearing. The committee was told that Swan did not mean any discourtesy by not appearing; he was then at Broadmoor and likely to remain there for some time (Judson, 1973).

The days when questionable prescribing practices could go unnoticed had ended. By the mid-1980s, the GMC and the police had become much more active in investigating doctors whose behaviour was considered irresponsible or unsafe. By the time the 70-year-old Dr Kobina Arba Taylor came under scrutiny, the regulatory environment had changed significantly (Home Office. *Misuse of Drugs Act*, 1971).

Taylor was no ordinary practitioner. A former Nigerian diplomat, he carried himself with the air of someone accustomed to authority and public life. However, that did not shield him when he was caught in a sting operation. Undercover officers, posing as desperate patients in need of medication, approached him, and Taylor complied. What he did not realise was that every encounter was being meticulously recorded and prepared for court.

In 1987, he was convicted at Aylesbury Crown Court on four counts of prescribing controlled drugs in breach of the Misuse of Drugs Act. Evidence demonstrated that, over 7 months from December 1984 to June 1985, he had issued prescriptions to more than seventy individuals. The court sentenced him to a 1-year conditional discharge, a lenient outcome, but one that left his professional reputation in ruins.

This was not his first encounter with the law. A few years earlier, Taylor had been involved in a much larger operation: a £1 million scheme supplying passports to illegal immigrants. That case was tried at the Old Bailey, and although the scale of the fraud was enormous, Taylor received a 4-month suspended sentence. The judge, when passing sentence, said he was being merciful, citing Taylor's years of service to his community and his poor health.

Over the next few years, to the present day, the GMC has become more prominent, often stepping in after high-profile patient deaths. National headlines echo public sentiment, with newspapers depicting doctors as villains rather than healers: "Doctors who Trade in Misery" and "Victims of Pusher Doctors" have become common refrains. Alongside requests from professionals for stricter prescribing controls, the media launched its own campaign against prescribing doctors. The tone was established by headlines such as the *London Standard*'s 1982 accusation: "How Doctors Feed the Heroin Black Market."

Yet, this did not deter some doctors and the idea that a prescription pad could be as potent a tool for drug supply as any smuggler's network persisted.

If earlier cases showed how prescribing had become a matter for the police and the courts, then the case of Dr Sudesh Madan revealed what could happen once any semblance of providing care was entirely removed from the equation.

In 2012, Madan was not officially registered as a doctor. She had already been removed from the medical register in 2001 for reckless prescribing of amphetamines. However, losing her licence did not stop her. She continued to exploit her medical authority by posing as a doctor and operating nationwide slimming pill clinics. Police searches later uncovered nearly 25,000 phentermine tablets and over 13,000 capsules of diethylpropion, both potent amphetamine-based appetite suppressants. To her patients, many of whom knew her as "Dr Ahmed," she appeared to be a genuine doctor. After brief consultations, she would hand out prescriptions. A week's worth of pills, promising weight loss, typically costs £20. Madan's operation was first exposed not through medical channels, but during a police investigation into a fatal car crash in Hatfield in 2009. One of the drivers involved told officers she had been taking slimming pills supplied by Madan. Although the tablets were not found to have caused the crash, the investigation uncovered a loose thread that led to a national inquiry. The lead detective described what they found: "*Sudesh Madan ran a large-scale operation across the country, callously posing as a doctor and, without regard for her patients, prescribing these slimming pills, which could have endangered them. We believe her motivation was greed, and we are determined to use our powers to seize any profits she made from her actions.*" Madan earned over £1 million through her clinics. She was eventually convicted, imprisoned for 18 months, and ordered to repay her illegal gains or face a longer sentence.

Where doctors like Dally had once advocated for compassion in prescribing, Madan abandoned even the semblance of medical duty. Her "Easy Slim" empire reduced the act of prescribing to a mere commercial transaction.

What had begun as the British System, an experiment in humane care for dependent patients, had within a generation fallen into outright criminality disguised as medicine.

By the end of the twentieth century, Britain's era of liberal prescribing had largely come to an end. The cases of Dally, Frankau, Petro, Taylor, Swan, and Madan showed how fine the line could be between genuine care and commercial interests. Nonetheless, the scale of these scandals remained quite limited, kept in check by the UK's stricter drug supply chains and a culture of professional regulation that, although not perfect, generally intervened before issues could escalate into the large pill mill crises that later devastated the United States.

AMERICAN PILL MILLS

The factors influencing Britain's early pill mills, such as individual prescribers, willing patients, and an illegal market, were intensified by something the United Kingdom never fully experienced: the influence of the pharmaceutical industry's marketing machine. American doctors had long maintained closer, more transactional links with drug companies. Add to this direct-to-consumer advertising, which was unthinkable in Britain, and you get a perfect storm where patients were encouraged to request, or even demand, specific branded opioids.

In the United States, pill mills, clinics that dispense large quantities of opioids with minimal medical oversight, have been at the centre of some of the most serious abuses. Often operating under the guise of legitimacy, they exploit gaps in monitoring systems, with doctors occasionally moving between states to avoid detection. For patients desperate for relief, these clinics offer easy access to medication but little in terms of holistic care or follow-up. For some prescribers, this model proves especially profitable (Dickson-Gomez et al., 2022).

However, the line between a busy pain clinic and a pill mill can be dangerously thin. Chronic pain remains notoriously difficult to treat, and opioid prescribing guidelines, whether from the Centers for Disease Control and Prevention (CDC) in the United States or the National Institute for Health and Care Excellence (NICE) in the United Kingdom, are often interpreted differently depending on the clinician's training, the patient population, and local attitudes. This creates fertile ground for both genuine clinical disagreement and, unfortunately, deliberate exploitation. In this environment, the pill mill was no longer just a side venture for a few rogue doctors. It grew into an industrial operation, functioning on a scale never seen before. In America, clinics emerged in states with relaxed regulations, selling not only prescriptions but also a complete illusion of pain-free living. Waiting rooms became overcrowded, cash-only payments kept the paper trail minimal, and queues of cars outside certain clinics became as common as drive-through fast food outlets.

What followed was an opioid crisis of historic proportions, driven not only by individual greed but also by a coordinated system involving prescribers, distributors, and manufacturers. The cases that follow demonstrate how individual doctors can breach legal and ethical boundaries in pursuit of money, attention, or control. The story of Operation Pilluted highlights a more systemic and industrialised form of medical crime (Kennedy-Hendricks et al., 2016). This operation, involving nearly 1,000 law enforcement officers, was a 15-month investigation in 2015 into rogue prescribers, pharmacists, and other intermediaries involved in illegally supplying potent medications, particularly in opioid-affected states such as Arkansas, Alabama, Louisiana, and Mississippi. As a result, vehicles, weapons, and cash were seized, and 73 warrants led to the confiscation of more than $10 million and millions of dollars' worth of real estate. It also resulted in the arrest of 280 individuals, including twenty-two doctors, nurses, and pharmacists. Some of these individuals had become involved in sophisticated rackets alongside non-medical criminals, demonstrating that the white coat can serve as a shield for large-scale trafficking.

The case of Dr Oscar Lightner, aged 73, is a notable example. With his stepson, he operated a Texas pill mill. According to evidence presented at his trial, Lightner, 73, and Andres Martinez Jr., 29, ran a Health and Wellness clinic functioning as a pill mill. Lightner, who owned and practised at a medical clinic, prescribed combinations of controlled substances, including hydrocodone, carisoprodol, and alprazolam, to patients without legitimate medical reasons in exchange for cash payments ranging from $250 to $500. He prescribed over 600,000 opioid pills in just 14 months, earning more than $1.2 million in cash. Martinez, the office manager and Lightner's stepson, recruited homeless and vulnerable individuals through "runners" who brokered the exchange of prescriptions for cash, and coordinated efforts to bring multiple people into the clinic to pose as patients and obtain prescriptions for opioids and other controlled substances. He received a 7-year jail sentence.

Similar cases happened across America, where owners of pain clinics were convicted of giving addicts and dealers pre-signed prescriptions, sometimes without seeing the patient, covering their tracks with false medical records. A judge called one such case "*drug traffickers in white lab coats*," a phrase that highlights both the betrayal of professional duty and the level of harm.

Other individual cases came to light.

Dr Joel Smithers ran a pill mill in West Virginia, one of the states hardest hit by the opioid epidemic. Over 2 years, he received more than $700,000 in cash and card payments, prescribing over half a million highly addictive opioid pills, including oxymorphone, oxycodone, hydromorphone, and fentanyl, to nearly every patient who entered, with many travelling hundreds of miles for his services. His practice lacked even basic medical equipment, functioning more like a drug dealer's outlet. In 2019, Smithers was sentenced to 40 years in prison for illegally prescribing controlled substances and causing the death of a patient.

Dr Gordon Freedman engaged in another corrupt scheme: collaborating with pharmaceutical companies. Paid through a fake "speakers bureau" to promote a fentanyl spray, Freedman's speaking fees increased directly with the number of prescriptions he issued. These so-called educational events often amounted to little more than expensive restaurant dinners, with attendance lists forged to create a misleading impression of legitimacy. Freedman was amongst the leading prescribers in the country and received a prison sentence of over 27 years for accepting bribes and kickbacks in exchange for prescribing millions of dollars' worth of fentanyl.

Dr Rodney Moret, a 67-year-old American doctor, was involved in over-prescribing and large-scale healthcare fraud. His crimes included more than $15 million worth of prescription drugs and an additional $6 million in healthcare fraud. Operating under the guise of a pain management and HIV infusion clinic, he distributed over 700,000 hydrocodone tablets, 240,000 alprazolam tablets, and more than 2 million millilitres of promethazine with codeine cough syrup, whilst billing Medicare for unnecessary or fictitious procedures. He employed "patient marketers" to direct individuals to his clinic for prescriptions, which were then sold illegally on the street. Moret also exploited the situation to harass and sexually assault female patients. He was sentenced to over 6 years in prison.

An FBI spokesman said, "*Rodney Moret, a former physician, intentionally fuelled the local opioid epidemic by overprescribing addictive medications to patients for his gain.*" and went on to say:

> The message should be clear: any doctor or healthcare professional who prioritises profit or does harm to their patients under the guise of providing health care will be subject to the full investigative resources of the FBI and our law enforcement partners.

These examples demonstrate that prescription-drug-related crime amongst doctors varies from those involved in organised pill mills to those secretly connected to industry, and to those combining drug diversion with insurance fraud and sexual exploitation. There are many more examples that could have been included in this chapter. Since 2007, Federal Strike Forces have charged thousands of medical professionals who collectively billed insurers and government programmes more than US$27 billion, saving lives as they root out rogue doctors (Kennedy-Hendricks et al., 2016).

BALANCING ACCOUNTABILITY WITH CLINICAL FREEDOM

Much blame has been attributed to the pharmaceutical industry for its aggressive marketing and the financial incentives offered to doctors to promote opioid use in pain management. Evidence indicates a clear link between industry payments to physicians and their prescribing habits. A 2020 study found that such payments were associated with increased prescribing of the paying company's drug, higher overall prescribing costs, and greater use of branded medicines. Similarly, a joint CNN and Harvard analysis of prescriptions issued in 2014–2015 revealed that doctors wrote over 811,000 prescriptions for Medicare patients, nearly half of which contained at least one opioid, and more than 54% of those doctors (over 200,000) had received payments from companies manufacturing opioids.

STANDARD OF PROOF

Until recently in America, prosecutors did not need to prove that doctors knew or intended their prescriptions to be misused to secure a criminal conviction. It was sufficient to demonstrate that their practices diverged from accepted norms, effectively equating poor or risky prescribing with the intent to act as a drug dealer.

This change occurred following a significant Supreme Court ruling in March 2022. The Court determined that during the trials of two convicted doctors, the jurors had not been properly instructed to consider a "good faith" defence. Both doctors, sentenced to 21 and 25 years respectively, believed their prescribing practices adhered to accepted medical standards. The Court confirmed that the prosecution's duty was to prove beyond a reasonable doubt that a defendant "knowingly or intentionally acted in an unauthorised manner." In criminal law, both *mens rea* (the "guilty mind") and *actus reus* (the "guilty act") must be established. Simply demonstrating that a doctor deviated from guidelines, especially if they genuinely believed they were acting correctly, was insufficient for a conviction.

The decision was more than just a legal and technical change; it acknowledged the importance of safeguarding clinical autonomy whilst ensuring accountability. For many doctors, it provided reassurance that practising in good faith would not automatically be mistaken for criminal intent. For prosecutors and regulators, it emphasised the need for stronger, evidence-based standards when building cases. Many individuals in both the medical field and patient communities welcomed the change, especially given the previous uncertainty in opioid-related prosecutions and the potential detrimental effect on legitimate pain management.

EMERGING PILL-MILLS

In recent years, the prescribing scene in the United Kingdom has shown troubling similarities to the early stages of the opioid crisis, especially regarding Attention Deficit Hyperactivity Disorder (ADHD) medications, ketamine for depression, and cannabis-based products. ADHD prescriptions in England have increased by about 18% each year since the COVID-19 pandemic, rising from around 25 items per 1,000 people in 2019–2020 to over 41 items in 2023–2024, with lisdexamfetamine use growing by 55%. Notable regional differences have also appeared, with a 28% yearly rise in London compared to just 13% in the North East and Yorkshire (Khan & Hasan, 2025). This rise, partly driven by greater awareness, particularly amongst young women exposed to symptom-sharing on platforms like TikTok and Instagram (Kirkpatrick & Lawrie, 2024), raises concerns about overdiagnosis, hurried assessments, and private clinics sidestepping strict clinical standards (Foster & Ellis, 2024).

At the same time, ketamine, which was once strictly controlled as an anaesthetic or used sparingly for treatment-resistant depression, is becoming more accessible in private clinics, raising concerns of a "wild west" regulatory environment, fragmented care, and unregulated prescribing outside appropriate oversight. Meanwhile, non-prescribed ketamine use has increased significantly: in 2023–24, 3,609 people sought treatment for ketamine addiction, an eightfold rise compared to 2014–15, highlighting a worrying increase in recreational misuse amid limited therapeutic regulation (GOV.UK, 2024; Guerrini et al., 2025).

On another note, prescribing of medical cannabis has risen markedly: the Care Quality Commission in England has expressed serious concerns about practices in the private sector following a dramatic 130% increase in prescriptions of cannabis-based medicinal products, from roughly 150,000 items in 2022–2023 to 346,000 in 2023–2024, often for conditions with limited clinical justification and lacking clear regulatory oversight (Care Quality Commission, 2025).

Some countries where prescribing cannabis has become widespread advertise clinics outside arrival at airports, recreating the drug-tourist trade seen in London during the 1960s.

Whilst each of these therapies, ADHD medications, ketamine, and medical cannabis, has real therapeutic potential, their integration into a commercial model, driven by media attention, private prescribing, and regulatory delays, resembles a new "pill mill" era. Without stricter regulation, standardised diagnostic criteria, transparent prescribing practices, and integration with established NHS pathways, we risk a system guided by profit rather than patient needs, with consequences that may only become clear in the future.

The death of actor Matthew Perry in 2024 has reignited public debate about fraudulent and illegal prescribing practices. Dr Mark Chavez, a physician based in San Diego, has agreed to plead guilty to conspiracy to distribute ketamine. According to his plea, he sold the drug to another doctor after obtaining it through a fraudulent prescription and made false representations to a wholesale distributor.

The main challenge remains how to enable clinicians to treat patients effectively without encouraging misuse or addiction, and how to distinguish between those acting in genuine clinical judgement and those exploiting the system for personal gain. Following high-profile cases, whether involving Hollywood celebrities or small-town pain clinics, this debate continues to influence public perception, professional behaviour, and the regulatory landscape.

SPORT, DOCTORS, AND DRUGS

The misuse of medical authority extends beyond addiction treatment; it has also sullied the sporting world. Misuse of doctors' prescribing powers has damaged athletes' health, harmed teams, and undermined the fundamental principle of fair competition. These doctors, tasked with protecting the well-being of those they care for, became central figures in scandals that shifted the sporting narrative from stories of victory to tales of deception.

Cycling, long marred by systemic doping, proved particularly susceptible to unethical medical involvement. Dr Michele Ferrari, once a celebrated sports physician, became synonymous with cycling's darkest era. He devised complex doping schemes for leading athletes, most notably Lance Armstrong. His 2004 conviction for sporting fraud resulted in a suspended sentence, yet Ferrari remained defiant and continued his activities. Years later, another suspended sentence for supplying banned substances confirmed that his shadow endured long after the sport aimed to move forward.

Dr Eufemiano Fuentes, the mastermind of *Operación Puerto*, expanded his reach further. His blood-doping network stretched beyond cycling into athletics and other sports, implicating hundreds of athletes. In 2013, he was convicted of endangering public health and received a 1-year suspended sentence, a punishment many found far too lenient considering the extent of harm. The ongoing secrecy surrounding many athletes' identities showed just how deeply his influence infiltrated top-level sport.

Even state-run programmes have used medicine as a weapon to gain a competitive edge. In Cold War East Germany, Dr Lothar Kipke played a key role in systematically doping young swimmers and track athletes, many of whom were unaware of what they were given. His conviction years later revealed the human cost of a nationalist pursuit of dominance: long-term health issues faced by athletes who had little choice in their participation.

What connects these cases is not just the professional sanctions or criminal convictions but also the culture of complicity that allowed them to thrive. Teams, sporting organisations, and even governments sometimes protected offending doctors to safeguard reputations. Weak regulation and legal loopholes meant that even the worst offenders often avoided meaningful criminal punishment.

CONCLUSION

Whether in pain clinics or Olympic arenas, the misuse of medical authority has consequences that extend far beyond the individuals directly involved. In the clinical setting, overprescribing and unethical financial ties with pharmaceutical companies have contributed to addiction crises. In sport, doping programmes have harmed athletes' health, undermined fair play, and caused entire disciplines to struggle for credibility.

REFERENCES

Alamy. (n.d.). Dr John Petro held at Frost TV show, January 1, 1968 [Photograph]. Alamy. https://www.alamy.com/jan-01-1968-dr-petro-held-at-frost-tv-show-dr-john-petro-was-arrested-image69433129.html

The British Medical Journal (1970). General Medical Council: Disciplinary Committee. *The British Medical Journal, 1*(5696). www.jstor.org/stable/20382932

Care Quality Commission. (2025). The safer management of controlled drugs: Annual update 2024 (Key issues). https://www.cqc.org.uk/publications/controlled-drugs/2024/issues

Dickson-Gomez, J., Krechel, S., Spector, A., Weeks, M., Ohlrich, J., Green Montaque, H. D., & Li, J. (2022). The effects of opioid policy changes on transitions from prescription opioids to heroin, fentanyl and injection drug use: A qualitative analysis. *Substance Abuse Treatment, Prevention, and Policy, 17*(1), 55. https://doi.org/10.1186/s13011-022-00480-4

Foster, A., & Ellis, N. (2024). TikTok-inspired self-diagnosis and its implications for educational psychology practice. *Educational Psychology in Practice, 40*(4), 491–508. https://doi.org/10.1080/02667363.2024.2409451

GOV.UK. (November 28, 2024). Adult substance misuse treatment statistics 2023 to 2024: report. Office for Health Improvement and Disparities. https://www.gov.uk/government/statistics/substance-misuse-treatment-for-adults-statistics-2023-to-2024/adult-substance-misuse-treatment-statistics-2023-to-2024-report

Guerrini, I., Kalk, N., Jelen, L., & Strang, J. (2025). Non-prescribed ketamine use is rising in the UK. *BMJ, 389*, r1167. https://doi.org/10.1136/bmj.r1167

Home Office. Misuse of Drugs Act 1971 - Section 13: Direction Prohibiting Exercise of Powers in Relation to Controlled Drugs: Dr Kobina Arba Taylor. The London Gazette. 22 May 1987; (50926): 6646

Judson HF. (1973). *The British and Heroin. The New Yorker*. 17 September and 1 October 1973.

Kennedy-Hendricks, A., Richey, M., McGinty, E. E., Stuart, E. A., Barry, C. L., & Webster, D. W. (2016). Opioid overdose deaths and Florida's crackdown on pill mills. *American Journal of Public Health, 106*(2), 291–297. https://doi.org/10.2105/AJPH.2015.302953

Khan, M. U., & Hasan, S. S. (2025). Socioeconomic status and prescribing of ADHD medications: A study of ICB-level data in England. *BMJ Mental Health, 28*(1), e301384. https://doi.org/10.1136/bmjment-2024-301384

Kirkpatrick, C. E., & Lawrie, L. L. (2024). TikTok as a source of health information and misinformation for young women in the United States: Survey study. *JMIR Infodemiology, 4*, e54663. https://doi.org/10.2196/54663

Mars, S. (2003). Heroin addiction care and control: The British system 1916 to 1984. *Journal of the Royal Society of Medicine, 96*(2), 99–100.

Stimson, G., & Oppenheimer, E. (1982). *Heroin Addiction: Treatment and Control in Britain*. Tavistock Publications.

Strang, J., & Gossop, M. (2005). *Heroin Addiction and The British System. Treatment and Policy Responses* (Vol. 2). Routledge.

Strang, J., Ruben, S., Farrell, M., Witton, J., Keaney, F., & Gossop, M. (2005). The History of Prescribing Heroin and Other Injectable Drugs as Addiction Treatment in the UK. In *Heroin Addiction and the British System. Treatment and Policy Responses* (Vols 1–2, pp. 1–16). Routledge.

12

Sexual misconduct in medicine

CLARE GERADA AND ZAID AL-NAJJAR

Amongst all crimes committed by doctors, those involving sexual misconduct are some of the most difficult to address because they are so damaging to the doctor–patient relationship. Whether murder, manslaughter, or fraud, the same disturbing patterns recur. A doctor's professional status acts as a shield. Institutions often fail to act, and so the abuse persists unchecked for years, sometimes decades. These are deliberate, intimate violations carried out by individuals entrusted with the power to heal, leaving lasting scars long after the acts themselves.

This chapter will discuss the general issues of sexual misconduct in medicine. The next chapter will examine specific cases.

BOUNDARIES AND BREACHES

Professional sexual misconduct (PSM) involves breaching sexual boundaries within the professional–patient relationship. This includes sexual contact, sexual harassment, or unnecessary physical examinations, whether conducted verbally, physically, or virtually. It also encompasses expressions of thoughts and feelings or gestures that are of a sexual nature or that a patient or surrogate may reasonably interpret as sexual.

PSM rarely starts with a single, catastrophic error. More often, it stems from a series of small boundary violations that may seem harmless at first. A doctor might extend an appointment, agree to see a patient after hours, or allow a consultation to continue into an after-hours conversation. Someone else might accept a modest gift of thanks. A person may offer a hug during a moment of distress. None of these actions, on their own, may appear overtly unethical. However, collectively, they can form a slippery slope in which professional boundaries weaken, increasing the risk of exploitation.

DOI: 10.1201/9781003781066-12

Take, for example, the GP who began visiting an anxious patient at her home after evening surgeries. He convinced himself it was more convenient for her and avoided the fuss of the clinic. She, however, experienced his presence in her private space as an intimacy that drew them closer. What he regarded as therapeutic became, in her mind, something much more personal.

Breaches of time and place are often the first cracks. A shared meal, an invitation to a social event, or a home visit outside usual boundaries subtly shifts the encounter into personal territory. Gifts also blur these boundaries; what starts as a token of thanks, like a bottle of wine at Christmas, can come to symbolise a special relationship. Physical contact carries particular risks. Whilst a handshake is rarely questioned, gestures such as a hug, a hand on the shoulder, or a brush of the arm can be misinterpreted. In boundary matters, perception is everything. What a doctor perceives as kindness may, for the patient, seem romantic or sexual, and once that line is crossed, it cannot be easily defended.

One psychiatrist described hugging a patient after a breakthrough session. "She was crying, I felt moved," he later reflected. "But the next week, she arrived with a card describing me as her soulmate." What he had seen as compassion, she had experienced as an invitation.

Money and language each pose their own risks. Lending or borrowing, exchange fees, and business dealings can turn interactions into purely transactional ones. Likewise, speech and presentation are crucial. Being overly familiar, dropping professional titles, dressing casually, or sharing personal issues all weaken the framework that defines the clinical role.

A doctor once confided in a patient about his failing marriage, hoping to explain his distracted mood. She, however, felt singled out as a confidante, "the only one who really understood him." The professional balance had been lost in a single disclosure.

Sexual contact with patients is *always* harmful. Doctors might justify it as consensual, but the imbalance of power means genuine consent can *never* truly be given. Such misconduct cannot only destroy a patient's trust but also harm a doctor's career. Sexual violations are not mistakes; they are deliberate acts that exploit the doctor–patient relationship. They cause psychological harm and compromise ongoing medical treatment. Violations breach not only professional standards but also the core principles of medicine. As the Hippocratic Oath declared in 274 AD:

> Into whatsoever houses I enter, I will enter to help the sick, and I will abstain from all intentional wrongdoing and harm, especially from abusing the bodies of man or woman, bond or free.

Modern regulators uphold the same standard. The General Medical Council states:

> You must not use your professional position to pursue a sexual or improper emotional relationship with a patient or someone close to them. You must make sure that your conduct justifies your patients' trust in you and the public's trust in the profession.

Doctors often live in the same communities as their patients, meet them in social settings, and increasingly engage with them on social media. Navigating these shifting roles, professional, personal, and local, is a complex task. However, none of these challenges justify breaches.

HOW PREVALENT IS PROFESSIONAL SEXUAL MISCONDUCT?

Understanding the accurate scale of such misconduct is difficult because there is no comprehensive global database of cases. However, research from around the world reveals a troubling reality of sexual misconduct in medicine.

Anonymous surveys of American doctors revealed that 3% to 9% of respondents, mainly men, admit to past sexual contact with a patient (Sansone & Sansone, 2009).

Analysis of the (American) National Practitioner Data Bank shows that between 2003 and 2013, 862 doctors had at least one report of sexual misconduct lodged against them. These figures probably underestimate the actual prevalence, as misconduct often remains unreported or unrecorded (Skipper & Schenthal, 2012).

In Canada, reports indicate that disciplinary actions against doctors for sexual misconduct are more than twice as frequent as in the United States. Researchers suggest this reflects stricter enforcement rather than a higher prevalence, but it highlights how regulatory systems influence what becomes visible (AbuDagga et al., 2019).

In the Netherlands, a 2002 study of general practitioners found that just over 3% admitted to having had sexual contact with a patient, with the figure rising to around 4% for the male doctors (for women, the figure is about 0.8%). The same research indicated that although these encounters were sometimes described as consensual, the power imbalance between doctor and patient questions this claim (Leusink & Mokkink, 2004).

Men are responsible for 80% of incidents involving sexual boundary violations in the therapeutic relationship (Garrett, 2002). Whilst female practitioners rarely commit sexual boundary violations, when they do, it is usually with female patients.

In the United Kingdom, collecting accurate data is also challenging. Reports indicate that a small but consistent percentage of criminal convictions involving doctors relate to sexual offences. Records from the General Medical Council show that, year after year, dozens of doctors are disciplined for proven misconduct of this nature. However, the true extent of those who never come to the authorities' attention remains impossible to determine.

A study conducted in Germany involved a public survey. The study used a probability sample (representative of the German adult population aged 14 years and above) to gather reliable and generalisable data. Between February and April 2020, the researchers sent questionnaires to over 2,500 individuals. The study found that nearly 5% of women and over 1% of men reported experiencing PSM (this was perpetrated by any health professional, not just doctors). Almost all the perpetrators were men.

The nature of the misconduct included:

- Sexual contact (contact of a sexual nature, presumably beyond routine medical necessity).
- Sexual harassment.
- Unnecessary physical examinations.

Amongst those reporting sexual contact, about one-third of these incidents occurred *before the age of 18.*

Qualitative studies also illuminate patterns of abuse. An exploratory analysis of 101 American cases published in 2017 found that the most common forms of abuse were inappropriate touching (33%), sodomy (31%), rape (16%), child molestation (14%), and purportedly "consensual" sex (7%). Specific patient characteristics, such as being female and young, were linked to a higher risk, as were certain physician traits, including being male, over 39 years old, and often examining patients alone in non-academic settings. The authors concluded bleakly that there were no necessary conditions for abuse beyond the sexual urges of the physician concerned, and that it would be impossible to predict who might become a predator.

The Atlanta Journal-Constitution (AJC) conducted an in-depth multistate analysis of cases of sexual misconduct in the United States, under the title "Doctors and Sex Abuse." The effort involved collecting more than 100,000 disciplinary documents and regulatory records from across all 50 states in order to reveal patterns that are typically hidden.

The series was recognised nationwide (it was a Pulitzer Prize finalist) and drew attention for raising public awareness and pressuring regulatory authorities. The AJC study identified **over 3,000** doctors publicly accused of sexual misconduct between 1999 and 2015; of these, more than 2,400 had cases clearly involving patients. A significant proportion of doctors disciplined for sexual misconduct were later permitted to practise again.

The AJC's follow-up investigations (2017 onwards) found that in just 2 years (2016–17), more than 450 doctors faced regulatory or court action for sexual misconduct.

Taken together, these findings show that sexual misconduct in medicine is neither a rare anomaly nor limited to a single country or culture. It remains a persistent issue, influenced by opportunity, power, and failures in oversight, and official disciplinary records only reflect a small portion of the problem (Clemens et al., 2021).

THE CULTURE OF SILENCE AND REPORTING BARRIERS

As mentioned, incidents of sexual misconduct by doctors are almost certainly underreported (AbuDagga et al., 2019). This is hardly surprising, given the silence surrounding it (Singh, 2024). Few doctors are willing to report a colleague whose behaviour raises concerns (Campbell et al., 2007; DesRoches et al., 2010). This is partly due to professional loyalty and partly because the system rarely makes it easy to complain. Complaints are often dismissed as misunderstandings; for example, as a doctor described in Chapter 13, who claimed his erect penis pushed against a patient he was examining was a set of keys in his pocket. Perhaps the most disturbing of all were the cases in which complainants against Larry Nassar, the American doctor to Olympic gymnasts who were either threatened with removal from the team or told they should be grateful for the care they were receiving (his case is discussed in the next chapter). For some, a doctor under suspicion is quietly moved on rather than confronted.

It is not just colleagues who fear retribution for reporting misconduct. Many patients also do not report what has happened to them. Some are paralysed by shock, shame, or disbelief. Others fear they will not be believed; after all, how could a respected doctor possibly be accused of such behaviour? The imbalance of power is so great that many victims feel it is safer to say nothing rather than risk being dismissed or humiliated. Even those who do come forward often find the process punishing, dealing with medical boards or other regulators, reliving trauma during interviews, and enduring legal proceedings. Some withdraw their complaints to avoid further distress.

Hospitals and healthcare organisations add another layer of concealment. Reporting requirements are often ignored or circumvented, especially when the accused is a senior or well-paid doctor whose reputation enhances the institution's prestige. It is simpler to "manage" the issue discreetly than to risk a scandal.

Moreover, even when cases are brought to authorities, outcomes remain inconsistent at best. Unless there is strong evidence or multiple witnesses (which is unlikely), complaints are often dismissed. One American study found that only a small number of complaints ever advanced to a formal hearing. The rest were handled informally, perhaps with a warning letter or a private discussion, leaving patients unprotected whilst the doctor continued to practise (DuBois et al., 2019).

The *AJC* examined several cases in which professional sex offenders received remarkably light sentences for their crimes. For example, the New York doctor, Dr Dilip Kumar Roy was sentenced to just 28 days in jail after being accused of raping a patient during a medical examination.

Dr Robert Anthony Hadden, a Manhattan obstetrics and gynaecology specialist, was accused of multiple instances of oral sex and unwanted sexual touching of patients. He was charged with abusing five women. In a 2016 plea deal, he admitted to a felony criminal sexual act and a misdemeanour of forcible touching. Hadden was required to surrender his medical licence but received no jail time or probation. His "time served" amounted to only part of a single day in jail following his arrest.

In 2017, Dr Jorge Burgos was sentenced to 7 days in jail, served at weekends so that he could continue his medical practice. He had originally faced 16 counts of open and gross lewdness, accused of groping and kissing at least seven patients during examinations. In a plea deal, 13 of the counts were dropped.

A paper published in 2025 on sanctions imposed on UK doctors facing the regulator for sexual misconduct highlighted inconsistencies in penalties and argued that some sanctions were not severe enough to reflect the actions of the doctors. The researchers looked at the outcome for doctors who had faced action by the GMC. They found that all perpetrators were male doctors, with more than 80% holding positions of authority. Several cases involved multiple patients, demonstrating repeated and systematic abuse. One case involved a medical consultant guilty of rape, but he was given only a 12-month suspension rather than being erased, because it was deemed to be a "one-off event." Another doctor was found to have "pursued and groomed" a vulnerable patient from the age of 14 but was only suspended from the register for 12 months, with the tribunal panel citing evidence of "insight, remediation and remorse" as the reason he was not struck off the register (Dixon et al., 2025).

Behind these statistics lies a simple truth: medicine remains reluctant to confront its own predators. Instead of robust accountability, there are loopholes, compromises, and evasions. Abusive doctors are moved elsewhere, quietly reprimanded, or even allowed back into practice with little assurance that patients will be protected. The message to victims is clear: you may not be believed, and if you are, little will change. The message to perpetrators is equally clear: you may be caught, but the consequences are survivable (AbuDagga et al., 2019).

DISBELIEF

There is a long history of women not being believed, particularly in medicine, where practitioners have sometimes assumed that female patients were prone to making false allegations of sexual misconduct, often for perceived financial gain.

Across time, the relatively unrestricted access doctors had to patients, combined with insufficient caution in conducting intimate examinations, was thought to expose practitioners to the risk of false accusation. In the nineteenth century, this perceived risk of false allegations of sexual crimes by patients was thought to be heightened by the introduction of chemical anaesthesia. Sexual fantasies were soon described as a common side effect, with previously unconscious thoughts said to surface because of the disinhibition caused by the anaesthetic agents.

These anxieties shaped the way doctors understood and managed the boundaries of professional conduct. The notion that women were unreliable narrators of their own bodily experience reinforced existing gender hierarchies within medicine, legitimising a paternalistic stance in which the practitioner's authority was presumed to outweigh the patient's testimony. Fear of false accusation became a powerful psychological and institutional defence, serving to protect not only individual reputations but also the collective image of the medical profession as rational, honourable, and beyond reproach.

Over time, this defensive posture contributed to a culture in which women's discomfort, pain, or protest could be reinterpreted as misunderstanding, hysteria, or fantasy. The doctor's word became unassailable, whilst the patient's voice was marginalised. The residue of this imbalance remains visible in contemporary scandals, where professional solidarity and deference to authority continue to impede the recognition and redress of sexual abuse within medical settings.

There are, sadly, cases that illustrate the human cost of investigative processes themselves. One such tragedy is that of Dr Sridharan Suresh, a consultant anaesthetist who died by suicide after he came under police investigation following an allegation from a teenage patient (see Chapter 14).

ADDRESSING THE PROBLEM

Addressing physician sexual misconduct is complex, but several strategies can help reduce its occurrence. Preventive education is essential and should be integrated throughout the different stages of medical training and practice. Medical students, trainees, and practising doctors need guidance on what constitutes misconduct, how to report it, and how to establish and maintain professional boundaries (Dowling & Steele, 2023).

Sensitive examinations, such as intimate or invasive procedures, should be performed in the presence of a trained and authorised chaperone. Chaperones must be able to recognise inappropriate behaviour, document their attendance, and, where appropriate, confirm their presence in the medical record. Public education is also vital, as it helps patients understand what constitutes professional misconduct and how they can raise concerns through the proper regulatory channels.

Enhanced data collection remains a key priority. Allegations of sexual misconduct should be systematically documented, analysed, and published in anonymised form to enable meaningful national and international surveillance.

Only through cultural change and education can we hope to reduce the occurrence of such cases in the future.

REFERENCES

AbuDagga, A., Carome, M., & Wolfe, S. M. (2019). Time to end physician sexual abuse of patients: Calling the U.S. Medical community to action. *Journal of General Internal Medicine, 34*(7), 1330–1333. https://doi.org/10.1007/s11606-019-05014-6

Campbell, E. G., Regan, S., Gruen, R. L., Ferris, T. G., Rao, S. R., Cleary, P. D., & Blumenthal, D. (2007). Professionalism in medicine: Results of a national survey of physicians. *Annals of Internal Medicine, 147*(11), 795–802. https://doi.org/10.7326/0003-4819-147-11-200712040-00012

Clemens, V., Brähler, E., & Fegert, J. M. (2021). #patientstoo – Professional sexual misconduct by healthcare professionals towards patients: A representative study. *Epidemiology and Psychiatric Sciences, 30*, e50. https://doi.org/10.1017/S2045796021000378

DesRoches, C. M., Rao, S. R., Fromson, J. A., Birnbaum, R. J., Iezzoni, L., Vogeli, C., & Campbell, E. G. (2010). Physicians' perceptions, preparedness for reporting, and experiences related to impaired and incompetent colleagues. *JAMA, 304*(2), 187–193. https://doi.org/10.1001/jama.2010.921

Dixon, F., Pouncey, A. L., Ali, R. K., Vitish-Sharma, P., Bengtzen, M., & Nortley, M. (2025). *Sexual misconduct: UK medical practitioners tribunal service is not fit to practise. BMJ, 390*, e086867. https://doi.org/10.1136/bmj-2025-086867

Dowling, T., & Steele, S. (2023). Is sexual misconduct training sufficient in the UK's medical schools: Results of a cross-sectional survey and opportunities for improvement. *JRSM Open, 14*(9), 20542704231198732. https://doi.org/10.1177/20542704231198732

DuBois, J. M., Walsh, H. A., Chibnall, J. T., Anderson, E. E., Eggers, M. R., Fowose, M., & Ziobrowski, H. (2019). Sexual violation of patients by physicians: A mixed-methods, exploratory analysis of 101 cases. *Sexual Abuse, 31*(5), 503–523. https://doi.org/10.1177/1079063217712217

Garrett, T. (2002). Inappropriate therapist-patient "relationships". In R. Goodwin, & D. Cramer (Eds.), *Inappropriate relationships: The unconventional, the disapproved, and the forbidden* (pp. 147–170). Lawrence Erlbaum Associates Publishers.

Leusink, P. M., & Mokkink, H. G. (2004). [Sexual contact between general practitioner and patient in the Netherlands: Prevalence and risk factors]. *Nederlands Tijdschrift Voor Geneeskunde, 148*(16), 778–782.

Sansone, R. A., & Sansone, L. A. (2009). Crossing the line: Sexual boundary violations by physicians. *Psychiatry (Edgmont (Pa.: Township)), 6*(6), 45–48.

Singh, R. (2024). Sexual misconduct in the health services: Tip of the iceberg. *Sushruta Journal of Health Policy & Opinion, 16*. https://doi.org/10.38192/16.1.8

Skipper, G. E., & Schenthal, S. (2012). Sexual misconduct by professionals: A new paradigm of understanding. *Missouri Medicine, 109*(3), 184–186.

13

Specific cases of professional sexual misconduct

CLARE GERADA AND ZAID AL-NAJJAR

In this chapter, we have been careful not to become voyeuristic by cataloguing the distressing details of the abuse committed by doctors against their patients. Whilst it has been necessary to provide some information to illustrate the issues, we have kept these details to a minimum. Our aim is to highlight the underlying patterns rather than focus on the specifics.

We have a separate chapter discussing the use of drugs in facilitating sexual abuse, which explores in greater detail how some doctors misuse substances to overpower or silence their victims.

PATTERNS OF ABUSE

Although each case has its unique circumstances, certain elements recur: access, opportunity, and power imbalance. When these align, the conditions for abuse are established. Every case discussed in this chapter typifies this convergence.

We have categorised the cases into four main groups, although they frequently overlap.

1. Child and youth abuse – when doctors abuse their privileged access to children and adolescents.
2. Abuse disguised as medical treatment – intimate assaults carried out under the guise of legitimate procedures.
3. Exploitation of vulnerable adults – patients targeted because illness, poverty, or trauma made them less able to resist or report abuse.
4. Voyeurism and indirect abuse – breaches of privacy or dignity without direct physical contact. Though less visible, such acts exploit the same dynamics of power and access and can leave lasting psychological harm.

 DOI: 10.1201/9781003781066-13

The following cases illustrate each of these patterns.

CHILD AND YOUTH ABUSE

Some of the most troubling cases in this chapter involve paediatricians who used their position to access children for sexual purposes.

In September 2014, **Dr Myles Bradbury**, a 42-year-old paediatrician, pleaded guilty to 25 charges, including sexual assault, voyeurism, and possession of 16,000 indecent images of boys aged between 10 and 16. Bradbury qualified from the University of Birmingham in 1996 and, after a series of training posts, began working as a consultant in paediatric haematology and oncology in November 2008 at Addenbrooke's Hospital.

Bradbury would carry out unnecessary examinations, such as checks for pubertal development, often with the parents present but separated from the child by a curtain. Behind that flimsy partition, he committed his offences. He also secretly recorded patients using a pen equipped with a hidden camera. In some cases, he exaggerated the children's medical conditions so that he could see them more frequently and conduct more examinations. Concerns had been raised about his behaviour, but no action was taken.

In July 2012, Child Exploitation and Online Protection (CEOP) was alerted that Bradbury was purchasing suspect videos from the internet. On 27 November 2013, Canadian police discovered that Bradbury had bought an indecent video of children online. They shared this information with Suffolk Police, the same day the first complaint about Bradbury's behaviour was reported to Addenbrooke's. The complaint came from a grandmother who said her 11-year-old grandson had been asked to strip naked and examine his own genitals.

Bradbury was immediately suspended from the hospital and arrested on 18 December 2013. In September of the following year, he admitted to abusing his patients. Police say they will never know how many children Bradbury harmed because he destroyed his laptop's hard drive.

Before his arrest, there were several warning signs regarding Bradbury's behaviour, but colleagues accepted his excuses and did not suspect misconduct. Staff noticed he was seeing patients outside normal hours, excluding medical students from observing, and even holidayed with a patient's mother. Concerns were also raised about his obsession with puberty in seriously ill children. One mother witnessed him inappropriately touching her daughter but felt unable to challenge his professionalism.

The trial judge described him as the worst paedophile he had ever encountered. "*In many years' experiences on the bench, I have never come across a more culpable or grave course of sexual criminality which has involved such a gross and grotesque breach and betrayal of your Hippocratic Oath and trust reposed in you by your patients, their families and colleagues.*"

The judge went on to say:

> As I have said, for a doctor to attack gravely ill children in this way is one of the most serious forms of sexual offending imaginable,

> even if it does not involve physical violence, which goes beyond the abuse itself or penetrative activity.

Reviews of his actions revealed several recurring issues, many of which resonate with those discussed in Chapter 12.

https://www.judiciary.uk/wp-content/uploads/2014/12/bradbury-sentencing-remarks.pdf

These were systemic weaknesses in the hospital's oversight structure, including weak reporting channels and inadequate checks within the paediatric oncology service. Bradbury also discovered methods to bypass chaperone policies and manipulate hospital rules to be alone with patients. Bradbury leveraged his position and reputation (including portraying himself as a devout Christian in some reports) to gain the trust of parents and colleagues. He used excuses to conceal his actions when recording his examinations. Colleagues missed numerous clues that might have flagged his abuse earlier. There was a culture of deference in medical settings that could discourage scrutiny of senior doctors.

Around the same period, another disturbing case emerged. **Dr Michael Salmon**, a former paediatrician at Stoke Mandeville Hospital, was found guilty in 2015 of sexual offences against patients dating back to the 1970s and 1980s. Salmon received an 18-year prison sentence for one of the rape charges, with 14 years for the second rape and 2 years for each of the nine indecent assaults, all to run concurrently. At the time of his imprisonment, he was 80 years old.

He was convicted in 1990 of molesting young patients and admitted to indecently assaulting three girls in the 1980s, all aged 12 to 16 at the time. This misconduct was uncovered in 1987 during an audit at the hospital, when detectives searching his office for evidence of fraud found love letters from young female patients and launched a further investigation into his conduct. He was sentenced to 3 years for "breaking the trust" placed in him as a doctor and served about 18 months in Grendon Underwood Prison before being removed from the medical register.

Throughout his career, Salmon exploited his position to target vulnerable young patients, often separating them from their parents under the pretence of medical examinations. Behind a screen, whilst parents sat in the waiting room, he carried out assaults he later claimed were legitimate clinical procedures.

The details are shocking. A 14-year-old girl was tied to a couch and raped, told by Salmon that the assault was part of her treatment. A 16-year-old, seeking help because she thought she was pregnant, was tricked into a sham procedure and then coerced into sex with the phrase: "*one favour deserves another.*" In court, victims described lifelong trauma, nightmares, and a lasting inability to trust doctors. Judge Johannah Cutts QC called him a "predatory paedophile" whose actions were cold, calculated, and a profound abuse of medical trust.

Salmon believed himself to be untouchable, "bomb-proof," in his own words, convinced that no one would believe a child over a doctor. For decades, he was right. His conviction only changed after Operation Yewtree, the police investigation into Jimmy Savile, which prompted other victims to come forward. The parallels with Savile were unavoidable: both operated within the same hospital, exploiting a culture of deference and institutional silence. There was no evidence of collusion, but the similarities lay in how each was enabled by the same system of unquestioned authority and lack of oversight.

Across the Atlantic, another paediatrician, **Dr Johnnie "Jack" Barto**, built his career and reputation in a small community in Pennsylvania whilst carrying out a campaign of abuse that lasted four decades. In 2019, at the age of 71, he was sentenced to at least 79 years in prison for sexually assaulting 31 children, most of whom were patients. Allegations had been made as early as 2000, but the case was dismissed, and the community rallied in support of him. He continued to practise, protected by disbelief in his guilt, until his arrest in 2018. At sentencing, the judge made it clear that justice had finally caught up with him. Barto showed no remorse and did not appeal, pleading no contest to the charges.

Some cases reveal as much about evolving social attitudes as they do about the doctor's crimes. In 1987, Professor Oliver Brooke was head of paediatrics at St George's Hospital in London when he was found with thousands of images of child sexual abuse in his office cupboard. He admitted that he had been sharing them with a small group of friends for 15 years. He was sentenced to 12 months in jail and told by the trial judge that society had to be protected from people who "*peddle this dangerous filth.*" However, on appeal, his sentence was reduced to 6 months, with a further 6 months suspended. Lord Lane, the Lord Chief Justice, compared his behaviour to "*a schoolboy collecting cigarette cards in olden times*" and described him as "*a wonderful man*" apart from these offences. That leniency, almost unimaginable today, reflected an era in which such crimes were still minimised if the offender held status and had the right connections.

In recent years, police have sometimes acted pre-emptively to prevent abuse, as with **Dr Salman Siddiqi**, a locum paediatrician convicted in 2023 for attempting to meet a minor for sex at her hospital. The "minor" was an undercover police officer. During online conversations that led to his arrest, Siddiqi repeatedly referenced his role as a doctor, fully aware of the power and authority it conferred. The sentencing judge described the offence as deeply troubling and highlighted that Siddiqi's awareness of the potential harm such conduct could cause made it even more serious.

It is, of course, not only paediatricians who have been known to abuse children in their care, nor only doctors working in the United Kingdom or North America. France was shaken by the case of **Dr Joel Le Scouarnec**, a former surgeon who admitted to sexually abusing hundreds of patients, most of whom were children, over a period spanning 1989 to 2014. In 2024, he was sentenced to a maximum of 20 years in prison, though under French law, he may be eligible for parole as early as 2030, having already served 7 years. Le Scouarnec, now 74, stood in court dressed in black, silent and expressionless as Judge Aude Burési read out the verdict. In March 2024, he confessed to the abuse of 299 victims. Judge Burési noted that he had deliberately targeted the most vulnerable: children who were unwell, sedated, or under anaesthesia.

Le Scouarnec had already been jailed once before. In 2020, he was convicted and sentenced to 15 years for the rape and sexual assault of four children, including two of his own nieces. He later admitted that throughout his career, he had abused patients whilst they were anaesthetised or recovering from operations. His handwritten diaries, in which he recorded the assaults in disturbing detail, helped police identify victims, many of whom had no memory of the events until confronted with the evidence. For some, the trauma proved too much: two of his victims ended their lives in adulthood, unable to escape the legacy of what they had endured as children. The trial sparked national outrage, not only at the scale of the crimes but also at the silence and failures that allowed them to continue unchecked. Le Scouarnec was allowed to continue treating children even after a conviction in 2005 for downloading images of child sexual abuse. The prosecuting lawyer accused the medical establishment of turning a blind eye, whilst civil parties highlighted a system that failed to act even as rumours about him spread.

One victim's words captured the heart of the scandal: "*No one acknowledged responsibility, whereas all the victims said it's not only a man who did that, but also the system which let him do it.*" This is a theme that has recurred throughout this book.

ABUSE DISGUISED AS MEDICAL TREATMENT

The doctors discussed in this chapter conceal their abuse behind a façade of legitimate medical care. They utilise their knowledge to justify intimate examinations, making it difficult for patients to question what is happening. The environment, the language, and the white coat all work together to suppress doubt. In such cases, the usual safeguards of medicine, consent, and explanation are undermined. Instead of protecting the patient, these elements become tools to silence them. A rehearsed routine of medical jargon, a confident tone, or a casual remark about "routine practice" can allay suspicion and disarm resistance. The authority of the doctor is so ingrained that patients often feel unable or even ashamed to challenge what is occurring. What makes this form of abuse particularly insidious is its plausibility. To the outside world, and even in the patient's own memory, the examination can seem medically justified. This ambiguity not only shields the perpetrator from scrutiny but also causes the victim to doubt their own perceptions. The following example demonstrates a doctor who took this façade to its extreme, creating a pseudoscience to conceal his abusive behaviour. This doctor is Larry Nassar, the former USA Gymnastics (USAG) team doctor.

Dr Larry Nassar

Some doctors have committed crimes so heinous that they are forever remembered in history. Harold Shipman is one of these, recognised as one of the most prolific serial killers, whilst Larry Nassar is infamous for the decades of abuse he inflicted on girls and young women.

Nassar disguised his assaults as legitimate medical treatments, supported by the complicity or silence of those around him. Over three decades, he abused more than 400 children and young adults: some were assaulted only once, whilst others were victimised dozens or even hundreds of times. His victims included Olympic athletes assaulted in hotel rooms, primary school-aged gymnasts in local gyms and in the basement of his family home, athletes treated at his clinic's office, and even the daughter of family friends, whom he began abusing when she was just 6 years old. To world-class athletes, he presented himself not just as a doctor but also as a friend and caring confidant. He also groomed families of athletes and other adults into believing he was an exceptional physician committed to the health and well-being of others (McPhee & Dowden, 2018).

Nassar had worked with gymnasts for most of his adult life. He started in high school as a coach for his school's gymnastics team. After earning a degree in osteopathy from the University of Michigan in 1985, he became a graduate assistant coach at Wayne State University. During this time, he also volunteered with the American Gymnastics Association and was soon appointed to the medical staff for the 1987 Pan American Games.

In 1988, he participated in other USAG events, including the pre-Olympic trials and the post-Olympic tour. One witness recalled that he "practically lived in the gym," being there almost every day for hours, arriving early to tape ankles and staying late to treat pulled muscles.

He was a multiple award winner for his care of athletes and by the mid-1990s, after completing medical school, Nassar had established himself as a leading figure in the treatment of gymnastics injuries, making him the ideal doctor for these young athletes.

His first Olympics were in 1996, when he served as team doctor for the Women's National Team, benefitting from the spotlight of the Women's Team's historic achievement: winning the nation's first-ever team gymnastics gold medal. Following the success of these Games, Nassar was appointed National Medical Coordinator, a role he held for nearly 20 years. He volunteered at the National Team training camps at the Karolyi Ranch and served on the medical staff at the Women's Artistic Gymnastics World Championships and Olympic Games over many years. These roles increased his influence and allowed him to become deeply involved in the world of elite gymnastics.

Nassar's abuse was disguised as legitimate medical procedures, such as vaginal examinations, often done without the use of gloves. He frequently gave academic lectures, authored clinical guidelines, and created PowerPoint presentations emphasising the importance of the pelvic floor for core strength. He used various abusive methods, but the common thread was his ability to normalise his behaviour, convincing athletes that these intimate and uncomfortable procedures were part of proper medical treatment. To justify interventions involving the pelvic area, Nassar customised his explanations to fit the athlete's complaint. For hip pain, he claimed that an "intravaginal adjustment" was necessary to reposition the hip bones. For back issues, he mentioned pressure points in the pelvic floor that could relieve discomfort or suggested that the spine needed "realignment." When dealing with a hamstring problem, he argued that "you have to get up in there to massage."

He also often touched athletes' breasts, claiming it was necessary to treat rib, shoulder, or upper body issues.

He crafted an image as "a miracle worker," someone regarded as capable of fixing almost any injury or problem. He was perceived as a doctor who genuinely cared about his patients' overall well-being and as a kind, supportive presence amid the high-pressure environment of gymnastics. Many gymnasts described him as the "good cop," the one who shielded them from harsh coaches and who, in their words, "literally and metaphorically put us back together."

Nassar strengthened this persona by giving tokens of kindness: Olympic pins for the young athletes he treated, or small gifts of bread and snacks that were forbidden at training camps for the Olympians. This mix of professional prestige and apparent compassion fostered a particularly strong form of trust. To the gymnasts, he was not just another doctor; they were told he was the best, their best chance to find relief from pain. As a result, many believed that whatever he did must be medically justified.

This crafted image of exceptional expertise and selfless care boosted his authority and granted him unusually unrestricted access to athletes, with minimal oversight of his practices. However, as we now know, what was happening under the guise of treatment was systematic sexual abuse conducted openly.

In late summer and autumn of 2016, following an *Indianapolis Star* investigation into sexual abuse within gymnastics, the first survivor publicly accused Nassar, soon followed by many others. As allegations increased and the investigation tightened, Nassar tried to cover his tracks. He took his work laptop to a repair shop and paid to have it wiped clean. The next day, he disposed of several hard drives filled with thousands of files in his roadside rubbish. When waste collection was delayed, law enforcement seized the discarded devices.

The hard drives revealed that, beyond the abuse he personally committed against girls and women, Nassar had collected over 37,000 images and videos depicting child sexual exploitation, including material involving infants.

On 21 November 2016, prosecutors charged him with multiple counts of first-degree criminal sexual conduct. Just weeks later, on 14 December, a federal grand jury indicted him on child pornography offences. His combined sentences amounted to a minimum of 140 years and a maximum of 360 years in prison. Today, under prisoner number 21504-040, he is incarcerated in a high-security federal facility in central Florida.

Given the number of survivors, the extent of abusive acts, the many adults and organisations that failed to intervene, and the decades during which he operated, Nassar's record of serial sexual abuse is staggering.

Elite gymnastics and the Olympic landscape more broadly fostered conditions that enabled his crimes to thrive. The sport predominantly involved young girls and normalised, even mandated, intimate physical contact during training and treatment, making athletes particularly vulnerable. Additionally, the culture of elite gymnastics entailed its own dangers: strict discipline, unquestioning obedience, and the acceptance of pain and discomfort as standard parts of achieving success. These norms not only removed typical barriers to abuse but also discouraged survivors from speaking out.

Young gymnasts were often separated from their parents during training and travel, and the intense demands of competition left them socially isolated, living much of their lives within the closed world of the gym. Add to this the relentless expectation of perfection, every day, every moment, and these athletes quickly learned to endure hardship, stay silent, and avoid "rocking the boat" for fear of losing their chance at success after years of sacrifice by themselves and their families.

Whilst Nassar is solely responsible for his predatory actions, it is crucial to recognise that doctors who commit such crimes seldom act alone. They function within systems that, knowingly or not, facilitate abuse. In Nassar's case, numerous individuals and institutions permitted his misconduct to persist unchecked: coaches at both club and elite levels, trainers and fellow medical staff, administrators at Michigan State University, officials at USAG, and the United States Olympic Committee. Some ignored clear warning signs, others dismissed or downplayed reports, and in the most troubling instances, they failed to act even when victims' disclosures of abuse were explicit.

Law enforcement also missed crucial chances to intervene effectively. And when survivors started speaking publicly, many encountered disbelief, stigma, or outright rejection from their own communities.

Dr Manish Shah

In East London, GP Manish Shah exploited the need for medical examinations as a tactic to target women and girls. He told them that intimate examinations were essential to rule out serious disease, referencing high-profile cases to support his claim. He cited the death of Jade Goody, a TV celebrity who died from cervical cancer, and actress Angelina Jolie's preventive mastectomy to instil fear and secure compliance. Many of his victims were young, inexperienced patients who trusted his authority. He falsified medical records to conceal the unnecessary nature of the examinations and groomed and flattered some patients, referring to one 15-year-old as his "star" and "favourite." Complaints arose when a young patient reported inappropriate behaviour during an appointment. More women came forward, leading to multiple trials. By 2023, he had been convicted in three separate proceedings, receiving three life sentences with a minimum term of 15 years. The judge told him, "You selected young and vulnerable women, gained their trust and preyed on their fears. You regularly abused your position of power for your sexual gratification."

Dr Jaswant Rathore

Another GP, Dr Jaswant Rathore, described his abuse as "manipulative therapy." He performed intimate procedures on women without clinical justification, often without a chaperone. Rathore offered little or no explanation for his actions and failed to keep proper records, steps the court concluded were intended to conceal his misconduct.

On some occasions, he pretended to check for cancer or ectopic pregnancy when, in reality, the examinations were merely a guise to assault his patients. Respected within his community and holding senior roles in local primary care, he leveraged his professional reputation to shield himself from suspicion. In 2018, he was sentenced to 12 years' imprisonment for multiple sexual assaults. The judge described his actions as "of no practical use at all" other than for his own gratification.

What makes these cases particularly troubling is how fear in medicine can be weaponised to establish control. The rhetoric of the need for early detection of serious disease as real and urgent instils anxiety and becomes almost impossible for the vulnerable patient to refuse. The abuse not only lay in the physical act but in the calculated engineering of fear.

Dr Clifford Ayling

Dr Clifford Ayling worked in the East Kent area in 1973, having previously worked at various hospitals in and around London since qualifying in 1963. From 1974 to 1988, he served as a part-time clinical assistant in obstetrics and gynaecology at the Kent and Canterbury Hospital and in another hospital in Margate. In 1981, he began practising general medicine in Folkestone, initially in partnership, but from 1983 as a sole practitioner. In preparation for his retirement at the age of 70 in 2001, he rejoined a partnership in 1998.

From 1984 to 1994, he also worked part-time as a clinical assistant in colposcopy in Ashford. Whilst practising as a GP, Ayling also took on locum medical sessions in family planning clinics across East Kent. In 1998, he was arrested and charged with indecently assaulting his patients. By 2000, he was found guilty on 12 charges of indecent assault involving 10 women and was sentenced to 4 years in prison. He was acquitted of a further nine charges. Over 60 women eventually came forward with similar accounts of abuse. The allegations leading to Ayling's convictions broadly involved inappropriate touching or examinations of women's breasts or gynaecological organs. The earliest incident considered in the criminal trial occurred in 1991, with most cases linked to events in the general practitioner's surgery rather than hospitals. A significant part of Ayling's defence was that the contested examinations were medically necessary or justified and adhered to guidelines accepted by a responsible medical community. The jury's verdict on the 12 counts he was found guilty of indicated they rejected this defence, concluding the examinations were conducted for his personal gratification.

Ayling's methods were alarmingly routine. Women were told to undress completely, often without chaperones, and were subjected to unnecessary intimate examinations, including repeated breast checks, smears, and internal procedures. Vulnerable women were targeted, such as teenagers seeking contraception, women in difficult life situations, and those reliant on medication controlled by Ayling. He used this power to pressure compliance, dismissing objections as hysteria or rudeness. Even in his early career, staff and patients expressed an unwillingness to be seen by him, in part due to his keenness to do vaginal examinations. Several midwives reported being asked by patients to make a clear note to that effect in their medical records. In the late 1970s, the midwives at Thanet Hospital wrote a petition stating that they could no longer work with him and that he was harming patients and conducting unnecessary vaginal examinations.

In August 1984, a midwife complained about Ayling after he made a crude sexual remark whilst delivering a baby. Despite all these concerns, no firm action was taken. In subsequent years, concerns about his behaviour continued to surface. At one postnatal examination, a nurse entered the room to find Ayling masturbating whilst carrying out a vaginal examination. She pulled him away from the patient and reported him to the senior staff. He was referred to a psychiatrist and later allowed to return to work. In 1991, a young patient complained to Kent Police that Ayling had carried out an internal examination without consent, prolonged it unnecessarily, made sexual comments, insisted she strip naked, fondled her breasts, and pressed his leg against her. She described feeling "dirty and abused." Although he was later convicted of indecent assault in 2000, at the time the Crown Prosecution Service decided not to prosecute and referred the matter to his GP employers. Throughout this period, Ayling was investigated by a panel of senior doctors known as "The Three Wise Men," and by psychiatrists, all of whom concluded that he did not suffer from any identifiable mental illness. One complaint from a student midwife in 1992 led to Ayling receiving a warning letter. A manager at William Harvey Hospital in Ashford investigated another incident in 1993. The medical director interviewed the patient, who claimed that the "erection" the patient was complaining of was a large bunch of keys in his pocket, which he produced during the meeting. This explanation was accepted.

Despite repeated warnings, he was allowed to continue practising until his eventual conviction years later.

Although Ayling's hospital contract was not renewed, his lawyers successfully argued that there should be "no stain on his professional character." Astonishingly, he even obtained a reference from Dr Rodney Ledward and another consultant attesting that he provided "an entirely satisfactory service."

Rodney Ledward was later struck off for gross incompetence, having harmed numerous women through reckless gynaecological surgery.

Consequently, Ayling was able to keep practising as a GP and to assault women for years afterwards.

Eventually, victims were believed and their testimonies revealed the emotional toll they were subject to. Many were left humiliated, powerless, and confused about whether procedures were medically necessary.

He often targeted vulnerable patients, including teenagers.

One recalled:

> I was 16 and naive and never had any previous doctor. I'd been brought up to trust my doctor.

She described undergoing numerous breast and internal examinations until she finally gained the confidence to resist.

> The last time I went to him, he asked to examine my breasts again. I said, 'No, you have already shown me how to do that myself.' He insisted, but for the first time, I became self-conscious. I thought there was no breast cancer in my family, and I'm young and fit and healthy. I let him go through with the routine, but after that, I left his surgery and never returned.

Ayling would insist on conducting a breast examination ahead of prescribing emergency contraception. Another patient was refused repeat prescriptions for anti-anxiety medication without first undergoing an intimate examination. One patient underwent an internal examination every 2 weeks and a smear each month for 3 years. Each time, she was required to strip naked. She testified, "The more he abused me, the more medication I took."

With hindsight, the signs of Clifford Ayling's abuse seem obvious. But for his patients, isolated, vulnerable, and conditioned to trust their doctor, leaving felt impossible. Each believed she was alone; each was too frightened to complain (Pauffley, 2004).

Dr Roy Murray

Dr Roy Murray, a GP in St Helens, Merseyside, was described as a "healer turned predator" by a judge when he was sentenced to 6 years in prison for indecently assaulting women patients. Convicted of 23 counts of indecent assault, Murray abused women under his care between 1981 and 1998, often claiming it was for necessary intimate examinations.

During his 9-week trial, jurors learned that consultations sometimes lasted up to 40 minutes. Women arriving with minor complaints, coughs, or earaches were told to disrobe and undergo painful and embarrassing internal examinations. Some recalled him patting them on the bottom or making comments about their bodies. Victims described him as "cold, arrogant, and acting like God." (contemporary Press Association report in The Guardian (17 September 2004). Full ref: Press Association. (2004). 'Predator' GP jailed for abusing patients. The Guardian, 17 September 2004).

Although police eventually gathered over 40 allegations, the crimes only came to light after one woman confided her experiences to a psychotherapist in 2000.

Murray argued that his actions were clinically justified, often citing contraception checks, but his reasoning was not consistently recorded in the notes. The judge told him:

> You cynically preyed upon trust for your own sexual gratification. Over a period of 14 years, in an appalling inversion of your role, you were healer turned predator. You have shown no remorse.

Like Clifford Ayling in Kent, Murray exploited the unique vulnerabilities of general practice: patients seen alone, often distressed, accustomed to accepting intimate examinations without question, and socialised to defer to the authority of the family doctor. All relied on the "*you trust your doctor*" culture, where refusal seemed unthinkable and complaints were dismissed as misunderstandings. In both cases, the GP's surgery, imagined by patients as a place of safety and care, became the site of repeated sexual abuse, protected by the respectability of the medical role and the silence of institutions unwilling to challenge it.

ABUSE TOWARDS VULNERABLE WOMEN

Some doctors target adult patients whose circumstances make them less able to resist or speak out. Vulnerability can take many forms: youth, poverty, illness, pregnancy, or trauma. For the doctor intent on abuse, these are not obstacles. They are opportunities.

Dr Krishna Singh

Dr Krishna Singh was a GP honoured nationally (MBE) for his contributions to healthcare. He also served as a police surgeon from 2005 to 2010, examining individuals in police custody. These roles brought him into contact with women at moments of significant vulnerability. Amongst his cases was a woman who visited him after being raped. Others included pregnant women seeking routine care.

Over 35 years, Singh assaulted 47 women and girls, some younger than 16. His victims later explained why they had not reported him sooner. He was a senior partner in the practice, and his wife was the practice manager.

Younger women feared they would not be believed. His crimes only came to light after one woman spoke out during the surge of disclosures following the Harvey Weinstein scandal. More women came forward, and the extent of his abuse became clear. In 2022, at the age of 72, Singh was sentenced to 12 years in prison. The trial judge told him, "You used your position manipulatively to carry out unnecessary physical examinations of a sexual nature, including intimate examinations without a chaperone or any prior explanation, in circumstances where there was no clinical justification."

Dr Angus Brooke

Even after being convicted of causing or inciting sexual activity with a patient in 2022, Brooke, a GP since 1996, denied any wrongdoing. The patient was a woman diagnosed with "sex and love addiction" and a personality disorder. During a consultation, Brooke exposed himself and encouraged her to masturbate him. At sentencing, the judge described the offence as "*a massive and considerable breach of trust.*" Brooke attempted to shift blame onto the patient, claiming their interaction was consensual and influenced by her behaviour. The court was not persuaded. The judge reminded him that his role was to protect and support, not to exploit. The woman's vulnerabilities were known to him, and he had deliberately abused them, causing her significant psychological distress and physical symptoms triggered by the stress of the assault.

In these situations, the power imbalance is evident.

VOYEURISM AND EXPLOITATION

Some doctors do not physically touch their victims at all. Instead, they breach their privacy for sexual gratification, abusing their position to access spaces and moments that most people consider safe.

Dr Barend Delport

Dr Barend Delport, a GP initially trained in South Africa but practising in the United Kingdom, used intimate medical examinations as a chance to photograph his patients. His victims included children as young as two.

When police searched his home, they found over 5,500 inappropriate images of children amongst more than half a million pornographic and voyeuristic pictures. Delport, like many others in this chapter, hid his actions behind a "cloak of professionalism," conducting unnecessary and invasive examinations that appeared routine to the untrained eye.

In 2019, he was sentenced to 6 years in prison, finally admitting to 26 offences including sexual assault and making, taking, and possessing indecent images of children over 10 years.

The judge observed that even in a society becoming more conscious of professional misconduct, the medical profession still holds a special level of trust, and Delport had taken advantage of this to commit his crimes.

Although there is no physical contact, the violation remains just as serious when it occurs indirectly. The harm comes from the deliberate exploitation of access, breaching privacy, and the realisation that something as routine as a medical check-up could be exploited for someone else's sexual gratification.

THE IMPACT

Sexual misconduct by doctors has deep and lasting effects. Patients who experience sexual abuse in a medical setting, like other survivors of sexual assault, face increased risks of developing conditions such as anxiety, depression, substance misuse, and post-traumatic stress disorder (AbuDagga et al., 2016). Their relationships with partners, family, and close friends may also suffer. Additionally, public trust in doctors can be seriously damaged. This loss of confidence becomes even more serious when severe cases of physician sexual abuse appear to go unpunished.

REFERENCES

AbuDagga, A., Wolfe, S. M., Carome, M., & Oshel, R. E. (2016). Cross-sectional analysis of the 1039 U.S. physicians reported to the National Practitioner Data Bank for sexual misconduct, 2003–2013. *PLoS ONE*, 11(2), e0147800. https://doi.org/10.1371/journal.pone.0147800

McPhee, J., & Dowden, J. P. (2018). *Report of the Independent Investigation: The Constellation of Factors Underlying Larry Nassar's Abuse of Athletes*. Ropes & Gray LLP. (Published December 10, 2018).

Pauffley, A. (2004). *Committee of Inquiry: Independent investigation into how the NHS handled allegations about the conduct of Clifford Ayling* (Cm 6298). London: The Stationery Office.

14

Sex, drugs, and doctors

CLARE GERADA AND ZAID AL-NAJJAR

This chapter deals with one of the darkest intersections of medicine: the misuse of drugs to facilitate sexual abuse. Unlike simple addiction, where dependence is the main factor, these cases are characterised by intent: drugs are stolen, prescribed, or diverted not for personal use, but as a form of currency, leverage, or to facilitate sexual behaviour. They breach two profound boundaries: the misuse of medical authority and the violation of trust, creating a particularly toxic and disturbing mix.

DRUGS, DOCTORS, AND POWER

> The theatre lights dazzle, the disinfectant smell is sharp, and the hum of machinery is strangely comforting. A woman reclines, sleepy, as a voice tells her she will soon drift off to sleep. She trusts this man; he is the doctor, the one who knows what the drugs will do. As the sedative courses through her veins, she feels her limbs relax, her vision blurs. There is a moment of floating, a slip between waking and nothingness. But then, a hand where it shouldn't be, a sense of violation, a terrible confusion. She cannot move or protest. She is at the mercy of the very person she sought care from. Few betrayals cut so deep.

This is a fictional case, but one based on many of the doctors described in this chapter.

When doctors misuse drugs to cross the sexual boundary, the betrayal becomes even more severe. Medicine has always involved substances that can dull pain, induce sleep, or loosen inhibitions. For unscrupulous practitioners, drugs may be exploited not for healing but for control. They abuse their authority by administering substances and then exploiting the helplessness these substances cause. These crimes are not committed in alleyways or dark

DOI: 10.1201/9781003781066-14

streets, but in surgeries, clinics, and homes, places where patients feel they are safest.

THE NATURE OF THE BOUNDARY

Sexual misconduct, as we have seen in Chapter 12, by doctors can take many forms. Drugs can exacerbate this abuse in two ways.

First, they remove agency. A patient who is sedated, intoxicated, or rendered unconscious cannot give consent.

Second, they obscure evidence. Victims may have no memory of events, or may doubt themselves, unsure whether what they recall was real or a dreamlike hallucination. In legal terms, this makes prosecution more difficult, and in psychological terms, it deepens the trauma of uncertainty.

Therefore, the drug/sex transgressor is doubly abusive: by abusing their professional authority to administer a drug under the pretence of care, and by exploiting the vulnerability it causes to satisfy sexual desire or to demonstrate dominance.

VICTORIAN ANXIETIES: CHLOROFORM AND ETHER

In the nineteenth century, the widespread availability of opium, chloroform, and ether sparked fears about their potential misuse in medicine. When James Young Simpson introduced chloroform anaesthesia in Edinburgh in 1847, it was celebrated as a miracle, enabling surgery without pain. However, almost immediately, darker concerns arose. What if unconscious patients were vulnerable to assault? What if the doctor, alone with an insensible woman, was tempted to exploit her? Soon after the introduction of chloroform as an anaesthetic agent, sexual fantasies were flagged as a common side effect.

Allegations began to surface of surgeons and anaesthetists abusing their positions to assault patients, especially in obstetrics. In the 100 years from 1780 to 1890, 22 cases arose when an assault was alleged to have occurred whilst the patient was unconscious or under anaesthetic; some apparently involved the application of a speculum (Tomkins, 2017).

Victorian courts were hesitant to believe such claims, but they entered the cultural consciousness, fuelling gothic stories of doctors capable of rendering women insensible at will. Writers such as Mary Elizabeth Braddon incorporated doctors and drugs into tales of domestic menace, whilst Wilkie Collins's fiction often hinted at the blurry boundary between medical authority and abuse. Gothic stories thrived on depicting sinister surgeons, whose mastery of chemistry enabled them to manipulate consciousness at will. More established works echoed these fears indirectly. Stevenson's Dr Jekyll and Mr Hyde used chemical self-experimentation as a metaphor for professional duplicity. At the same time, Stoker's Dracula portrayed unconscious heroines surrounded by doctors administering blood transfusions; interventions that hinted at sexual violation. These stories reveal how the miraculous promise of painless surgery through chloroform was quickly overshadowed by darker imaginings: that the unconscious patient was vulnerable, and even the doctor could become a predator.

Although there were whispers of abuse in the nineteenth century, courts were reluctant to take them seriously. Victorian reverence for the medical profession meant juries almost always sided with doctors. One case that did result in a conviction, although it was later overturned, involved Robert Hunter, an American doctor who had travelled to Britain to promote his claimed cure for tuberculosis. Whilst in London, he also established a practice and began treating patients. One of these, Annie Merrick, accused Hunter of raping her whilst she was under general anaesthetic. She did not report the assault for 2 weeks, a delay that juries of the time considered damaging to her credibility. Nonetheless, Merrick's husband and brother attacked Hunter, leading to two criminal trials: one for the alleged rape and another for the assault on Hunter. Hunter was acquitted, causing the courtroom to erupt in applause, with colleagues and the wider medical community offering him enthusiastic congratulations.

A few years later, Richard Freeman, an obstetrician, was accused twice of assaulting female patients whilst they were under anaesthetic, in 1867 and 1870. On both occasions, he was found not guilty.

It took over a 100 years before a proven case of such abuse finally came to court.

BARBITURATES AND SEDUCTION

By the mid-twentieth century, the widespread medical use of sedatives and "truth serums," such as sodium amytal and sodium thiopental, created conditions conducive to abuse.

In the United States, psychiatrists used sodium amytal or pentothal in narcoanalysis, which led to patients having blurred memories, a vulnerability that, in documented cases, was exploited for sexual purposes. Women who later reported hazy, half-remembered assaults were often dismissed because their drug-clouded recollections were deemed unreliable.

Across the Atlantic, the General Medical Council from the 1960s to the 1980s disciplined GPs and psychiatrists for giving barbiturates or Valium (diazepam) to female patients under the guise of calming them, then making sexual advances.

MODERN SCANDALS: BENZODIAZEPINES AND ANAESTHETICS

Recent decades have uncovered cases of doctors using benzodiazepines, ketamine, and anaesthetic agents to incapacitate patients for sexual purposes. Unlike the vague suspicions of the Victorian era, these crimes are now documented in chilling detail, sometimes captured on hidden cameras placed by investigators.

In several cases across the United Kingdom, the United States, and Europe, anaesthetists and GPs have stockpiled sedatives and then invited patients for unnecessary procedures or "private consultations" where they administered drugs that rendered victims unconscious or unable to resist. These cases often only came to light when brave victims persisted with complaints or when forensic examinations found traces of drugs inconsistent with legitimate treatment.

ASSAULT UNDER ANAESTHESIA

In California, Dr Jeffrey Joel Abrams pleaded guilty in 2015 to eight counts of sexual penetration of an unconscious person, three counts of sexual battery, and one count of child pornography. All the counts involved assaults at his low-income clinic, where many patients were Hispanic immigrants who spoke little English. Abrams sexually assaulted unconscious patients and took more than 1,300 explicit photos of patients, including one of an 8-year-old girl.

He was not sentenced to imprisonment for his convictions. Instead, a California court in September 2015, noting that he had renal cancer, placed him on 1 year of house arrest and 5 years' probation (Medical Board of California, 2014).

The Attorney General of California at the time was Kamala Harris.

Anaesthetist, Dr Leng Ky, operated a pain management clinic in America and was sentenced to 17 years in prison for his guilty plea to sexually assaulting female patients whilst they were under anaesthesia. The victims were administered drugs like ketamine and propofol and told their memories were drug-induced hallucinations (DA NewsCenter, 2023).

In 2022, in New York, gastroenterologist Zhi Alan Cheng transformed the hospital ward into his hunting ground. Behind his composed bedside manner lay a secret archive of videos: sedated and helpless patients filmed as he assaulted them. At least seven women were identified, three of whom were under his medical care when he administered anaesthesia. In this apparent investigation, investigators found vials of liquid sedatives. Confronted with the evidence, Cheng entered guilty pleas and now faces up to 24 years in prison.

The abuse by Roger Abdelmassih in Brazil occurred on a massive scale. A celebrity fertility specialist, honoured by politicians and the wealthy, Abdelmassih built a public reputation of brilliance and kindness. Behind closed doors, he was raping women entrusted to his care, women sedated for fertility treatments, women rendered unconscious by drugs intended to give them hope of motherhood. For years, his victims' voices were ignored, their testimonies dismissed amid the glow of his reputation.

But when the weight of evidence finally pressed home, the extent of his immorality became clear. In 2010, Abdelmassih was convicted of 52 rapes and 39 attempted assaults, many involving unconscious women. The court sentenced him to 278 years in prison, a number so enormous it seemed more a public reckoning than a punishment.

Together, Cheng and Abdelmassih stand at the far end of the spectrum: doctors who used sedation not as a means to healing, but as a mask behind which they committed the most personal betrayals. They demonstrate with clarity how the doctor's unique power, the ability to induce unconsciousness, can be turned into a weapon.

TRADING SEX FOR DRUGS

Across Britain and America, disciplinary hearings have revealed doctors who used drugs as a form of currency. For example, women were given Valium (diazepam) or temazepam "to help with nerves," only to find themselves ensnared in exploitative relationships. Some were coerced into sex in exchange for prescriptions; others were groomed into dependence, then exploited whilst drugged.

In America, Dr Joseph Santiamo, a 65-year-old elder care expert in New York, was convicted of exchanging prescriptions for oxycodone for sexual favours from young women. Sentenced to 57 months in prison, he faced harsh remarks from the presiding judge, who stated that the only difference between Santiamo and a street dealer was "the white coat he wears."

If Santiamo blurred the line between physician and drug dealer, Dr Thomas Edward Radecki obliterated it.

A psychiatrist, once known as a campaigner against violence in the media, was revealed to have been running what prosecutors described as a "prescription-for-sex" racket. Radecki supplied opioids and other controlled substances to vulnerable female patients, exploiting their addictions to bind them to him. The exchanges were sordidly transactional: a prescription for painkillers in return for a sexual act. Some women, already dependent on the drugs, found themselves trapped in a cycle of exploitation, returning again and again, not for therapy but for pills they could not live without. Far from protecting the vulnerable, Radecki created dependency and then weaponised it for his own gratification. Convicted on multiple counts, he received an 11- to 22-year prison sentence.

Another psychiatrist – and perhaps the most high-profile case in the United Kingdom involving sex and drugs – was that of Dr Adam Osborne, the younger brother of former Chancellor of the Exchequer, George Osborne. In 2016, he was struck off the medical register by the Medical Practitioners Tribunal Service after being found guilty of having a 2-year relationship with a vulnerable patient he was treating privately for anxiety and depression. When the patient reported this to the General Medical Council (GMC), Osbourne begged her to retract her statement and threatened her in emails, stating that it would "destroy" his family and adding: "I will make sure you pay." A medical tribunal concluded that Osborne's behaviour was "profoundly unacceptable" and determined that his fitness to practise was impaired due to misconduct.

This was not Osborne's first misconduct. In 2010, he was suspended for 6 months for prescribing medication to a £150-an-hour escort with whom he had been in a "relationship." They reached a different arrangement. Instead of paying her hourly, Osborne agreed to pay her £795 a month in rent in exchange for what she described as "sex on tap." The woman, who was 21 at the time, had a cocaine habit that was spiralling out of control. His misconduct came to light when she was admitted to the hospital with psychotic symptoms linked to cocaine's side effects. The woman had been taking quetiapine, used to treat schizophrenia, which she admitted had been supplied by Osborne.

THE COMMON THREADS

Across these cases, specific themes recur. Drugs were used as tools of control; what was presented as medical care was a deliberate removal of a patient's autonomy. Whether given as intravenous sedatives or pills, the outcome was always the same: helplessness.

For survivors, the aftermath was profoundly distressing. Memories of what had occurred were often hazy and fragmented, leaving many unsure whether their experiences were real or imagined. This corrosive uncertainty intensified the trauma and, in turn, made prosecutions more challenging. Within the profession, silence often prevailed. Colleagues occasionally noticed irregularities, strange prescribing patterns, unusual requests for sedatives and stockpiles that seemed difficult to justify, but speaking out was rare. Even when suspicions arose, the legal system posed significant obstacles. Many of the substances used left the body swiftly, erasing the very evidence that might have led to a conviction. In practice, successful prosecutions often relied on multiple victims coming forward or on physical evidence such as videos.

Medicine has taken steps to prevent repetition, such as stricter drug controls, chaperones, and whistleblower procedures. Yet, as long as drugs exist that can alter consciousness, and as long as patients must entrust themselves to doctors in vulnerable states, the risk remains.

FALSE ALLEGATIONS

However, there are also many untold stories of doctors who have faced grave accusations, only for the allegations to later collapse. By this time, the damage to their lives is irreparable. One such tragedy is that of Dr Sridharan Suresh, a consultant anaesthetist who came under police investigation following an allegation from a teenage patient. The patient, who had undergone dental sedation, claimed she had been touched inappropriately.

Dr Suresh had administered midazolam and fentanyl, sedative agents known to cause hallucinations and disinhibition. The patient's description did not match his appearance, and there was no evidence placing him in the recovery room at the time of the alleged incident. He strenuously denied any wrongdoing throughout the enquiry.

Despite his employer's assurances that the GMC would not be notified unless he were charged, the police made a referral to the regulator. Shortly after receiving the GMC's notification email, Dr Suresh took his own life. The criminal investigation was subsequently dropped due to insufficient evidence.

REFERENCES

DA NewsCenter (March 2023). "Doctor who Sexually Assaulted Patients Sentenced To Prison". https://danewscenter.com/news/doctor-who-sexually-assaulted-patients-sentenced-to-prison/

Medical Board of California. (2014, October 31). *Stipulation of the parties re interim order of suspension and order.* In the matter of the accusation against Jeffrey Joel Abrams, M.D., Case No. 800-2013-003018, OAH No. 2014101000. Office of Administrative Hearings, State of California. https://www.documentcloud.org/documents/2925502-combined-16-pdf/

Teegardin, C., Robbins, D., Hart, A., & Ernsthausen, J. (2016, July 6). *Doctors & sex abuse*. The Atlanta Journal-Constitution. https://doctors.ajc.com/table_of_contents/

Tomkins, A. (2017). Medical misadventure in an age of professionalisation, 1780–1890. Manchester University Press.

15

Why do doctors transgress sexual boundaries?

CLARE GERADA AND ZAID AL-NAJJAR

SEXUAL BOUNDARY VIOLATIONS IN HEALTHCARE: INSIGHTS FROM PRACTICE

Working with doctors and other health professionals who have crossed sexual boundaries is uncommon in the United Kingdom. One of the few experts in this area is Jonathan Coe, who has been involved since the early 2000s. He is a specialist in professional boundaries, with a focus on the prevention of violations.

He started this work in the voluntary sector, working with advocacy groups for patients harmed by therapists. He later led the charity Prevention of Professional Abuse Network and developed intensive courses for clinicians accused of sexual and other boundary violations. His perspective, developed over two decades, provides a rare insight into how such behaviours occur, how systems respond, and what can be done to prevent reoffending.

DEVELOPING A UK APPROACH

Early research on health professionals who cross professional boundaries began in the United States, where boundary training was already well established. However, Coe quickly realised that American programmes, often dominated by didactic lectures and PowerPoint slides, did not translate well to the UK context. Instead, he designed small group interventions, no more than five participants at a time, that emphasised reflection, dialogue, and the exploration of personal responsibility. The goal was not merely to impart knowledge about rules, but to help participants confront the realities of their behaviour: how they understood it, how they rationalised it, and what it meant for their professional values.

DOI: 10.1201/9781003781066-15

PATTERNS OF VIOLATION

The cases Coe has handled range widely. At one extreme are serious, repeated abuses: doctors photographing children or exploiting patients through sexualised behaviour. At the other end are less obvious violations, but still harmful actions, such as inappropriate jokes, "banter" in surgical theatres, unwanted touching, or misinterpretations of normal interactions. He notes that such behaviour often persists publicly, justified by colleagues and shielded by the authority of the medical profession. For instance, he describes a doctor who believed that a colleague's dress signalled sexual interest and made flirtatious approaches until a complaint was made.

THE ROLE OF POWER AND RATIONALISATION

A recurring theme amongst perpetrators is the misinterpretation of cues and the denial of power imbalances. For example, a female doctor who entered a relationship with a recently divorced patient insisted there was no vulnerability involved, despite the clear imbalance and that she felt she was merely offering support. Support should not extend to candlelit dinners for two, and her interaction clearly crossed a professional boundary, made worse by the timing of her interventions. In many cases, clinicians convince themselves that their patients or colleagues are consenting adults, overlooking how illness, dependency, and professional authority create vulnerability.

SYSTEMIC FAILURES

Egregious cases also expose systemic blind spots. Staff often collude, intentionally or not, in downplaying concerns: a doctor photographing a child is dismissed as "doing research"; a consultant's sexualised humour is tolerated until a student nurse breaks down in tears. The protective shield of professional status remains strong. Coe recounts an American case where a doctor exposed himself from his office window; when questioned, he was seen as a reliable witness to the "real" culprit rather than a suspect himself, the assumption by law enforcement being that doctors do not transgress in this manner.

PSYCHOLOGICAL AND DEVELOPMENTAL UNDERPINNINGS

Many offenders have histories of trauma. Research has shown higher rates of childhood and adult trauma amongst clinicians referred for sexual boundary violations, and Coe's life experience supports this. Unresolved bereavement, marital breakdown, professional stress, and untreated mental illness often serve as background factors (Spickard et al., 2008). One study examined whether individuals attending a professional boundaries course (mainly physicians) shared certain personal risk factors. The researchers focused on three areas: attachment style, childhood trauma, and maladaptive beliefs.

The study indicates that childhood adversity may contribute to boundary difficulties, partly by affecting attachment and belief patterns. It also shows that boundary education and professional wellness programmes could be improved by addressing the influence of childhood trauma, attachment issues, and maladaptive thinking styles (MacDonald et al., 2015).

Yet trauma is not an excuse: most bereaved or traumatised doctors do not offend. Rather, such contexts may weaken boundaries, promote validation, and discourage help-seeking.

The American psychiatrist and psychoanalyst Glen Gabbard, internationally renowned for his work on the treatment of personality disorders, studied more than 70 psychotherapists who became sexually involved with patients. He identified four broad categories: those driven by psychosis (rare), the predatory and narcissistic, those caught in misguided "lovesickness," and those whose own vulnerabilities led them to masochistic surrender. The most concerning are the predatory and narcissistic, consisting of doctors who behave with entitlement, exploiting their position, sometimes repeatedly, with their behaviour often noticed early but too frequently ignored. For some, misconduct is not driven by lust but by a desire for power. The ability to render a patient unconscious, to strip them of choice, fuels a darker need for control. For others, the line is crossed gradually, judgement clouded by alcohol, drugs, or the slow erosion of professional boundaries. Doctors who misuse substances are particularly vulnerable, as behaviour once considered unthinkable becomes excused in their own minds (Gabbard, 1999).

At the time of writing, only a limited amount of data addresses the attributes of physician offenders. One large study analysed reports submitted to the American National Practitioner Data Bank (NPDB) between January 2003 and September 2013. In total, 1,039 physicians had at least one report related to sexual misconduct. Ninety per cent were aged 40 or older. Most cases (75.6%) involved only licensure (excluding criminal) reports. Sexual misconduct cases were more likely than other offences to result in serious licensure sanctions (89% vs 68.1%) and revocation of clinical privileges (29.3% vs 18.8%). In malpractice payment reports, 87.4% of victims were female. The most common type of harm recorded was *emotional injury only*. Strikingly, 70% of physicians who had clinical privilege restrictions or malpractice fines for sexual misconduct were never disciplined by state medical boards for this behaviour (AbuDagga et al., 2016).

A study of 101 physician licensees deemed to have committed sexual misconduct (DuBois et al., 2019) examined common characteristics amongst the doctors, patient victims, practice settings, types of sexual violations, and consequences for the perpetrator. In each case, a criminal law framework was used to investigate how motives, means, and opportunity combined to produce sexual misconduct. Finally, cross-case analysis was conducted to identify clusters of causal factors that explain specific types of sexual misconduct. Most cases involved a combination of five factors: male physicians (100%), age older than 39 (92%), lack of board certification (70%), non-academic practice settings (94%), and always examining patients alone (85%). Only three factors, suspected antisocial personality, physician board certification, and vulnerable patients, differed significantly across the types of sexual abuse: personality disorders were most frequently suspected in cases of rape, physicians were more often board certified in cases of consensual sex with patients, and patients were more often vulnerable in cases of child molestation.

Lastly, a study of 761 US physicians disciplined for sex-related offences revealed that between 1989 and 1996, the number of physicians disciplined for such offences increased significantly from 42 to 147, with these cases representing a growing proportion of all disciplinary actions (2.1% to 4.4%). These offences attracted considerably harsher penalties than others, with nearly three-quarters resulting in licence revocation, surrender, or suspension. Most incidents (75%) involved patients, ranging from sexual intercourse to rape and exploitation. The offending doctors were more likely to work in psychiatry, obstetrics and gynaecology, or family practice. They tended to be older than average, although rates of board certification were similar (Dehlendorf & Wolfe, 1998).

Therefore, there is no single characteristic of a doctor who crosses sexual boundaries other than perhaps being male. The reasons are varied, shaped by personality, circumstance, and culture.

POWER AND ENVIRONMENTAL FACTORS

Silence has allowed abuse to continue. For decades, colleagues closed ranks, regulators hesitated, and courts often sided with doctors, the courtroom erupting in applause if the doctor was found not guilty, as if the profession itself had been vindicated. Protecting medicine's reputation mattered more than listening to patients.

Gendered power dynamics worsened the problem. Throughout much of the nineteenth and twentieth centuries, medicine was predominantly male, whereas many of those most vulnerable, patients in gynaecology, psychiatry, or general practice, were female. Women who dared to speak out often faced disbelief and stigma, especially if drugs had blurred their memories. These forces, power, opportunity, professional exceptionalism, and silence, created fertile ground for misconduct. And they endured well into modern times.

REGULATORY AND CULTURAL SHIFTS

Attitudes have shifted significantly. Until the 1980s, the GMC's guidance regarded affairs with patients mainly as a moral failing, but only if they led to adultery. Nowadays, regulators view even a single sexual boundary violation as grounds for erasure. Guidance by the GMC issued in 2006 warned doctors to think long and hard before embarking on a sexual relationship even with a former patient (Eaton, 2006; Sheather, 2006).

The #MeToo movement has sped up this change, drawing new attention to behaviours once dismissed as "banter." Clinicians who previously defended sexualised humour as part of medical culture now find themselves unable even to quote their own comments, as they sound extremely inappropriate when read back verbatim.

REMEDIATION AND REHABILITATION

Most cases Coe encounters are not serial offenders but one-off or short-term violations. Regulators increasingly recognise that remediation is possible: with insight, therapy, and structured reflection, clinicians may resume safe practice after suspension. The key, Coe emphasises, is genuine ownership of behaviour and understanding its impact. When practitioners remain defensive or do nothing during suspension beyond online training, panels are unlikely to be convinced. However, if they can demonstrate reflection, therapy, and behavioural change, regulators may consider that a safe return is achievable.

CONCLUSION: FACING THE BETRAYAL

In the 1980s, Clifford Ayling, a Kent GP, assaulted numerous female patients during unnecessary examinations. Complaints were ignored or dismissed until his eventual conviction. Around the same time, Michael Haslam, a Yorkshire psychiatrist, engaged in sexual relationships with vulnerable women, claiming they were therapeutic. His conviction in the 1990s revealed what some colleagues had long suspected. Krishna Singh, a GP admired for his charisma, used his reputation to conceal decades of abuse. More recently, Myles Bradbury, a paediatric haematologist, exploited boys with cancer, protected by the privacy of the consulting room and the trust families placed in him.

From Robert Hunter's trial in the nineteenth century (he was accused but then acquitted of raping Annie Merrick whilst she was under anaesthetic) to Bradbury's in the twenty-first, the same themes persist: access to the vulnerable, authority that suppresses dissent, narcissism that fosters entitlement, and institutions prioritising reputation over safety.

What has shifted is less the psychology of perpetrators than society's willingness to listen to victims. Where Annie Merrick's testimony against Hunter in 1872 was met with scepticism, women and children who spoke out a century later found their voices more likely to be heard. Even so, the road from disclosure to conviction remained long and painful.

REFERENCES

AbuDagga, A., Wolfe, S. M., Carome, M., & Oshei, R. (2016). Cross-sectional analysis of the 1039 U.S. Physicians reported to the National Practitioner DataBank for sexual misconduct, 2003–2013. *PLoS ONE*, 11(2), E0147800. https://doi.org/10.1371/Journal.Pone.0147800.

Dehlendorf, C. E., & Wolfe, S. M. (1998). Physicians disciplined for sex-related offenses. *JAMA*, *279*(23), 1883–1888. https://doi.org/10.1001/jama.279.23.1883

DuBois, J. M., Walsh, H. A., Chibnall, J. T., Anderson, E. E., Eggers, M. R., Fowose, M., & Ziobrowski, H. (2019). Sexual violation of patients by physicians: A mixed-methods, exploratory analysis of 101 cases. *Sexual Abuse*, *31*(5), 503–523. https://doi.org/10.1177/1079063217712217

Eaton, L. (2006). Doctors are warned against sex with former patients. *BMJ (Clinical Research Ed.), 333*(7574), 876. https://doi.org/10.1136/bmj.333.7574.876

Gabbard, G. O. (1999). Psychodynamic approaches to physician sexual misconduct. In J. D. Bloom, C. C. Nadelson, & M. T. Notman (Eds.), *Physician sexual misconduct* (pp. 205–223). American Psychiatric Press.

General Medical Council. (2024). "What to do if you think you have been subject to sexual misconduct by a doctor: A resource for patients and colleagues." https://www.gmc-uk.org/-/media/documents/sexual-misconductby-a-doctor-a-resource-for-patients-and-colleagues-english-version_pdf-108554760.pdf

MacDonald, K., Sciolla, A. F., Folsom, D., Bazzo, D., Searles, C., Moutier, C., Thomas, M. L., Borton, K., & Norcross, B. (2015). Individual risk factors for physician boundary violations: The role of attachment style, childhood trauma and maladaptive beliefs. *General Hospital Psychiatry, 37*(5), 489–496. https://doi.org/10.1016/j.genhosppsych.2015.06.002

Sheather, J. (2006). Sexual relationships between doctors and former patients. *BMJ: British Medical Journal, 333*(7579), 1132. https://doi.org/10.1136/bmj.39042.529641.BE

Spickard, W. A., Swiggart, W. H., Manley, G. T., Samenow, C. P., & Dodd, D. T. (2008). A continuing medical education approach to improve sexual boundaries of physicians. *Bulletin of the Menninger Clinic, 72*(1), 38–53. https://doi.org/10.1521/bumc.2008.72.1.38

16

Doctors, fraud, theft, and corruption

PALLAVI BRADSHAW

Corruption and fraud in medicine may not cause the visceral shock of murder or sexual assault, but they are no less a betrayal. Corruption generally means the misuse of entrusted power for personal gain. It can include bribery, nepotism, embezzlement, kickbacks, conflicts of interest, and favouritism. Not all corruption is illegal under criminal law; for example, cronyism or bending rules for personal connections can be unethical and harm institutions. It often involves power relationships, where someone in a position of authority misuses funds.

The amounts involved in healthcare are staggering, with estimates suggesting that at least 10% to 25% of global spending is lost directly through corruption.

In Australia, Medicare fraud is estimated to cost billions each year. In the United Kingdom, the NHS is thought to lose nearly two billion pounds annually to fraud, bribery, and corruption. Almost £750 million of the potential losses identified relate to losses in primary care. Of this amount, almost half is linked to patient fraud, whilst the rest is attributed to potential fraud by dental, optical, pharmacy, and general practice contractors.

In the United States, tens of billions of dollars are lost each year due to false claims, kickbacks, and other schemes. These figures are not just numbers; they represent medicines not purchased, treatments not funded, and patients not cared for. The perpetrators are not always shadowy figures operating on the fringes. They can be respected professionals, well-known within their communities. Some act out of greed, others under financial pressure, and a few claim they are bending the rules for their patients' benefit. Whatever the motive, the outcome remains the same: public money and trust are being misused.

Transparency International, a global non-governmental organisation (NGO), aims to fight corruption and promote transparency, accountability, and integrity across all levels of government, business, and society. It has identified six of the most common types of corruption in health service delivery.

DOI: 10.1201/9781003781066-16

These are:

> Bribery, which can happen when patients are asked, either openly or secretly, to pay "under-the-table" fees to access services that should be free or to skip queues for tests, surgery, or hospital beds. These payments take advantage of the vulnerability of the ill and their families, and they promote inequality because those with resources can buy their way to the front of the line, leaving the poor waiting.

Embezzlement and theft are yet another way corruption damages fragile systems. Medicines, vaccines, or equipment bought with public funds might be siphoned off and sold privately. Hospital budgets meant for community health projects can quietly vanish, diverted to enrich administrators. What is lost in these thefts is not just money but also the chance to provide care for those most in need.

Fraud is more subtle but just as damaging. In some systems, doctors or managers can create "ghost patients" by submitting claims for treatments that were never provided. Others inflate insurance claims or prescribe drugs unnecessarily to make a profit.

Abuse of power occurs when those in authority misuse their position for selfish benefit. This could include a surgeon recommending unnecessary procedures to increase profit or a senior doctor leveraging their influence to exploit junior colleagues. Power imbalances in healthcare are genuine, and when they are exploited, they undermine the principles of mentorship, honesty, and patient-centred care.

Conflicts of interest are another, often underappreciated, form of corruption. A doctor may prescribe an expensive branded drug not because it is clinically superior, but because of pharmaceutical company incentives. Procurement officials may direct contracts to firms in which they or their associates hold shares. On the surface, the care may appear legitimate, but hidden interests distort decisions and erode trust.

Nepotism and clientelism damage institutions from within. When jobs, promotions, or access to specialist training are awarded not on merit but on family ties or political loyalty, the health system is weakened. Capable candidates are excluded, and patients ultimately suffer from a culture that values connections over competence.

Alongside these six categories sits absenteeism, a practice that extends beyond doctors legitimately absent due to illness.

Taken together, these forms of corruption form a spectrum of harm. They differ in size and visibility, but all share one trait: they divert limited resources and undermine the trust on which medicine relies.

What follows are some specific examples of doctors who have faced criminal charges for fraud, theft, and corruption. This chapter will not deal with crimes relating to "pill mills," which will be covered in Chapter 11.

STEALING TIME AND FAKING TIME SHEETS

Absenteeism in healthcare is not simply a matter of staff being unwell or legitimately unavailable. It often refers to something more insidious: health professionals drawing public salaries whilst failing to deliver the services they are contracted to provide. This practice can take different shapes. In many countries, doctors and nurses employed in government hospitals spend their contracted hours working in private clinics instead, diverting patients away from the public system. Others, particularly those with political or personal protection, can skip work without fear of disciplinary action, setting a tone of impunity that normalises the behaviour for colleagues. In some cases, the problem is even more brazen, with so-called "ghost workers" appearing on payroll lists, phantom employees whose wages are siphoned off by managers or officials.

The extent of absenteeism is remarkable. Global estimates indicate it impacts between one-third and one-half of all health workers, yet it remains one of the least studied forms of corruption in the healthcare sector. However, its effects are highly visible to patients and communities. Rural clinics are often found closed during regular hours because the sole doctor is absent, working elsewhere for private profit. Hospital departments may operate with unsafe staffing levels because senior doctors seldom attend, leaving junior staff to manage unsupported. Patients, frustrated by long waits and poor service, may be compelled to make informal payments or visit absent staff in their private practices, where they must pay again for care that should have been freely available.

The effects spread further. Waiting times rise, quality of care drops, and health inequalities grow as those with money can buy access whilst the poor are left behind.

Absenteeism, therefore, is not merely a minor workplace problem but a form of corruption that threatens both fairness and safety in healthcare. It shifts the costs and responsibilities onto patients and communities, thereby eroding the principle of universal care.

Despite its damaging effects, absenteeism in healthcare is usually regarded as an administrative or disciplinary issue rather than a criminal offence. Staff may face suspension, disciplinary action, or quiet tolerance, but prosecution is uncommon.

One such case involved consultant John Coffey, who pleaded guilty at Preston Crown Court to defrauding Lancashire Teaching Hospitals of nearly £24,000. Coffey had agreed to help reduce a backlog of X-ray scans by reviewing them outside his regular working hours for £4 per film. However, an investigation revealed that he completed much of the work during his usual working hours and then submitted the reports after 5 pm, falsely claiming overtime. He was suspended, resigned from the trust, and has since repaid the full amount.

FRAUD

Fraud in medicine can sometimes be quite simple: lying about hours worked. Doctors have been caught falsifying timesheets, forging signatures, and even claiming payment for shifts. At the same time, on annual leave, this has led, for some, not only to the loss of their licence to practise but also to criminal charges.

This large-scale falsification occurred in 2014, when four doctors were convicted of fraud at Basildon Hospital. Doctors Ann Clements, 51, Tom Cumberland, 42, John Mulholland, 41, and Martin Oliver, 37, were all blood circulation experts who operated heart-lung bypass equipment during surgery.

On paper, they worked a typical full-time week. In reality, they did little more than half of that, whilst moonlighting in lucrative private hospitals, mainly in London. Over 4 years, they worked 14,000 fewer hours than paid for, pocketing an extra £700,000, of which around £420,000 was fraud. Between them, they had formed a company, contracting themselves to work privately as well as working for the NHS.

The ringleader, John Mulholland, was an internationally renowned heart surgeon with an extensive list of publications. Court documents revealed that the group openly disdained the NHS: they mockingly called Basildon "Bas Vegas," and Mulholland wrote he avoided NHS duties "unless it's going to make cash or make our lives easier." The judge, David Owen-Jones, condemned the fraud as "systemic, well-planned, organised and executed," adding, "You gravely abused the trust placed in you… I feel these offences were motivated purely by greed." Mulholland was sentenced to 3 years in prison; his colleagues, described as "medium-scale players," faced career ruin. Whilst no patients suffered direct harm, the scandal demonstrates how senior doctors can exploit the system for personal gain.

A decade later, history repeated itself. In 2024, Dr Kifayat Ullah, a hospital consultant and well-known social media influencer, was convicted of defrauding Kingston Hospital NHS Foundation Trust of over £50,000 by submitting false timesheets. Having been brought in to help with the post-COVID backlog, Ullah soon reduced his hours to part-time but continued to submit 29 forged timesheets claiming full-time hours. Some had altered signatures, whilst others were completely fabricated. At sentencing, the judge remarked: "His actions stem from greed; he has brought disgrace on himself and his profession." Ullah received a 24-month suspended sentence, but like Mulholland and his colleagues before him, his reputation and career are now in ruins.

A doctor was jailed for 4 years after being found guilty of swindling up to £4m from hospitals in the biggest one-man fraud ever perpetrated against the NHS.

Dr Dimitri Padelis, 45, was sentenced to 4 years in prison after being convicted of one of the largest individual frauds against the NHS, estimated to have involved theft of between £2 and £4 million. Operating through his locum agency in South Norwood, he systematically falsified invoices by double-billing hospitals, inflating doctors' hours, and submitting fake expenses. Hospitals affected included Great Ormond Street, which was targeted 90 times. His fraud was uncovered when an audit at Gwynedd Hospital identified repeated payments to his company, leading to a broader investigation across multiple trusts. The judge condemned Padelis's actions as a serious breach of trust and stated he exploited weaknesses in NHS accounting out of greed. Padelis repaid the money in the cases prosecuted, but the investigation uncovered a widespread pattern of overcharging. The prosecution described the fraud as subtle, relying on small amounts taken repeatedly so it would go unnoticed.

In 2015, a 63-year-old Texas doctor, Dr Tariq Mahmood, was convicted of conspiracy to commit health care fraud. He received a sentence of 135 months in federal prison and was ordered to pay restitution of $599,128.02. Mahmood, a general practitioner who owned and operated several hospitals in Texas, engaged in a scheme over several years to defraud Medicare and Medicaid by submitting false claims. He and others added, altered, and incorrectly sequenced diagnostic codes that did not accurately represent patients' diagnoses and conditions, often without reviewing medical records.

This case was one of many brought by the nationwide Medicare Fraud Strike Force (n.d.) that charged 16 people from Detroit and included charges filed across the country against 243 people, including 46 doctors, for schemes involving $712 million in false billing.

The Medicare Fraud Strike Force, operating in nine cities nationwide, has charged nearly 2,000 defendants who have collectively billed the Medicare programme more than $6 billion since its inception in 2007.

Not all fraud involves complex accounting, long-term deception, or large sums of money. Some are simple acts of opportunism that are particularly damaging because of their timing. In 2020, as the COVID-19 pandemic overwhelmed the NHS, there was a desperate shortage of personal protective equipment (PPE). Frontline staff worked in fear, with some reusing masks or improvising protections. Against this backdrop, Dr Attiya Sheikh, a 46-year-old hospital doctor, and her husband Omer Sheikh saw not just a duty but an opportunity. Between May and October 2020, they sold stolen NHS Scotland PPE using four different eBay accounts, earning just under £8,000. A total of 56 transactions took place between 6 June 2020 and 2 October 2020. At the trial, both admitted handling stolen goods, and they were sentenced to 10 months in prison and their actions were described as "sheer greed."

CORRUPTION IN SERVICE PROVISION

This form may be the most insidious because it directly affects the care that patients receive. In the United Kingdom, cardiologists have faced investigation for inserting stents into patients who did not need them, procedures driven more by financial incentives and professional prestige than by clinical necessity.

Across Europe, unnecessary caesarean sections are so common that they are now seen as a systemic form of over-treatment. Conversely, under-treatment also occurs in Peru; doctors resisted allowing trained midwives to perform procedures such as colposcopy, not to protect patients but to defend their own income streams. Whether due to excess or neglect, when medical decisions are motivated by money rather than medical need, it is the patients who suffer as a result.

FAVOURITISM AND PREFERENTIAL TREATMENT

These practices undermine fairness, even when they are not illegal. In Spain and Italy, prosecutors have uncovered networks of doctors accused of manipulating waiting lists to fast-track friends, family, or political allies. In Australia, inquiries into rural hospitals revealed that limited dialysis slots were quietly reserved for well-connected patients, whilst others remained untreated. In the United Kingdom, critics have long highlighted the murky overlap between private and NHS practice: a patient who pays privately to see their consultant on Monday may find themselves fast-tracked onto an NHS theatre list by Tuesday, whilst poorer patients wait months.

MANIPULATION OF DATA

The most insidious form may be data manipulation, which hides corruption behind an illusion of success. In the NHS, doctors and managers have been implicated in reclassifying patients or adjusting waiting list figures to meet government targets. Across Europe, audits in Italy and Greece uncovered billing for procedures that were never performed, maximising reimbursements from public funds. In Mexico, doctors inflated maternal health data, claiming syphilis and HIV screenings that never occurred to meet performance targets. The result was preventable cases of congenital syphilis, concealed by glowing reports.

PRESCRIPTION FRAUD

Prescription fraud is a common way to enter into criminal activity. A GP who prescribes expensive medication on an NHS prescription for their child may think it's harmless because the child is genuinely ill. However, if no consultation took place and the GP is not the child's registered doctor, it still constitutes fraud. In one case, a doctor working in an accident and emergency department wrote two prescriptions for oestrogen cream using the names of random patients from the hospital database. The medication was for a friend overseas, who was not entitled to free NHS care. The deception was uncovered when a pharmacist noticed the irregularity and the unusual medicine prescribed as an emergency. The doctor was struck off and cautioned by the police.

Fraud can also occur in more subtle ways in private practice, where referral rings operate secretly. A doctor refers patients for unnecessary tests to a clinic in which they have a financial interest, or to a colleague who will return the favour. Kickbacks are paid discreetly, with the patient unaware that medical judgement has been influenced by profit.

MOTIVATION, PRESSURE, AND RATIONALISATION

Most doctors will never commit fraud. They face the same opportunities, access, and temptations without crossing that line. But for the few who do, the reasons vary. For some, the motive is straightforward greed. Extra income supports a lifestyle they cannot otherwise afford, fuels a taste for status, or funds expensive habits. The Basildon perfusionists, for instance, treated the NHS as a source to exploit, pocketing hundreds of thousands of pounds from private work. Others act under financial pressure. Debts mount, relationships break down, or obligations push their income to its limit. Addiction is another strong factor.

A smaller group acts under the guise of altruism. They may exaggerate symptoms so a struggling patient can access benefits or admit someone under false pretences to secure social support. In their view, this is compassion, not crime. Yet in law, the intent to deceive is enough to constitute fraud.

And then there are the rationalisers.

Fraud by doctors often hides behind the stories they tell themselves. They believe they are not criminals, but instead adjusting an unfair system, easing a path for patients, or taking what they are "entitled" to. A trusted GP or consultant can easily think their irregular payments are simply "professional fees." Kickbacks for referrals become just part of the business of medicine. Each step seems small, and each justification more straightforward than the last.

This mental reframing enables fraud to develop unchecked. By the time the behaviour becomes significant enough to attract scrutiny, the doctor may have convinced themselves they are still acting within acceptable limits. Even worse, when colleagues observe dishonest practices going unchallenged, it erodes the culture of honesty within the profession. What begins as a single rationalisation can spread, making it easier for others to cross the line.

FRAUD PREVENTION AND DETECTION

Healthcare fraud costs billions worldwide, and efforts to combat it have developed into a notable industry. Governments, insurers, and health authorities allocate resources to prevention and detection, but outcomes differ.

In the United Kingdom, the NHS Counter Fraud Authority leads investigations, recovers funds, and refers serious cases for prosecution. The Department of Health and Social Care's 2023 counter-fraud strategy aims to prevent, detect, and recover half a billion pounds over 3 years. In the United States, the Department of Justice targets large-scale scams through specialist units like the Medicare Fraud Strike Force, which uses data analysis to identify suspicious billing. Australia, South Africa, and many other countries have established similar teams, often working with private insurers.

Prevention depends on more than just rules. Strong governance, effective regulation, and secure systems are vital, but they are not enough. Fraud control also relies on a culture where whistleblowers feel safe to speak out without fear of retaliation. Anonymous tip lines, algorithmic analysis of billing data, and stricter supplier vetting are all part of the toolkit. However, much detection still occurs too late, once the fraud is deeply embedded and the losses are significant.

Barriers remain. Complex billing systems create loopholes that dishonest practitioners can exploit, disguised as coding errors or clinical discretion. Witnesses may be reluctant to testify, and institutions themselves might be conflicted, having benefited from the very fraud under investigation. Negotiated settlements can recover money, but too often they allow perpetrators to avoid the scrutiny of open court.

In advanced systems, many frauds are still uncovered the old-fashioned way: a vigilant pharmacist questioning a prescription, a colleague noticing a pattern, or a patient querying a bill. Supporting and promoting these voices may be the most effective way to detect fraud.

REFERENCE

Medicare Fraud Strike Force. (n.d.). U.S. Department of Health and Human Services, Office of Inspector General. https://oig.hhs.gov/fraud/strike-force/

17

Addiction, opportunity, and descent into crime: Reflections from Dr Namasivayam Thiagalingam

ZAID AL-NAJJAR

When doctors are convicted of committing fraud, the cases often make headlines; however, few speak openly about their experience. Dr Namasivayam Thiagalingam, a former emergency physician, is one of them. His story offers a rare insight into how personal crisis, addiction, opportunity, and professional status can all play their part in such a fall from grace, even in experienced clinicians.

Graduating in Sri Lanka and practising in Britain since the mid-1980s, Thiagalingam describes a career that began with pride and ended in prison. "I came here to build a life," he said. "I loved the work. Patients trusted me, but I lost everything because I stopped looking after myself."

He remembers how the deaths of both parents in quick succession, two failed marriages, and long hours spent on night shifts left him feeling isolated and depressed. He recalls even going to his local railway station with the intent of ending his life; however, it was his attachment to his dog "Mariah" that ultimately stopped him.

Alcohol, at first a comfort, became a necessity. "You start with a drink after work," he said, "then you drink to get through your depression, and you do your best to disguise your drinking so you can go to work."

Around this time, Dr Thiagalingam was also convicted of drink-driving offences and was banned. Despite the ban, he continued to drive and was subsequently convicted of driving whilst disqualified. He received a suspended sentence and 200 hours of community service but despite all of this, he continued to drink.

 DOI: 10.1201/9781003781066-17

When he attempted to stop drinking, withdrawal tremors and sleeplessness drove him to use benzodiazepines and sleeping pills to cope with his symptoms. That is when he began self-prescribing. "I thought I could handle it," he recalls. "When you're addicted, you think you're still functioning. You don't see the slide."

He explains that the fraud started almost coincidentally because his judgement and memory were so impaired – clouded by a cocktail of drugs and alcohol.

Rotas were on paper and not well checked. He began claiming payments for extra sessions he hadn't worked, justifying it by saying it balanced out because he had worked many shifts he hadn't claimed for. When no one spotted it, the behaviour continued. Over time, the claims added up to thousands of pounds: "At first, I thought it evened out. But once you cross that line, you stop seeing where it is."

Addiction complicated the deception. "When you are dependent," he explained, "you think only about survival and not right or wrong." He removed prescription pads, wrote false prescriptions under fictitious names, and "pharmacy-shopped" across London to sustain his supply of sedatives. "It wasn't about greed," he said. "It was survival. Without alcohol or tablets, I'd shake, sweat, and panic."

His position as a doctor both enabled and helped conceal his actions. "People trusted me automatically," he reflected. "No one questioned me; I knew the system, the forms, the pharmacies. I knew which questions wouldn't be asked. I knew what other drugs I needed to take to counteract the side effects of the ones I was self-prescribing." The shield of respect and sword of medical knowledge slowed detection, and the fall, when it came, was more complete.

The end came when a pharmacist noticed a prescription he had submitted for diazepam and reported the matter to the police because the amount prescribed was far beyond usual therapeutic doses. They later discovered blank prescription pads and empty medication boxes at his home. Despite the circumstances surrounding his deception, the judge at his trial stated there was no one to blame but him. He was convicted of fraud and related offences and received a sentence of 3 years' imprisonment.

Prison forced a reckoning, and he described his time there as very difficult. He recounted his experience of taunting and assaults from other inmates at the time; however, since then, he has maintained abstinence. Without alcohol or medication, he confronted the full reality of his dependence. "It was withdrawal and clarity at the same time," he recalled. He describes that period not as punishment but as an interruption – the point at which his denial of his addiction finally broke down.

He describes prison as both punishment and redemption. "For the first time in years, I was sober. It was agony, but it was the first time I could think clearly." During this sentence, he read law books, helped other inmates with appeals, and began to understand the full extent of what he had done. "You can be intelligent and still lose all judgement when your brain is soaked in alcohol," he said. "Addiction pollutes the frontal lobe – you can't tell right from wrong."

Released after 18 months, he lost his home, savings, and medical registration. Yet he remained abstinent and gradually rebuilt his life through volunteering and community work. He describes that period as one of humility and perspective. "Now I live in a small flat, when I used to live in a house with a jacuzzi and have a personalised car number plate. However, I have had enough. I help at the foodbank, and I'm part of the community again. It keeps me grounded." He also supports others in recovery. "I can't undo what I did," he said, "but I can warn others before they fall."

His message to younger doctors is stark but compassionate. "Don't isolate yourself. When things start to go wrong, financially, emotionally, or professionally, talk to someone. Alcohol won't fix it. Shame kills doctors faster than drink or drugs."

He also warns against the illusion of invulnerability that can accompany seniority. "Being a doctor gives you access, authority, and trust. That's powerful and dangerous. You can convince yourself that rules are flexible because you're saving lives. But the same status that protects you will destroy you when you fall."

He believes the NHS has learned from incidents like his: e-prescribing and electronic timesheets would have made his fraud much more difficult. But he insists that prevention isn't only about systems; it's about culture. "We need to make it normal to say 'I'm not coping'. I was terrified to admit weakness. If I had asked for help, I'd still be a doctor."

UNDERSTANDING THE PATTERN

His account reveals familiar themes found in the literature on professional misconduct. Substance misuse and burnout heighten vulnerability to ethical collapse, especially in isolated practitioners lacking support or oversight. Opportunity, in his case, unsecured prescription pads and paper claims systems, provided the means. Rationalisation did the rest.

Thiagalingam sees the issue less as a moral failing and more as a convergence of impairment and systemic neglect. "The system trusted me completely," he reflected. "No checks, no questions. You just signed a form, and it went through."

He also raises uncomfortable cultural questions. As an international medical graduate, he feels his treatment by the regulator was harsher than that of his UK-trained peers and those who could afford top-class legal representation. Whether or not this is true, the perception itself matters, emphasising the need for transparent and fair disciplinary processes.

What emerges is not the story of a greedy man but of one consumed by dependence and shame. "I lied," he admits. "There are days I didn't work, I claimed. But I was already lost." His remorse is evident, but so too is his determination to use his experience constructively.

Addiction-driven frauds are often ignored in debates about medical crime, yet they question the profession's dependence on trust. They serve as a reminder that protecting patients and the public also involves safeguarding doctors' health.

As Thiagalingam put it: "If I had asked for help sooner, I'd still be a doctor. Instead, I became a warning." Looking back, he sees his story as a lesson in both human vulnerability and systemic failure. He does not excuse his actions but places them in the context of untreated illness and institutional blind trust. "The judge said it best," he remembered. "'A man who took up a job to look after others, failed to look after himself, and fell into dishonesty.' That's me."

Now, over a decade later, he still shares his experiences with others in recovery. "Show remorse. Show insight. Don't repeat mistakes. People will forgive you if you change."

For all his losses, he says, there is one gain: understanding. "I learned the hard way what addiction and shame can do. If my story makes one doctor ask for help before it's too late, then something good has come out of it."

18

Final thoughts

CLARE GERADA AND ZAID AL-NAJJAR

Judy sat in her GP's waiting room; the familiar sound of the call bell and murmur at the reception desk were usually reassuring. Today, however, she felt uneasy. Someone had left the local paper behind, and the front-page headline caught her eye: "Local Doctor Convicted of Sexual Assault." Beneath it was the image of an ordinary-looking, middle-aged man.

As she read the story, Judy's mind drifted back to her own consultations with Dr Smith, the GP she had known for years. She remembered the many times he had examined her at her most vulnerable. Everything had always seemed appropriate, but she could not shake the nagging thought: how could she really know? She wasn't a medic. Her thoughts were interrupted by her name being called to Room Two, where Dr Smith was waiting.

Judy's story is fictional, but it echoes many of the cases described in this book. Each scandal leaves a lasting mark.

Doctors embody not just technical expertise but also trust, wisdom, and moral authority. In ancient Greece, the Hippocratic Oath formalised this expectation: that those granted power over life and death must use it only for good. Yet, throughout this book, we have described doctors who betrayed their oath in the most profound ways. From Thomas Neill Cream's poisonings in Victorian London to Christopher Duntsch's catastrophic operations in Dallas, from Harold Shipman's lethal injections to the systemic fraud draining billions from healthcare systems, the methods and motives vary, but the patterns are disturbingly familiar.

In every case, the doctor's professional status provided both opportunity and protection. Whether it was Paolo Macchiarini exploiting the reverence given to "surgical geniuses," or Larry Nassar using his PowerPoint presentations to justify his actions, these doctors' white coats acted as camouflage as well as weapons. Patients trusted them. Colleagues hesitated to challenge them. Institutions shielded reputations rather than safeguarding patients. And their targets were often the most vulnerable: children, the elderly, the incapacitated, or those already struggling.

 DOI: 10.1201/9781003781066-18

Reflecting on the cases, we can see that warning signs were often evident: patterns of complaints, unusual behaviour, and poor results were frequently ignored or minimised. The very notion that a doctor might behave in such a manner was unthinkable to many, allowing perpetrators to go unchecked. Many of the doctors we studied moved easily between hospitals, regions, or even countries, often leaving with glowing references from employers eager to see them go.

A study on peer reporting found that only two-thirds of doctors with direct knowledge of an impaired or incompetent colleague reported this to the appropriate authorities (DesRoches et al., 2010). The most common reason for not acting was the "belief that someone else was handling the problem" – with 19% of respondents citing this reason. Nearly 12% of those surveyed cited fear of retaliation or the belief that "nothing would happen as a result of the report." Whilst this survey was on all types of professional misconduct, it is likely that similar concerns would also apply to reporting sexual misconduct by colleagues.

Scandals have prompted reforms. After Harold Shipman, the monitoring of controlled drugs and the investigation of deaths were overhauled. Cases of sexual misconduct led to the introduction of mandatory chaperone policies, even for non-intimate examinations. Electronic records now maintain audit trails that are more difficult to falsify. Most clinical systems enable tracking of medicines, making it easier to detect unusual prescribing patterns compared to previous years. Regulators are more prompt in acting, and data sharing between agencies and across international borders has improved. Whistleblowing policies and the "Freedom to Speak Up Guardian" in England reflect a growing awareness that silence can enable harm.

It is now routine for organisations to regularly scrutinise performance data, allowing for the earlier identification of outliers whose outcomes deviate from those of their peers.

But new vulnerabilities still arise. Telemedicine, accelerated by the pandemic, broadened access but also introduced new risks of inappropriate prescribing or exploitation. Globalised healthcare makes it easier for rogue doctors to move between jurisdictions. The rate of medical innovation continually surpasses regulatory systems.

Despite substantial changes to the regulation and oversight of medical practice, the conditions that enable medical criminality will always exist, offering an almost unmatched combination of intellectual challenge, social status, influence, and control over the futures of others.

The vast majority of those seeking to enter the profession are driven by a sincere desire to make a positive difference in the service of others. However, it will remain a tempting vocation for a minority motivated by malicious intent, hidden behind a white coat.

The English psychiatrist Dr Humphrey Osmond, remembered for coining the term *psychedelic*, once suggested that the medical role rests on three qualities: wisdom, authority, and charisma (Tanne, 2004). The first two are easily recognisable. Wisdom arises from knowledge, training, and clinical experience, the steady accumulation of judgement that patients expect from a seasoned practitioner.

Authority flows from the institutional position of the doctor: the white coat, the prescription pad, the sanction of the state, and of the profession itself.

However, it is the third trait, charisma, that demands closer examination when assessing doctors who cross ethical or criminal lines. Charisma is what extends a doctor's influence beyond mere reason. It is the capacity to inspire trust, elicit devotion, and persuade others to accept one's judgement without question. Charisma functions on an emotional level: patients may feel *seen*, *understood*, or *special* in the presence of a charismatic doctor, and colleagues may also be drawn into their sphere.

Psychoanalysis helps us understand why charisma has such influence. The doctor–patient relationship is prepared for transference: patients project onto their doctors' feelings rooted in early experiences of parental care. The doctor may become an unconscious symbol of protection, authority, or omnipotence. A charismatic doctor, knowingly or not, enhances this dynamic. Their warmth, confidence, or apparent certainty can strengthen dependency and diminish scepticism. Likewise, doctors themselves are not immune to countertransference. They may enjoy being idealised, feeling uniquely capable or specially chosen, and this gratification can impair their own judgement.

In most medical encounters, these forces are balanced by professional discipline, reflection, and systems of accountability. But when charisma dominates, the equilibrium tilts. Patients may collude with their own exploitation, rationalising away doubts or suspicions. Colleagues, too, can fall under the spell: a persuasive doctor can bend the perceptions of peers, nurses, or administrators, creating a protective shield around their actions. Institutional structures, far from containing such power, may at times reinforce it, mistaking charisma for leadership or vision.

History shows that some of the most serious medical transgressions have been committed not by colourless officials but by doctors who wielded this charismatic authority. Harold Shipman's elderly patients trusted him implicitly, even as he betrayed that trust fatally. Michael Swango in the United States dazzled colleagues with apparent brilliance, whilst concealing a murderous pathology. Larry Nassar was considered to be a miracle worker. Less extreme but still corrosive examples, doctors who exploit patients sexually, financially, or emotionally, often rely on the same alchemy of transference and charisma to silence doubts and override safeguards.

Seen in this light, Osmond's triad provides a lens on the inherent risks of the medical role. Wisdom and authority can be monitored, audited, and checked. Charisma, by contrast, is intangible and elusive. It slips past formal regulation, operating in the hidden space of unconscious expectation and interpersonal influence. And yet it is often what patients most desire in a doctor: someone who radiates certainty, compassion, and conviction.

To understand the criminal doctor, we need to examine not only their personal pathology but also the psychological currents of transference, dependency, and misplaced trust that run through the medical relationship itself.

Understanding the nature of these criminal acts helps us better support victims and improve systems for detecting and reporting misconduct. Preventing such cases is not solely about perfecting control measures, as criminal masterminds will almost always find ways to bypass them; it instead involves fostering a culture of accountability, transparency, courage, and truly listening to what our patients are saying. Fear is the weapon so effectively wielded by those discussed in this book, and it is a culture of fear in healthcare that we must work to dismantle.

More can be done to empower and educate patients about warning signs and to equip them with the confidence to speak to someone if they suspect a problem.

ENGAGE, EDUCATE, EQUIP, EMPOWER

One benefit of modern technology and social media is the ease of access to information. Enter a doctor's name into any search engine, and you are likely to find reviews from previous patients, details about their medical registration, and their background. Patients should be encouraged to carry out their own research and learn about those they plan to consult.

In the end, the shadows in which these perpetrators of harm hide are not dispelled by infallible systems, regulations, or perfect practitioners, none of which exist. They are dispelled by the ability to shine a light when such darkness is encountered, unencumbered and without fear.

REFERENCES

DesRoches, C. M., Rao, S. R., Fromson, J. A., Birnbaum, R. J., Iezzoni, L. I., Vogeli, C., & Campbell, E. G. (2010). Physicians' perceptions, preparedness for reporting, and experiences related to impaired and incompetent colleagues. *JAMA, 304*(2), 187–193. https://doi.org/10.1001/jama.2010.921

General Medical Council. (n.d.). "Intimate Examinations and Chaperones". https://www.gmc-uk.org/professional-standards/the-professional-standards/intimate-examinations-and-chaperones/intimate-examinations-and-chaperones

Tanne, J.H. (2004). Humphry Osmond. *BMJ, 328*(7441), 713. https://doi.org/10.1136/bmj.328.7441.713

Index

Absenteeism, in healthcare, 156
Abuse
  child and youth, 128, 129–132
  disguised as medical treatment, 132–138
  patterns of, 128
  towards vulnerable women, 138–139
  voyeurism and exploitation, 139–140
Adams, David Jackson, 36–37; *see also* Swango, Michael
Adams, John Bodkin, 15
Addiction, 7–8, 95–100
  factors contributing to, 96–97
  hospital culture and, 97–98
  nineteenth-century normality and, 98–100
The Adventure of the Speckled Band (Doyle), 51
American pill mills, 112–114
Anaesthesia, assault under, 144
Anaesthetics, 143–144
Angel of Mercy, 30
Assault, in medicine, 74–93
  Bailey, Harry, 84–89
  Duntsch, Christopher, 75–78
  Fata, Farid, 89–91
  Macchiarini, Paolo, 78–82
  Patel, Jayant, 82–83
  Paterson, Ian, 83–84
  under anaesthesia, 144
Atlanta Journal-Constitution (AJC), 123
Ayling, Clifford, 136–138
Azeez, Nadeem, 71–72
Bailey, Harry, 30, 84–89
Baker, Richard, 17, 18, 23
Ballet, Hippolyte, 52
Banks, Alan, 10, 22
Bawa-Garba, Hadiza, 70–71
Beddoes, Thomas, 99
Belaney, James Cockburn, 100
Benzodiazepines, 143–144
Births and Deaths Registration Act 1874, 57
Bleak House (Dickens), 51
Bradbury, Myles, 129
Bramhall, Simon, 91–92
Brooke, Angus, 139
Burgos, Jorge, 124
The Butcher of Paris (Petiot Marcel), 4, 47–48

Care-Assisted Serial Killing (CASK), 27–28
Castaing, Edme, 52–53, 54
The Chelmsford File (documentary), 87–88
Child and youth abuse, 128, 129–132
Child Exploitation and Online Protection (CEOP), 129
Chloroethyl-Cyclohexyl- Nitrosourea CCNU (lomustine), 60–61
Chloroform, 142–143
Church of Scientology, 87
Clark, Ronald E, 48–49
Clinicide, 27, 28
Cocaine, 97, 98
  recreational use of, 107

Coda, Giorgio, 29
Collins, Wilkie, 51, 99
Compartmentalisation, 31
Conflicts of interest, 155
Convictions, 35–36
  high bar for, 67–69
Cook, John Parsons, 53–54
Corruption, in medicine, 154, 158
Cream, Thomas, 4
Cream, Thomas Neill, 41–46, 51
  birth of, 41
  career, 42–43
  education, 41–42
  marriage, 42
  trial of, 45
Crime scenes, 29
Cultural shifts, 151
Culture of silence, and reporting of sexual misconduct, 123–125

Dally, Ann, 109
Data manipulation, 159
Deep Sleep: Harry Bailey and the Scandal of Chelmsford (Fife-Yeomans and Bromberger), 88
Deep sleep therapy (DST), 30, 85–87
Dehumanisation, 31–32
Delport, Barend, 139–140
Dickens, Charles, 51
Doctor Glas (Söderberg), 51–52
Doctor–patient relationship, 2
Donneybrook House, Hyde
  Shipman at, 8–9
Doyle, Conan, 51
Drug of choice, 19
Drugs
  addiction, *see* Addiction
  misuse of, *see* Misuse, of drugs
  and money, 105
  trading sex for, 145
Duntsch, Christopher, 4, 30, 75–78

Embezzlement, 155
Esmail, Aneez, 19
Ether, 142–143
Exploitation, 139–140

Fata, Farid, 4, 89–91
Faulkner, Mary Ann, 43
Favouritism, and preferential treatment, 158–159
Fife-Yeomans, Janet, 88
Fifth Report *(Safeguarding Patients: Lessons from the Past – Proposals for the Future)* (Smith), 22–23
First Report of the Shipman Inquiry, 17–18
Frankau, Lady, 107–109
Fraud, in medicine, 154, 155–158
  prevention and detection, 160–161
Freedman, Gordon, 114
Freud, Sigmund, 97
Froggatt, Clive, 97

Gadgil, Prabhaker, 67
Gardener, Katherine "Kate," 43
Garg, Sudhanshu, 68–69
General Medical Council (GMC), 8, 20, 22–23, 92, 109, 121, 143, 151
Gorton, Alice, 17
Grinspoon, Peter, 97
Gross negligence manslaughter (GNM), 64–65
  Azeez, Nadeem, 71–72
  Bawa-Garba, Hadiza, 70–71
  early cases of, 65–66
  high bar for conviction, 67–69
  Mamman-Aka'Aba, Isyaka, 72
  Sellu, David, 69–70
Grundy, Kathleen
  death of, 11–13

Hadden, Robert Anthony, 124
Halsted, William Stewart, 99
Hazzard, Linda, 46
Hazzard, Linda Burfield, 46–47
Hedonistic Killers, 29
Heroin, 107
Holmes, Ronald M., 29
Holmes, Stephen T., 29
Hurwitz, Brian, 24

Jennings, Oscar, 99
Jung, Carl, 2

Kaplan, Robert, 27, 29
Ketamine, 115, 116
Knock ou le Triomphe de la médecine (play), 2
Kwan, Thomas, 62–63

Lambeth poisoner, *see* Cream, Thomas Neill
Lamson, George, 57–58
Landon, Letitia Elizabeth, 50
Lewin, Louis, 99

Macchiarini, Paolo, 78–82
Mack, Hattie, 43
Magical drug, 97
Mahmood, Tariq, 158
Main, Thomas, 2
Mamman-Aka'Aba, Isyaka, 72
Massey, Alan, 10
Mattison, JB, 99
McQuade, Barbara, 89
Medical Act, 1858, 55
Medical serial killers
- classification of, 29–30
- motivation behind, 28–29
- personality disorder/psychopathy and, 30–31

Medical terrorist, *see* Ortiz, Raynaldo Rivera
Medicare fraud, 154
Medicare Fraud Strike Force, 158
Medicine as weapon, 50–52
- Castaing, Edme, 52–53
- Kwan, Thomas, 62–63
- Lamson, George, 57–58
- Ortiz, Raynaldo Rivera, 61–62
- Palmer, William, 53–56
- Pritchard, Edward William, 56–57
- Vickers, Paul Richard Jarvis, 60–61
- Warder, Alfred William, 58–60

Mental illness, 28
Menzies-Lyth, Isabel, 31
Mercy Killer, 30
#MeToo movement, 151
Mission-Oriented Killers, 29
Misuse, of drugs
- benzodiazepines, 143–144
- chloroform, 142–143
- ether, 142–143
- sedatives, 143

Modus operandi, 19
Money, drugs and, 105
The Moonstone (Collins), 51
Moret, Rodney, 114
Morphine, 98
- recreational use of, 107

Murray, Roy, 138

Nassar, Larry, 124, 132–135
National Practitioner Data Bank (NPDB), 40
Nepotism, 155
Nineteenth-century normality, 98–100

Opium, 98
Ortiz, Raynaldo Rivera, 61–62
Our Mutual Friend (Dickens), 51

Paget, James, 99
Palmer, William, 4, 51, 53–56
Patel, Jayant, 30, 82–83
Paterson, Ian, 83–84
Personality disorder, 30–31
Pethidine addiction, Shipman and, 7–8
Petiot, Marcel *(The Butcher of Paris),* 4, 47–48
Pill mills, 24, 105
- American, 112–114
- from British system to, 106–112
- emerging, 115–117

Poisonings, 35–36, 50–51
Poisons Act, 1857, 55
Political Mass Killers, 30
Porter, Charles, 100
Power
- abuse of, 153
- and environmental factors, 151
- role, and rationalisation, 149

Prentice, Michael, 67–68
Prescription fraud, 159
Preston Crown Court, Shipman's trial at, 13–15
Pritchard, Edward William, 51, 56–57
Professional sexual misconduct (PSM); *see also* Abuse
  addressing, 126
  boundaries and breaches, 120–122
  prevalence of, 122–123
  reporting, 123–125
Psychological facilitators, 31–32
Psychopathy, 30–31
Public Inquiry, 15, 16–17
  areas of, 16
  extent of Shipman's unlawful activities, 17–18
  Fifth Report *(Safeguarding Patients: Lessons from the Past - Proposals for the Future)* (Smith), 22–23
  investigation about Shipman's long overlooked, 18–19
  Shipman becoming serial killer, 19–22
Pyatt, Frank, 44

Quiet Killing, 27

Rathore, Jaswant, 135–136
Rationalisation, role of power and, 149
Regulatory shifts, 151
Rehabilitation, 152
Remediation, 152
Reporting, of professional sexual misconduct, 123–125
Reynolds, Linda, 9–10
Romano, Jules, 2
Rugeley poisoner, *see* Palmer, William

Safeguarding Patients: Lessons from the Past – Proposals for the Future (Fifth Report by Smith), 22–23
Sedatives, 143
Self-medication, 99
Self-prescribing, 98
Self-regulation, 39
Sellu, David, 69–70
Serial killers; *see also specific killers*
  defined, 26, 27–28
  historical overview, 26–27
  medical, *see* Medical serial killers
  Shipman as, 19–22
Serial Murder (Holmes and Holmes), 29
Serturner, Friedrich W, 98
Sexual boundary violations, in healthcare, 148
Sexual misconduct in medicine, *see* Professional sexual misconduct (PSM)
Shah, Manish, 135
Shipman, Harold Frederick, 4–6, 29
  becoming serial killer, 19–22
  and death of Kathleen Grundy, 11–13
  at Donneybrook House, Hyde, 8–9
  and drug addiction, 7–8
  early life of, 6
  long overlooked, investigation regarding, 18–19
  signature, 19
  trial of, 13–15
  unlawful activities, extent of, 17–18
  victims, deaths of, 9–11
Signature, leaving, 91–93
Singh, Krishna, 139
60 Minutes (TV program), 87
Smerick, Peter, 30
Smith, Dame Janet, 8, 18, 19, 21
  Fifth Report *(Safeguarding Patients: Lessons from the Past – Proposals for the Future)*, 22–23
Smith, Kenneth, 17, 18
Smith, Richard, 4
Smithers, Joel, 114
Söderberg, Hjalmar, 51
Spencer, Paul, 9
Standard of proof, 115
Starvation doctor, *see* Hazzard, Linda Burfield
Stevenson, Robert Louis, 51

The Strange Case of Dr Jekyll and Mr Hyde (Stevenson), 51
Strychnine, 54
Sullman, Barry, 67–68
Swan, Christopher Michael, 109–110
Swango, Michael, 29, 33
  career resurrection, 36–38
  change in name, 36–37
  early life and medical career, 33–34
  education, 34
  first documented murder, 43
  international crimes, 36–38
  poisonings and convictions, 35–36
Systemic failures, 149

Taylor, Alfred, 55
Theft, 155
Thiagalingam, Namasivayam, 162–165
Transparency International, 154
Treatment Killers, 30

Ullah, Kifayat, 157
Unconscious phantasy, 2

The Venetian Bracelet (poem), 50
Vickers, Paul Richard Jarvis, 60–61
Violation patterns, 149
Visionary Killers, 29
Voyeurism, 139–140

Warder, Alfred William, 58–60
Williamson, Claire, 46
Wimbledon poisoner, *see* Lamson, George

Zarkin, Allan, 92–93

For Product Safety Concerns and Information please contact our EU representative GPSR@taylorandfrancis.com
Taylor & Francis Verlag GmbH, Kaufingerstraße 24, 80331 München, Germany

www.ingramcontent.com/pod-product-compliance
Lightning Source LLC
LaVergne TN
LVHW011234150926
848065LV00030B/328
* 9 7 8 1 0 4 1 3 1 8 6 1 3 *